1986

U.S. POLICY
TOWARD LATIN AMERICA

Also of Interest

†Available in hardcover and paperback.

About the Book and Author

Recent U.S. military involvement in Central America has sparked heated debate over U.S. policy in the region. To informed observers of U.S.–Latin American relations, however, Washington's actions reflect U.S. regional and global objectives that have evolved in the course of 150 years of U.S. involvement in Latin America.

This text provides students with the necessary tools for understanding and interpreting the substance of U.S. policy toward Latin America. To analyze the shifts in policy, Dr. Molineu establishes a framework defining U.S. interests as either region-specific or global and then discusses several policy approaches that have been employed within these categories.

From a regional perspective, the author identifies Latin America as a U.S. "sphere of influence," dramatized by such cases as the Spanish-American War, dollar diplomacy, and the Bay of Pigs. He then focuses on how regional economic concerns have influenced U.S. policy, exemplified by Washington's handling of the debt crisis. In his discussions of the global perspective, Dr. Molineu addresses the region in terms of dependency theory and the North-South conflict and in terms of the ideological issues of the cold war, the latter illustrated by the cases of the Cuban missile crisis, the overthrow of the Allende government in Chile, and the Reagan administration's posture toward Nicaragua. Finally, he examines the alternative global approach that focuses on the U.S. "democratic mission" to promote democracy and human rights in the region.

U.S. Policy Toward Latin America is both descriptive and analytical, giving students the facts about key events and a framework for interpreting them. In historical context, the book covers the breadth of U.S. policy toward Latin America. Emphasis on the most visible and controversial incidents of U.S. involvement helps students grasp U.S. policy in action and provides essential background for understanding the problems facing the United States in Latin America today. This text is ideal for courses on U.S.–Latin American relations and as a supplement in courses on U.S. foreign policy and international relations.

Harold Molineu is professor of political science at Ohio University. He is the editor of *Multinational Corporations in Latin America: An Annotated Bibliography* (1978).

U.S. POLICY TOWARD LATIN AMERICA

From Regionalism to Globalism

HAROLD MOLINEU

Westview Press • Boulder and London

To Connie, Doug, and Anne

Copyright © 1986 by Westview Press, Inc.

Published in 1986 in the United States of America by Westview Press, Inc.; Frederick A. Praeger, Publisher; 5500 Central Avenue, Boulder, Colorado 80301

Library of Congress Cataloging-in-Publication Data
Molineu, Harold.
  U.S. policy toward Latin America.
  Bibliography: p.
  Includes index.
  1. Latin America—Foreign relations—United States.
2. United States—Foreign relations—Latin America.
3. United States—Foreign relations—20th century.
I. Title. II. Title: US policy toward Latin America.
F1418.M72 1986   327.7308   86-1344
ISBN 0-8133-0272-2
ISBN 0-8133-0273-0 (pbk.)

Printed and bound in the United States of America

  The paper used in this publication meets the minimum requirements of the American National Standard for Permanence of Paper for Printed Library Materials Z39.48–1984.

10   9   8   7   6   5   4   3   2   1

CONTENTS

MAPS AND TABLES

PREFACE

This book grew out of a concern for interpreting the contemporary problems confronting the United States in Latin America. In 1983, former Congressman James W. Symington uttered a poignant plea for Americans to address "the one consideration that has frustrated earlier efforts in dealing with Latin America—our fundamental, dogged, appalling ignorance of the Latin mind and culture."[1] This book cannot claim to probe all aspects of the problem, but it does seek to illuminate major elements of Latin America's experience with the United States. Such an endeavor is one step toward reducing the persistent ignorance of the region referred to by Mr. Symington.

The book is an effort to put current events into a historical context and to illustrate how the United States has shifted from a regionalist definition of its interests to a preoccupation with global interests. Key events and issues that have shaped U.S. policy are discussed within the framework of two broad perspectives: the regional and the global. In addition, a critique based on noninterventionism is presented, and some attempt is made to identify the sources of U.S. policy.

Clearly, how one defines "the problem" in Latin America has an impact on how one judges U.S. policy in the region. Because of the partisan and often emotional overtones coloring the debate over the appropriate U.S. role, it is difficult to remain neutral. However, the events discussed here are presented so that the readers might have an opportunity to judge for themselves the wisdom and success of U.S. actions.

My own view is that any assessment of U.S. policy today requires a firm grasp of what has happened to generate so much friction between the United States and Latin America and of the rationale for U.S. intervention. Such an understanding suggests a path of caution and tolerance for U.S. policymakers.

Harold Molineu

NOTES

1. *New York Times*, September 23, 1983, 29.

ACKNOWLEDGMENTS

A number of people have contributed to the production of this work. First, my gratitude goes to Robert Gilmore of the University of Kansas, who first introduced me to Latin America, and to John Finan of American University for sustaining my interest. Of incalculable assistance has been my colleague Thomas W. Walker at Ohio University, who has read virtually the entire manuscript. Special thanks are also due to Stephen Ropp of the University of Wyoming for his valuable advice. Two graduate research assistants, William Wyss and Joel Ergood, provided hours of tedious and dedicated work, including preparation of the tables and maps. The tactful guidance of Barbara Ellington and Jeanne Campbell of Westview Press is likewise appreciated. The thorough and astute editing of Marian Safran rescued the manuscript from numerous problems in style and clarity and deserves more credit than can be given in this brief note. Errors of fact and matters of judgment, of course, remain my responsibility.

I am grateful to Pat Winebrenner and Dolly French of the Political Science Department at Ohio University for their help and to the university's College of Arts and Sciences for its financial support. I would also like to acknowledge the numerous students whose questions about U.S. policy in Latin America compelled me to tackle this project in the first place.

And finally, I owe my deepest gratitude to my wife, Connie, whose patience and encouragement sustained the entire enterprise.

Harold Molineu

U.S. POLICY
TOWARD LATIN AMERICA

INTRODUCTION

EXPLAINING U.S. POLICY

U.S. policy toward Latin America over the past 160 years has gone through a number of distinct phases and has shifted from neglect to intervention, from cooperation to conflict. In part, the policy has been characterized by a pattern: long periods of U.S. inattention followed by brief, intense periods of paternalistic involvement. And throughout the years, there has been a continuing debate over the precise nature of the relationship with Latin America. How, in other words, can we explain the often troubled but inescapable ties between the "colossus of the North" and the smaller, weaker states to the South?

Although Theodore Roosevelt treated the Caribbean Sea as an American lake and Ronald Reagan argued that Central America is the scene for another showdown between the United States and the Soviet Union, there has been little agreement among political leaders and scholars about the best way to view the U.S. role in Latin America. This study will explore the various perspectives on U.S.–Latin American relations that have been used to analyze U.S. involvement in the region. After all, how policymakers define the situation may well determine what their policies will be.

Current discussion of U.S. policy in Latin America is characterized by confusion and divergence over what approach or perspective is most useful. For example, Central America was important to the Reagan administration because the region was seen as a stake in the superpower contest. Therefore, certain policies were adopted and actions carried out that conformed to that assumption. In contrast, it has been argued that the recent turmoil in Central America resulted from internal factors, and thus a different set of responses was called for. In fact, because throughout the history of U.S.–Latin American relations there have been such persistent shifts in defining the problems, it is possible to provide different explanations for the same actions. Some explanations may, with the passage of time, have lost their

1

2

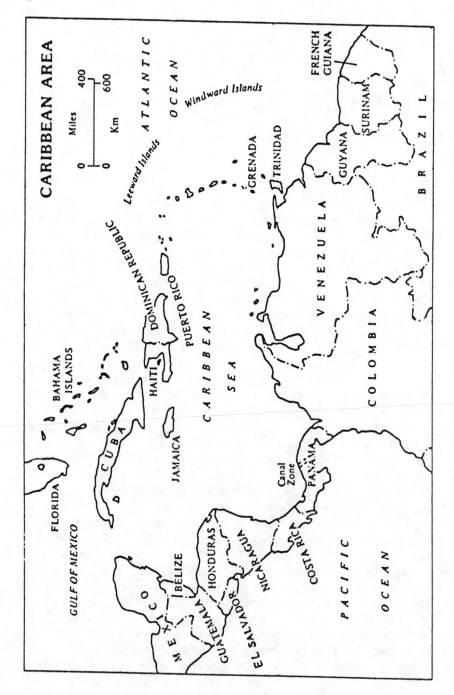

CARIBBEAN AREA

validity; others, however, continue to have considerable persuasiveness in Washington.

One point is very clear: Developments in Latin America, whether they be revolutions or elections, economic disruptions or economic growth, cannot be discussed without consideration of the role of the United States. Washington's direct interest in the future of the region dates back to the early nineteenth century and has been reinforced since then by intimate involvement in the economics, politics, and security of nearly every country in the hemisphere. Although it might be argued that the independence and security of most Latin American nations has been made possible by the protection of the United States, it can just as easily be asserted that the *lack* of independence and the *lack* of economic development are also attributable to the United States.

Consequently, the problems facing the United States in the region should be considered in the light of the historical influences and issues that underlie the contemporary scene. The erratic, well-meaning but frequently clumsy, and interventionist policies of the United States may seem to us as only minor inconveniences or setbacks, but to Latin Americans these actions have had a significant, even a determining, impact on their lives.

In order to grasp the dynamics of today's difficulties, therefore, it is necessary to divide the history of U.S.–Latin American relations into meaningful components. Instead of simply reviewing these events chronologically, this study examines them in the context of alternative or changing perspectives. Because the policymakers' choice of perspective can have an influence on policy, it is also important to consider the factors that might influence that selection. What is it, for example, that convinced President Reagan that Central America's revolutions were part of a global strategic struggle, although a number of Latin American scholars contended that the revolutions were linked to local factors or economic conditions?

The six perspectives presented here fall into two broad categories: regionalist and globalist. The region-specific category consists of the Western Hemisphere Idea, the sphere of influence, and regional economic dominance. The global category includes the democratic mission, the strategic approach, and dependency economics. I will also put forth a critique of U.S. policy based on the principle of nonintervention. No one of these perspectives is likely to provide a definitive explanation for U.S. behavior in Latin America. Instead, it should be clear that a variety of approaches have influenced U.S. policies and can be used to explain them.

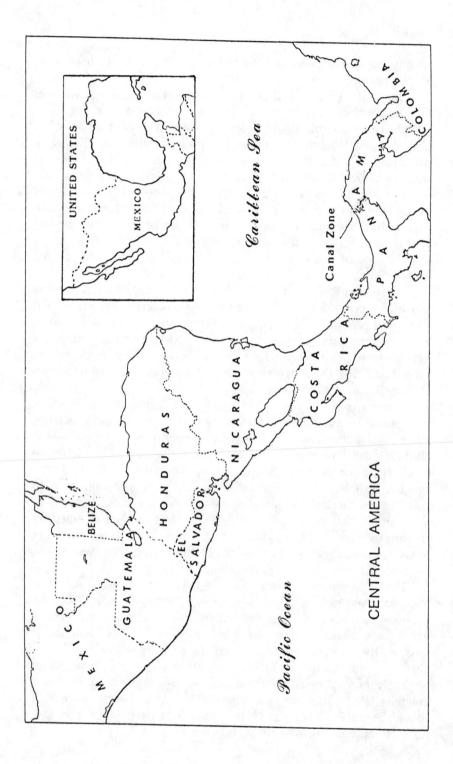

The particular perspective adopted by decisionmakers may depend very much on their beliefs and ideologies as well as on the policymaking process and the domestic political environment. In the final analysis, this review should enable the student of foreign policy to sort out the various aspects of U.S.–Latin American relations so as to have a more systematic and informed grasp of why these relations are today so entwined with misunderstanding, confusion, and conflict.

THE HISTORICAL IMPERATIVE

One of the reasons so much attention is paid to the roots of U.S.–Latin American relations in the following chapters is because of what might be termed the "historical imperative." This concept suggests that the historical process is such a major force in Latin America that the origins of crucial events in the region today are directly linked to the experiences of the past. The historical imperative does not mean that history predetermines events or that certain events, for example, revolutions, are inevitable but rather that a few key experiences can have a catalytic, even traumatic, effect on people, and the consequences of these experiences are likely to be felt for some time.

And yet, North Americans are chronic ignorers of history. Too often the United States deals with a problem, such as a civil war, as though it started yesterday when the first shots were fired. By this reasoning, all that is required is to identify the forces and issues currently at work and how they relate to U.S. interests and then proceed to negotiate (or fight) in the context of those immediate concerns.

To approach Latin America without a sense of the impact of history is to enter the arena with only one eye open; the perspective is likely to be distorted. The difficulties with Cuba, the friction with Allende in Chile, and the contest with the Nicaraguans did not begin in a historical vacuum. These issues did not simply emerge because of the arrival of one person—a Castro, for example—or because of the involvement of an outside power such as the Soviet Union. The presence of a Castro or Soviet aid may exacerbate a problem for the United States, but there would likely be trouble even if those two elements were removed. If the political upheaval is the consequence of a long-developing series of events, the solution will not be found in merely expelling a Castro or shutting off Soviet aid.

The United States has been a major historical influence on the political and economic developments in a number of Latin American countries. Thus, it is important to understand the nature of that involvement, even if it requires going back to the nineteenth century. Latin perceptions that U.S. interventions have consistently prevented them from working out their own political problems may or may not always be accurate. What counts, however, is not objective history but rather what people believe has happened. (It may not be co-incidental that the two cases of major revolution in Latin America in the last twenty-five years, Cuba and Nicaragua, were subject to some of the most intensive, prolonged U.S. intervention in the hemisphere.)

Other factors besides the history of relations with the United States may also shape events in Latin America. Some, such as the class system and landholding patterns, do have their origins in history; others, however, have arisen from more recent developments such as outside contacts and sudden political and economic changes. Moreover, internal factors, such as culture and geography, may further explain the course of events in a particular country, regardless of U.S. involvement. Consequently, to study U.S. policy in Latin America is to see only a part of the picture; in many cases, however, it may be the most important part.

A HISTORICAL OVERVIEW

Because this text is organized around key themes in U.S. policy toward Latin America, it is useful to sketch the broad historical trends and periods before proceeding with the thematic analysis.

The Monroe Doctrine

The "beginning" of U.S. interest in Latin America is typically marked by the announcement of the Monroe Doctrine in 1823. This statement identified the United States with the independence of the Latin American states and provided a basis for excluding European colonialism from the Western Hemisphere.

The Interventionist Period

The Spanish-American War of 1898 brought the United States into an active role in the future of a number of Latin American countries and launched the United States into a period of intervention in the Caribbean and Central America. Cuba became a protectorate of the United States. President Theodore Roosevelt's 1901 "Corollary" to the Monroe Doctrine sanctioned U.S. intervention in order to prevent European intervention in the area. Collaboration by U.S. officials and Panamanian rebels in 1903 brought the United States into possession of the Panama Canal.

The aggressive defense of U.S. investments and business interests in Latin America under the Taft administration led to a pattern of intervention known as "dollar diplomacy." The habit of using troops to protect business interests was continued through the 1920s, and it clearly established the perception of U.S. dominance over the political and economic life of much of the region.

The Good Neighbor

Under President Franklin D. Roosevelt, the United States embarked on a path designed to repudiate more than thirty years of military and political interference. Troops were withdrawn and agreements pledging nonintervention were signed. The policy of the "good neighbor" did establish more cordial relations between the United States and Latin America, but it did little to promote democratic procedures and reforms. Military governments and dictators were the prevailing forms of political rule in the region.

The Cold War Consensus

Following the generally close collaboration during World War II, the Western Hemisphere nations formed a military alliance in 1947 to deter external threats to the region. The Organization of American States (OAS) was created in 1948 to bring about political and economic cooperation and to provide machinery for keeping peace in the hemisphere. There was, among the various governments, a consensus that unity was necessary to deal with the growing worldwide communist threat. At this time, of course, the United States was emerging as a superpower with commitments far beyond the Western Hemisphere.

Containing Communism

Characteristic of U.S. policy in Latin America between 1954 and the present has been a concern for preventing what has been viewed as communist revolution. Recently declassified CIA documents indicate that covert U.S. action helped topple a supposedly communist government in Guatemala in 1954.[1] The proximity of Fidel Castro's Cuba as an ally of the Soviet Union shocked many people in the United States. The Cuban-Soviet alliance inspired U.S. officials to try to remove Castro from power and to prevent similar upheavals in the region. The 1961 Bay of Pigs invasion was a U.S.-sponsored attempt to bring Castro down; it failed, but intervention of the Lyndon Johnson administration in the Dominican Republic in 1965 did not. Dominican leftists were defeated, and groups friendly to the United States were brought to power.

As pressure continued against Cuba, the Richard Nixon administration extended the anticommunist campaign of the United States to Chile in the early 1970s. Determined to prevent the success of an elected Marxist president there, the United States engaged in what came to be known as a "destabilization" campaign to unseat Salvador Allende. Allende's fall in 1973 was presumably a message to Marxists that they could not succeed in this hemisphere.

Security and Human Rights

Under the Reagan administration in the 1980s, the campaign to contain communism continued. Active U.S. involvement in El Salvador was intended to prevent a "communist" revolution there. In Nicaragua, the victory of the Sandinistas in the 1979 revolution was seen as an extension of Cuban and Soviet influence and thus a direct threat to U.S. national security. Anti-Sandinista forces were supported by the United States in an attempt to prevent Nicaraguan aid to the Salvadoran rebels and to bring down the Sandinista government.

Sandwiched in with these assertive actions on behalf of U.S. strategic and security interests have been two major efforts to promote democratic reform and human rights in Latin America. John F. Kennedy's Alliance for Progress was an aid program tied to economic and political reform, and Jimmy Carter's human rights campaign was an effort to put some distance between the United States and the authoritarian and military governments of the region. Neither effort met with notable success. However, the debate between the demands of national security and the interest in human rights is a persistent feature of U.S. policy in Latin America even today.

U.S. INTERESTS IN LATIN AMERICA

Before reviewing U.S. actions in Latin America, we will look briefly at U.S. interests and goals as defined by Washington. Although what follows is not a comprehensive list, it does reflect the official view of Latin America. Also, any categorization of interests, goals, and means is likely to be tentative since situations change and different administrations have different priorities and values. In addition, these interests, goals, and means tend to overlap and to be intentionally vague.

In general, however, U.S. interests in Latin America are derived from

1. The geographic proximity of the region

2. The effect of Latin America on the world position of the United States
3. The presence of strategic resources
4. Traditional ties and associations
5. High levels of trade and investment
6. The potential influence of such countries as Brazil and Mexico
7. Humanitarian values

From this base, U.S. interests can be specified as follows: First, there are the obvious *security interests* arising out of the region's nearness. These are usually defined as keeping the hemisphere free from the influence of hostile powers. In fact, this particular interest has influenced U.S. policy since the early days of the nineteenth century. It is generally assumed that no coalition of Latin American states would be a security threat to the United States without outside help.

Because of its proximity, the Caribbean area is typically treated as a zone of influence, where U.S. tolerance of threats is very low. Brazil, because of its size, population, and resources is regarded as the single most important country, followed by Mexico, Venezuela, Colombia, and Argentina. Modestly important to Washington are Chile, Peru, and Jamaica. Cuba, because of its ties to the USSR, is accorded special notice, as are other countries, such as Nicaragua, when their activities take on strategic importance.

Political interests of the United States include a preference for supporting governments sympathetic to the U.S. global strategic position. It is in the U.S. interest to deal with stable governments that share the U.S. view of the threat from the Soviet Union. This has meant the application of a country-by-country, pragmatic judgment in assessing regimes, both democratic and authoritarian.

A less tangible political interest is how U.S.–Latin American relations reflect upon the worldwide reputation of the United States. The perception that the United States honors its commitments and stands by its friends is important to U.S. policymakers. If the U.S. will to act is lacking in an area where U.S. influence is preeminent, it is difficult to convince others in the world of the reliability of the United States. Thus events in the region may become important not because of their threat to the U.S. position in Latin America but because of their perceived impact on U.S. credibility in global politics.

Economic interests include continued access to strategically important raw materials, such as oil, copper, and bauxite. These interests also involve the activity of U.S. investors and exporters, essentially private interests. The U.S. government takes the position that it is in the national interest to promote the health of private commerce, but economic interests are not accorded the priority of security and political interests. In other words, the economic stake of the United States in the region and the strategic materials controlled by the Latin Americans are not vital to U.S. survival.

The most important *goals* of the United States in the hemisphere are (1) to maintain a region of independent states and (2) to prevent Latin America's being used as an area for strategic attack against the United States. The more specific *objectives* include:

1. Preventing a Soviet capability to launch strategic weapons against the United States via submarine and land bases
2. Preventing the establishment of hostile military bases in the region
3. Maintaining access to strategic resources
4. Maintaining access to the Panama Canal
5. Containing and/or destabilizing revolutionary forces and subversion
6. Encouraging the growth of U.S. trade and investment

The *means* to accomplish these objectives include:

1. Establishment of close ties with friendly governments and their military forces
2. Use of military and economic assistance to promote stability
3. Provision of training and material to countries threatened with subversion from outside
4. Resistance of efforts to nationalize U.S. private investments
5. Education of Latin Americans about the external threats to the hemisphere
6. Promotion of democratic processes

It should be kept in mind that U.S. officials, in dealing with Latin America, are attempting to work out relationships with more than thirty independent nations of various sizes and resources, with interests and goals often competitive with those of the United States. Because Latin America is such a complex region, oversimplifications about the people and their histories and politics should be avoided. At the same time, we must remember that the United States has a multitude of worldwide interests, many of which carry higher priority than those in Latin America. Nonetheless, the political, economic, and strategic importance of the region periodically asserts itself and reminds us of the folly of ignoring the forces at work there. As events in Latin

America can and do affect the security and influence of the United States and as they often intrude on domestic politics, it is critically important today to understand the sources and dynamics of the U.S.- Latin American relationship.

NOTES

1. Richard H. Immerman, *The CIA in Guatemala: The Foreign Policy of Intervention* (Austin: University of Texas Press, 1982).

PART 1
REGION-SPECIFIC APPROACHES

The assumption that there is something special about the relationship of the United States to Latin America is a *region-specific* perspective. Proponents contend that events in Latin America belong to a separate category of U.S. national interests and thus deserve a distinctive set of guidelines for responding. Part I first looks at the Western Hemisphere Idea in general, then examines the power-politics calculations inherent in the sphere-of-influence formula, and the implications of U.S. regional economic dominance, all variations of the regionalist perspective.

1
THE WESTERN
HEMISPHERE IDEA

That the Americas constitute a group of nations separate from the "Old World" of Europe is a concept of long standing. The history of North and South America is colored by the rejection not only of European colonialism but, presumably, of European political patterns as well. The idea of the "New World" as encompassing the entire Western Hemisphere dates back to the earliest days of colonial exploration and has given rise to perceptions that the area did in fact represent a new and distinctive way of life and that the countries and people of the Americas marched to a different drummer—primarily a democratic one. Especially in the United States, the early impulse for revolution—the very raison d'être of independence movements— was the rejection of European monarchies, religious persecution, economic deprivation, and political repression.

It was easy, in the 1820s, to draw parallels between the South American revolts from Spain and the U.S. revolt from Britain. Simón Bolívar was the George Washington of Latin America. The Latin heritage of Christianity (albeit Iberian Roman Catholicism) and of Western culture and languages, the search for representative government, and the factor of geographic proximity combined to form an image of common heritage, common values, and a common destiny with the young United States.[1]

THE MONROE DOCTRINE

For the United States, virtually from independence, the removal of a European presence in North America was a vital and continuing interest. Competition from the major European powers posed a continuing security and economic threat to the new nation. The Louisiana Purchase in 1803 eliminated the French from a vast area west of the Mississippi River. British territorial expansion was contained by the Peace of Ghent in 1815, and the Spanish were maneuvered, with some forceful pressure, out of Florida in 1819. Westward expansion and the systematic reduction of European colonization continued into the 1840s (the British were gently nudged out of the Oregon Territory in 1846).

The Monroe Doctrine of 1823 stands as a documentary manifestation of that deliberate policy of excluding Europe from the future of the New World.[2] This doctrine has been seen as a pillar of U.S. foreign policy in Latin America; it also is a symbol of the Western Hemisphere Idea. Its implications were clear: The destinies of the two Americas were inexorably linked; the persistence of European colonialism was a direct threat to the security of the United States. Because of the doctrine's importance in defining the Western Hemisphere, we need to review exactly what Monroe said and the consequences.

As the Latin American revolutions (1802–1822) promised to expel Spain from the hemisphere, there were concerns in Washington that other Europeans—the French in particular—would seek to restore colonial control over Spain's former possessions. Such a prospect not only offended the ideological sympathy felt for Bolívar and José de San Martín but also raised the specter of European power politics being fought out at the United States' back door. There was even fear of Russia acting on its territorial claims along the Pacific coast of North America.

The Message

At the urging of Secretary of State John Quincy Adams, President James Monroe issued his statement on December 2, 1823. It was not a message to Latin America but rather a declaration aimed at Europe. There were four main points:[3]

1. No further colonization: "The American continents, by the free and independent condition which they have assumed and maintain, are henceforth not to be considered as subjects for future colonization by any European power."
2. No transfer: territory belonging to one European power could not be assigned to another.
3. European noninterference: "We should consider any attempt" by the European powers "to extend their system to any portion of this hemisphere as dangerous to our peace and safety."
4. U.S. noninvolvement in Europe: "In the wars of the European powers in matters relating to themselves we have never taken any part nor does it comport with our policy to do so."

Thus, the United States had issued a warning to the Europeans to keep their hands off the Western Hemisphere and that any attempt to intervene or recolonize would be viewed as a threat to the United States itself or, as Monroe put it, "as a manifestation of an unfriendly disposition toward the United States." This doctrine made the first clear identification of Latin American independence with U.S. security. As we will see later, this statement had a continuing impact on the way in which the U.S. government perceived events in the Americas. Although the specific ultimatum about noncolonization and U.S. abstention from European affairs may seem archaic today, the tone and direction of the doctrine has, in more recent times, come to shape U.S. reactions to leftist and communist movements throughout Latin America.

The Application

The intrusion of "non-American" threats, including hostile ideologies, in the nineteenth and twentieth centuries resulted in the invocation of the Monroe Doctrine, both explicitly and implicitly. For example, the 1954 inter-American conference at Caracas adopted a resolution that conformed to the doctrine in spirit if not to the letter: "The domination of the political institutions of any American state by the International Communist movement, extending to this hemisphere the political system of an extra-continental power, would constitute a threat to the sovereignty and political independence of the American States."[4]

Such a resolution implied that there was a sense of hemispheric separation and a capacity for distinguishing "us" from "them." It was consistent with Monroe's declaration, which first drew the lines of demarcation between the political systems of the old and new worlds and which still stands as a cornerstone of the Western Hemisphere Idea. According to Monroe: "The political system of the allied powers is essentially different in this respect from that of America . . ." and the two hemispheres "are eminently and conspicuously different." It is likely that Monroe did not envision his words becoming enshrined as a doctrine or as a formula for U.S. policy in Latin America. In fact, one scholar contends that the statement was essentially a function of domestic politics in 1823, of Monroe's struggle to protect his political position, and not a result of a clearly thought-out strategy for dealing with Latin America.[5]

In addition to outlining a special relationship between the United States and Latin America, the Monroe Doctrine had the good fortune to become ingrained in U.S. history as a successful demonstration of

U.S. "toughness." The ultimatum had been given to the Europeans, and the popular perception over time was that they had not dared to defy it. Reality, of course was somewhat different.

First, the doctrine grew out of a British suggestion in 1822 that Washington and London issue a joint declaration against European intervention in the New World. Secretary of State Adams, however, insisted that the United States act alone, unfettered by an obligation to the British.

Second, two months prior to Monroe's statement, the British and French had reached an understanding (the Polignac Memorandum) denying any French intention of intervening in Latin America. When word of this arrangement reached Latin America, the impact of Monroe's warning was considerably diluted.

Third, the British government, committed as it was to Latin American independence and possessing the world's mightiest navy, was largely responsible for discouraging the recolonization of the hemisphere. Dedicated to free trade, the British preferred the open access to the New World, access resulting from the collapse of colonialism. Conveniently for Washington, these British interests coincided with those of the Monroe Doctrine.

Fourth, although there was no direct recolonization of Latin America, the Monroe Doctrine did not prevent the Europeans from interference during the nineteenth century. The record, for example, shows at least sixteen instances of direct European intervention. These ranged from a British and French naval blockade of Buenos Aires in 1843 to the British establishment of a protectorate over the Miskito coast of Nicaragua. In addition, there were a series of actions taken by the Germans, Italians, Spanish, French, and others from 1869 to 1897 to collect debts and settle economic issues in such places as Venezuela, Colombia, and Haiti.[6]

Perhaps the most flagrant defiance of Monroe's principle was the European move into Mexico in the 1860s while the United States was preoccupied with its Civil War. Britain, France, and Spain sent a joint military force to Veracruz in 1862 to force a settlement of claims against the Mexican government. The French remained in Mexico, caught up by the idea of expanding their empire, and despite heroic resistance from the Mexican army, announced in April 1864 plans for the installation of an emperor imported from Austria, Ferdinand Maximilian.

Maximilian was unable to establish effective control and when U.S. demands that he return to Europe were backed up by the mobilization of U.S. forces on the Rio Grande in 1865, the French called off their expedition. Maximilian himself was not finally deposed until 1867. For three years, however, French troops had been occupying a U.S. neighbor, apparently unmoved by the principles of the Monroe Doctrine.[7]

Another illustration of the active role Europeans were playing in the region in the 1800s arises from the widespread interest in a canal across Central America. U.S. officials acquiesced to the persistent efforts of the British to participate. According to the Clayton-Bulwer Treaty of 1850, Washington and London agreed to cooperate in the construction of a canal and to refrain from establishing exclusive control over it.

In the final analysis, the Monroe Doctrine has had two results: (1) the establishment of the concept of the Western Hemisphere Idea, and (2) the creation of a paternalistic attitude in the United States toward the countries to the south; after all, Washington had been the guarantor of Latin American independence. It was this role of self-appointed protector that led to a more aggressive and interventionist U.S. policy at the turn of the century.

THE PAN AMERICAN MOVEMENT

Blaine's Vision

During the nineteenth century there were a number of attempts to move the Western Hemisphere states toward some formal organization, or more explicitly, toward a "Pan American Union." As attractive as the rhetoric of this movement might have been, it took electoral politics and an appetite in the United States for commercial expansion to produce the first formal Pan American Conference in 1889. Secretary of State James G. Blaine, who for some time had been advocating a more aggressive trade policy, saw a Pan American union as a means to catch up with the economic growth of the imperialist powers. His vision of the United States as being on the verge of major power status in the 1880s, along with his interest in self-promotion, led to the convening of a conference in Washington to encourage trade in the hemisphere. Representatives from seventeen countries attended the 1889 meeting, and although little was agreed to, the idea of Pan Americanism did receive some concrete support.

The conference agreed to set up an International Bureau of American Republics, which in 1910 became known as the Pan American Union (PAU), with headquarters in Washington. Aside from serving as a vehicle for the promotion of U.S. commerce, the PAU's contribution to "union" was not discernible. For example, the U.S. secretary of state was the PAU's permanent chairman and efforts by Latin Americans to modify Washington's dominance proved uniformly unsuccessful.[8] Again, however, at least in the minds of the North Americans, the notion of a distinctive, separate Western Hemisphere received a symbolic boost from the PAU. Such an aura of union served to perpetuate the image that the peoples of the hemisphere shared common values and concurred with the U.S. leadership role. It also provided a palatable rationalization for U.S. intervention: We were all part of the same family.

Reality

The reality of trade and the rise of U.S. power in the late 1890s put into question the pretensions of equality and cooperation in the Americas. Demonstrations of U.S. power (against Chile, for instance) did not lend themselves to explanation on the basis of the Western Hemisphere Idea. The establishment in 1891 of a Chilean government openly hostile to Washington and apparently friendly to Britain induced President Benjamin Harrison to send the warship *Baltimore* to Valparaiso harbor as a symbol of U.S. concern. After two sailors died as a result of a brawl at a local saloon, the U.S. reaction was resentful and indignant—especially when the Chilean government refused to apologize. The refusal was considered an insult, and a belligerent, jingoistic mood took over Washington. The president threatened to take military action against Chile. Eventually a humbled Chilean government apologized in 1892 and paid a US$75,000 indemnity.[9] Such behavior may have been a triumph for U.S. power; it did not contribute to Pan Americanism, nor was it consistent with the Western Hemisphere Idea. Clearly, the reasons for U.S. action were not derived from a sense of community preservation but more from an assertion of power in keeping with a sphere of influence.

Although the Pan American movement emerged from initiatives taken by the United States, it is useful to examine the Latin American contribution to the movement. Such an examination suggests that there was not unanimous agreement that the creation of the PAU was the direction such a movement should take.

The Latin American Movement

Typically, credit for the first effort to bring together the states of the Americas is given to Simón Bolívar, who convened the "First International Congress" in the Colombian province of Panama in 1826. Bolívar's meeting gives credence to the assertion that Pan Americanism was as much a Latin effort as a U.S. one.

A closer examination, however, casts doubt on these beliefs and demonstrates the capacity for Washington to mislead itself about the nature of shared interests. For example, only four countries attended the Panama meeting (Colombia, Mexico, Peru, and the United Provinces of Central America, which in 1842 separated into the five modern states of Central America). The U.S. delegation was unable to attend because Congress failed to appropriate travel funds. Moreover, as the events of the next two decades demonstrated, inter-American relations were beset by incompatible interests, different priorities, and serious gaps in communication.

Bolívar's original concept of unity and cooperation was for *Spanish* America only, and in fact included the idea of ties to Great Britain, not the United States. Similarly, Mexican efforts toward collaboration in the 1830s focused on organizing the Latin Americans *against* the United States in order to contain U.S. imperialism. (Mexico at this time, of course, was beginning its losing battle with the United States over Texas and California.) An inter-American conference in Lima, Peru (December 1847–March 1848), was not attended by the United States. By this time, it was clear, as Arthur P. Whitaker so aptly put it, that "the marriage of the two Americas ended in divorce before there was even a honeymoon."[10]

The failure of efforts at political or even economic collaboration within Latin America indicates that the goal of Latin American unity was the ability to deal with Europe directly and without U.S. participation. Washington, however, had made it clear, by means of the Monroe Doctrine and support of the Pan American movement, that it viewed the future of both continents as inevitably linked and that, as the most powerful nation, the United States had a special obligation to lead the region. Thus, by 1900 there was a well-established and built-in tension between the two Americas. The United States was poised to defend its particular view of the world regardless of how this view corresponded to that of its neighbors or to the various proposals for hemispheric unity.

A Basis for Unity

The idea of a special relationship between the two Americas, based on their similar political cultures and their geographic insulation from Europe, provided the foundation for the belief that the national interests and political systems of the Latin American states would be modeled on those of the United States. As early as 1808, Thomas Jefferson voiced this assumption when he wrote of the Latin struggle for independence: "We consider their interests and ours as the same, and that the object of both must be to exclude all European influence from this hemisphere."[11]

Throughout the history of U.S.–Latin American relations there has been a persistent tendency for North Americans to take for granted that their values and goals were shared by the countries to the South. Although common interests do exist, the evidence of the past 160 years suggests that common interests do not translate into complete and total agreement on all counts. Efforts by the Latin American states in recent years to operate independently and to establish non-American ties have usually brought opposition from Washington. Cuba's ties to the Soviet Union and Nicaragua's identification with the Third World nonaligned movement, for example, have been treated as unacceptable deviance from the inter-American system.

Nevertheless, the Western Hemisphere Idea is not exclusively a U.S. proposition nor necessarily a devious attempt to disguise U.S. paternalism. There has been some Latin support for bringing the Americas together. In addition to Bolívar's 1826 congress, other Latin statesmen have noted the geographic and political inducements to unity. Argentina's noted foreign minister, Domingo Faustino Sarmiento, for instance, was well known for his support of a political-military alliance in the Americas, especially in the 1860s when much of Latin America was becoming concerned about French involvement in Mexico and Spanish intrusion into the Dominican Republic. In Sarmiento's eyes, the United States provided a model for the political development of Latin America, and thus close cooperation was essential.[12] As late as 1952, Mexican diplomat Luis Quintanilla acknowledged—albeit in a tone of resignation—that "to face the fact of America is to glance at any map. From pole to pole, from ocean to ocean, we are in the same boat, we were created to live together."[13]

THE GOOD NEIGHBOR POLICY

A third component of U.S. policy toward Latin America that may be explained by its appeal to the Western Hemisphere Idea is the Good Neighbor Policy of Franklin D. Roosevelt (FDR). This was a region-specific approach, couched in the language of hemispheric unity and the promotion of the common interests of all the Americas.

For thirty years prior to Roosevelt's inauguration in 1933, the United States had been deeply involved in the economic and political life of the Latin American nations (see discussion of dollar diplomacy and military intervention in Chapter 2). Roosevelt took immediate steps to repair the image of the United States, to pull back from blatant protection of U.S. foreign investment in the region, and generally to put U.S.–Latin American relations on a more even keel so that undivided attention could be given to fighting the Depression.

Roosevelt's strategy involved three prominent ideas: the abandonment of intervention, the return to a just and objective recognition policy, and the establishment of a new Pan Americanism of hemispheric solidarity, cooperation, and peace. It proved to be a dramatic turnaround in U.S. behavior, but because the rhetoric was stronger than reality, the policy of the good neighbor became another contributor to an illusion of hemispheric unity. For the United States, it was a way to confess the sins of the past, wipe them from memory, and pretend that history and growing U.S. power would be overlooked by the Latin Americans. The United States would now deal with its neighbors as equals and with respect for their sovereignty.

Actually, the United States had begun to modify its interventionist policies prior to Roosevelt's presidency. The Herbert Hoover administration had been responsible for the withdrawal of U.S. troops from Nicaragua in January 1933 and had set 1934 as the date for their withdrawal from Haiti. Nonetheless, it was FDR who gave the policy a name and dramatized the changes. He accelerated the pullout of marines from Haiti and negotiated with Cuba a new treaty repealing the Platt Amendment. (This amendment to the 1903 treaty with Cuba had given the United States the right to intervene in Cuba to protect Cuban security. The Cubans considered this provision an insult.) The United States, however, still maintained rights to the Guantánamo Bay naval base.

Nonintervention

To give official sanction to this new era of cooperation the Roosevelt administration first signed a pledge of qualified nonintervention at the inter-American conference in Montevideo, Uruguay, in December 1933. To the Latin Americans, the test of neighborliness was refraining from intervention, and thus it was quite a triumph to get the U.S. signature on a clause that read: "No state has the right to intervene in the internal affairs of another."[14] Secretary of State Cordell Hull, however, signed with a written proviso that the United States would continue to reserve the right to intervene according to the principles of international law. It was not until 1936, at the Buenos Aires conference, that the United States finally signed without reservation a promise not to intervene "directly or indirectly and for whatever reason, in the internal and external affairs of any other of the Parties."[15] Although not accompanied by the full-blown rhetoric of the Western Hemisphere Idea, this action did serve to generate a mood of hemispheric cooperation that carried into World War II.[16]

There was more to the Good Neighbor Policy—such as the arbitration of border disputes and development of inter-American peacekeeping procedures—but its major impact was to perpetuate the myth of a neighborhood of equals, sharing a common view of the world. Although the policy was a welcome change, it could not erase the record of military and economic intervention that had preceded it. Moreover, a close look at Roosevelt's actions toward Latin America indicates that despite FDR's refusal to send any troops into the region, the United States did not truly abandon its interventionist tendency. The Good Neighbor Policy contributed to the Western Hemisphere Idea but could not sustain it.

Impact on Cuba

Although relations with Latin America improved, the United States, with its disproportionate power and its economic interests, did not break the habit of getting involved in the internal politics of its smaller neighbors. The new attitude toward Cuba, symbolized by the repeal of the Platt Amendment, did not prevent Washington from attempting to bring democratic government to the island. Roosevelt's special envoy in Havana, Sumner Welles, supported the 1933 effort in Cuba to bring to an end the eight-year rule of an unpopular dictator, Gerardo Machado y Morales. Intervention on the side of democracy was termed "friendly advice" by Secretary Hull.[17]

Cuban democracy did not emerge, however. Welles's preference for acting president, General Alberto Herrera, failed to win the support of the army, so Welles selected another candidate, former Foreign Minister Carlos Manuel de Céspedes. In the wake of the political confusion, widespread rioting and strikes erupted, persuading the United States to send two warships to Havana harbor. Roosevelt explained the action as "solely for the purpose of safeguarding and protecting the lives . . . of American citizens."[18] Although the ships did seem to contribute to the restoration of order, the de Céspedes government lasted less than a month. Its collapse on September 5, 1933, resulted in an army rebellion led by a sergeant, Fulgencio Batista. Again, U.S. warships appeared off Havana—this time the force included thirty ships of various sizes. Most of the ships remained for five months until Batista had established control. No troops landed.[19]

Again, the pattern of not-so-subtle political manipulation continued. The new president, Ramón Grau San Martín, had intentions of revolutionary change, but he was not acceptable to Washington and survived only until January 1934. With U.S. "permission," Batista installed an acceptable president, Carlos Mendieta.[20] Elections were held in January 1936, but within a year Batista himself, with U.S. support, had taken overt control of the government. For the next six years, he was the dominant force in Cuban politics. Elected outright in 1940, Batista was a very popular president. He was responsible for a number of reform programs and openly cooperated with the Communist party. The constitution of 1940 was a liberal, social democratic document, and Batista adhered to its provisions, including the one against successive presidential terms.

In the 1944 elections Batista's longtime foe, Grau San Martín, was elected president. Reforms slowed and corruption increased as a series of conservative elected governments seemed unwilling and unable to implement the ideals of the 1933 revolt. Batista reappeared in 1951 as a candidate in the 1952 presidential election. Before the election could take place, however, Batista led a popularly supported coup that ousted the government of Carlos Prío Socorrás. Because the experience with the electoral process had been a discouraging one for the Cuban people, Batista's takeover was generally accepted.

Popular and reformist as he once was, Batista found the political, economic, and class divisions in the country beyond the reach of traditional politics. He became increasingly dictatorial and relied on the army to maintain control. The unsuccessful coup by a group of dissidents led by Fidel Castro on July 26, 1953, pointed to the problems confronting Batista as he attempted, rather brutally, to remain in power.

U.S. involvement in Cuban politics, despite noble intentions, did not produce a stable democracy. The interference did, however, become a unifying target for those Cubans determined to carry out a genuine revolution.

THE RIO PACT AND THE OAS

The unity of the Western Hemisphere that had emerged during World War II lingered in the postwar period. That unity, plus the perception that communism represented a threat to the West, led both to a military alliance between the United States and the Latin American countries and to regional political organization. These efforts have contributed to the Western Hemisphere Idea. Formal treaties and organizations do require some consensus and shared values, but whether they are sufficient evidence of "hemisphere-ism" remains in doubt.

The Inter-American Treaty of Reciprocal Assistance

Known as the Rio Pact, the Inter-American Treaty of Reciprocal Assistance was signed at Rio de Janeiro on September 2, 1947. The signers included the United States and, eventually, twenty-one other states in the hemisphere.[21] The idea of a mutual assistance treaty had been agreed to at a Mexico City conference in 1945, but the delay in making the accord final was due largely to disputes between the United States and Argentina's nationalist leader, Juan Perón. Although no fan of inter-American cooperation, Perón was unwilling to see Argentina left out of the regional grouping. Washington, too, finally came to see the importance of including Argentina in the agreement despite misgivings over Perón's leadership.

The Rio pact was the first joint security agreement entered into by the United States after the war. It preceded the North Atlantic Treaty by two years, but perhaps because of the Rio Pact's vague commitments the treaty did not generate nearly the interest and debate that surrounded the North Atlantic Treaty in 1949. The Rio Pact has been invoked a number of times, usually by the United States, to mobilize resistance to threats from communism.

The treaty gives the image of collaboration and equality: First, it declares that an armed attack against any American country will be considered an attack against all. Each state is to assist in meeting the attack. However, the nature of the assistance, which is to be collectively given, is not stated, nor is the response automatic. Action depends on a meeting of national foreign ministers. This also applies to aggression or threats to peace and security other than from an armed attack. These foreign ministers decide by two-thirds vote on the necessary response.

Given the history of U.S.–Latin American difficulties, an agreement on such a treaty, even with its uncertain obligations, was remarkable. Nonetheless, the Rio Pact was in keeping with the United Nations Charter; indeed, agreements that involved collective security were popular at that time. Of course, it was also consistent both with the U.S. policy of mobilizing anticommunist forces as quickly as possible and with U.S. efforts in the immediate postwar period to take advantage of its strong, successful image as the leader of the free world.

The Organization of American States

An attempt had been made at the 1928 inter-American meeting in Havana to elevate the Pan American Union to a formal organization based on a treaty. The time was not ripe for such a move because of the continuing unilateral U.S. interference in the hemisphere. By

1948, however, the atmosphere was much more conducive to setting up a regional organization. The cooperation during World War II, the lingering noninterventionist theme of the Good Neighbor Policy, along with the models of the United Nations and the Rio Pact, provided an appropriate consensus for creating a formal, treaty-based regional organization.

The Charter of the Organization of American States (OAS) was approved at the Bogotá conference in April 1948.[22] There were twenty-one original members; today there are thirty-one. The charter was an attempt to formalize rules and procedures that had developed in a rather informal and ad hoc fashion over the previous sixty years. Included were references to the basic principles of the inter-American system: (1) the obligation to settle disputes by peaceful means, (2) assistance to each other in the event of external aggression, (3) the importance of "representative democracy" to the "solidarity of the American states," (4) the need for economic cooperation, and (5) recognition of basic individual human rights without regard to race, nationality, creed, or sex.

Articles 15 and 16 of the charter deserve special attention for they reflect values so critically important to the Latin Americans. Article 15 explicitly says: "No state or group of states has the right to intervene directly or indirectly, for any reason whatever, in the internal or external affairs of any other state." Article 16 makes clear that nonintervention applies to more subtle means of influence as well: "No state may use or encourage the use of coercive measures of economic or political character in order to force the sovereign will of another state."

On the surface, adherence to the principles provided the basis for a political community. Awarding these principles the status of a treaty, which would have to be ratified by all governments, seemed to be the culmination of decades of struggle to give meaning to the Western Hemisphere Idea. For the Latin Americans, such an arrangement could be possible only when the United States went beyond the Montevideo (1933) and Buenos Aires (1936) declarations and formally accepted the principle of nonintervention in a treaty, which required approval by two-thirds of the U.S. Senate. For the United States, such an agreement was a mark of achievement in securing a mechanism for unifying the hemisphere without surrendering the opportunity for leadership. In fact, the United States would now have a forum for presenting its views and a device by which it could exert influence over the region.

The actual work of the OAS has not lived up to the expectations of its founders, but it is clear from the charter that the legal and organizational bases for formalizing the Western Hemisphere Idea exist. The reality, not surprisingly, is somewhat different. Members of the organization tend to use the OAS to suit their separate national interests. It can be, as mentioned, an instrument for the United States to give an image of multilateralism to its policies. It can also be used as a means of unifying Latin American opposition to the United States or, as Argentina did in 1982 in its struggle against Britain, as a way of mobilizing opinion behind a particular national cause. As is the case for other international organizations such as the United Nations, the role of the OAS is political: Its influence depends on what the members are willing to allow it to accomplish. With the political center of gravity in the hemisphere traditionally tilted toward the North, the effectiveness of the organization has depended considerably on what Washington is willing to tolerate.

THE ALLIANCE FOR PROGRESS

In President John F. Kennedy's 1961 speech announcing the Alliance for Progress, the idea of shared values formed a rationale for a program designed to promote economic development and political democracy in the hemisphere. With considerable eloquence, Kennedy declared:

> We meet together as firm and ancient friends, united by our determination to advance the values of American civilization. For this new world of ours is not merely an accident of geography. Our continents are bound together by a common history—the endless exploration of new frontiers. Our nations are the product of a common struggle—the revolt from colonial rule. And our people share a common heritage—the quest for dignity and the freedom of man.[23]

The Alliance was to be a $20 billion, ten-year cooperative effort among all American countries to bring political stability and representative government to Latin America. These goals were to be reached through vast reforms of corrupt political systems, a return to constitutional, nonmilitary government, and the political enfranchisement of the masses. The Alliance would promote economic reform by providing funds to improve the infrastructure for industrialization (such as roads and dams) and by collaborating in private investment projects. Economic and social justice would be encouraged by changing the inequitable tax systems, by promoting reform of the antiquated and unequal landholding system, and by providing for schools and health care facilities. It was a grand scheme, accompanied by visionary rhetoric.

Moreover, the Alliance would not be simply another U.S. bilateral aid program. A special committee of prominent economic and political leaders from throughout the hemisphere was established under the aegis of the OAS to review proposals for assistance. Aid was to be granted only when the applicants could show good faith efforts to implement political and economic reforms. It was a novel approach to aid, and by downplaying the U.S. role and by tying the aid, ostensibly, to reform instead of simply anticommunist security, the reputation of Kennedy and the United States improved dramatically in the region.

The endeavor ultimately failed, however. Although the rhetoric of the Alliance was one of cooperation and reform, the actions of the Kennedy administration showed that U.S. priority was being given to its own security interests. In fact, the rather clear premise of the Alliance was that economic and political injustices provided an opportunity for communism. The Cuban model was a glaring example: U.S. tolerance of poverty and suppression in the past and its support of rulers like Batista would lead invariably to Marxist revolutions such as Fidel Castro's. What was needed, Kennedy argued, was evolution, not revolution. But, in my view, a policy that grew essentially out of a fear of Castro and not out of a commitment to genuine political and economic change was bound to lose sight of those long-term objectives.

The other part of Kennedy's policy for containing Castroism was less publicized than the Alliance for Progress; it was military aid. The U.S. approach to revolutions worldwide in the 1960s was a combination of economic aid (the carrot) and military advice and assistance (the stick), and nowhere was this more visible than in Latin America. Because, in the view of the Kennedy administration, the wars likely to threaten the United States would be guerrilla-style movements, the Pentagon was instructed to develop a capacity for counterinsurgency warfare. The "Green Berets," or Special Forces, represented this effort in Southeast Asia. In Latin America the administration's policy primarily took the form of improving the training of local armies to fight guerrillas. An increase in U.S. military assistance, therefore, may have had more to do with the prevention of revolution than did the Alliance for Progress. For example, between 1953 and 1961, U.S. military assistance to Latin America averaged $65.58 million per year. In the first three years of the Kennedy-Johnson administration, military aid increased to an average of $172.3 million per year—more than double the previous rate. Economic aid also increased dramatically, going from an average of $204 million per year during the Dwight

Eisenhower administration to $1.3 billion per year in the 1962–1965 period.[24]

It is possible that the U.S. fear of a repeat of the Cuban revolution elsewhere may have been exaggerated. Although other countries may have had some revolutionary symptoms, their situations were not identical to Cuba's. In Bolivia, for example, efforts by one of Castro's closest advisers, Ernesto (Ché) Guevara, to mobilize Indian peasants into a revolutionary force failed, in part because of their lack of political consciousness. Conditions in northeast Brazil and in Peru might have been ready for revolutions, but the convergence of events that made the Cuban revolt a success was not duplicated. Among the factors that were crucial to the Cuban success was the collapse of the Cuban army; no comparable event occurred elsewhere in the region in the 1960s.

RECENT MANIFESTATIONS

The Caribbean Basin Initiative

In spite of the crumbling of community spirit in the 1960s, the Western Hemisphere Idea continued to be reincarnated. In President Reagan's 1982 speech announcing the Caribbean Basin Initiative (CBI), the sense of unity was bolstered by references to common goals, dreams, and religious values:

> We share a common destiny. We, the peoples of the Americas, have much more in common than geographical proximity. For over 400 years, our peoples have shared the dangers and dreams of beginning a new world. From colonialism to nationhood, our common quest has been for freedom. Most of our forebears came to this hemisphere seeking a better life for themselves; they came in search of opportunity and, yes, in search of God.[25]

Although the president went on to proclaim that the "peoples of the hemisphere are one," and that "we are brothers historically as well as geographically," it seems clear that his policy was largely a unilateral response to what he saw as a growing threat in the Caribbean area from Cuba and the Soviet Union. The CBI was a plan for meeting that threat by promoting economic development in the region through increased trade and private investment. It was an effort generated not through regional organizations, but from Washington itself. In this context, the rhetorical flourishes can be seen as a means of legitimizing U.S. policy. Whether the president's target was the U.S. domestic audience or Latin Americans, his evocation of the community theme perpetuated an image of U.S. benevolence that does little to enhance the credibility of U.S. policy.[26]

The Falklands/Malvinas Issue

Ironically, one of the most independent of the Latin American states, Argentina, saw fit to appeal to regional solidarity when it was locked in combat with Britain over the Falkland Islands (Las Malvinas) in May 1982. Washington's open support for the British was perceived as a virtual betrayal of its hemispheric colleague and of the anticolonialist traditions of the New World. Seldom had any inter-American issue generated so much emotion and frustration between North and South America.[27]

Argentina's suggestion that the Monroe Doctrine was being violated by the British attempt to hold on to its colony revealed the political power of the Western Hemisphere Idea as a symbol. Nations do react to symbols of alliance and friendship, even if those symbols are unsupported by reality, and the U.S. refusal to stand by Argentina undermined Latin American faith in the U.S. commitment to the declared ideal of hemispheric unity. Although the Western Hemisphere Idea did not influence U.S. policy in this episode, it did seem to mobilize the rest of the region. The vote at the OAS in support of Argentina was 17–0, with four abstentions (Chile, Colombia, Trinidad-Tobago, and the United States).

CONCLUSIONS

Other than some geographical proximity, there is little substance in the Western Hemisphere Idea. Even geography is a deceptive measure: Buenos Aires, for example, is farther from Washington than is Moscow. The Spanish-Portuguese political culture inherited by the Latin Americans is different from the Anglo-French republican principles that influenced the United States.[28] The racial, cultural, and class divisions that developed in Latin America as a result of colonialism have not, generally, mirrored the situation in the United States. The obvious differences in size, resources, and power also make it difficult to discern a basis for community between the Latin American nations and the United States. Moreover, the Latin American history of nondemocratic government, military intervention in politics, and vast economic gaps between rich and poor leads to misperceptions and misunderstandings by the United States.

It is important, nevertheless, to remember that Latin America has a Western orientation. Its experiences can be distinguished from those of other developing countries in Africa and Asia. The region's political thought and values, its prevalent religion, and its political and economic models generally reflect the Western tradition, which links Latin America not only with the United States but also with Western Europe. Thus, it is inappropriate to confuse allegiance to Western values and traditions with allegiance to the United States.

In spite of the theme of this chapter that there have been enduring and frustrating disagreements between the United States and Latin America, we cannot overlook the significant sympathy in the region for the values and policies of the United States. For many Latin Americans, the United States has long represented the ideals of political democracy and economic prosperity. The United States, as leader of the free world, has pursued policies throughout the globe that have coincided with the general anticommunist orientation of much of Latin America's populatioin. It is clear that the shared values are strongest among the political, military, and economic elites who have benefited over the years by their association with Washington. Rapport with the elites, however, does not mean that nonmembers of the elites reject U.S. ideals or see the United States as a ruthless piranha dedicated to devouring the hemisphere.

Nevertheless, this rapport does not eliminate the danger of over-estimating the operational effectiveness of the Western Hemisphere Idea. For example, the notion of a single hemisphere—or even a homogeneous Latin America—ignores the diversity of the region. Besides the visible disparities between the United States and Latin America, there are often overlooked, but still major, political, historical, economic, cultural, and racial differences among the Latin Americans themselves. The European heritage and culture of Argentina and Chile, for instance, help account for their traditional sense of independence. Argentina's reluctance to declare war against the Axis powers in World War II could be attributed to its substantial German and Italian ethnic identity.

Guatemala's continuing domestic problems are closely tied to its mountainous terrain and a largely Indian society dominated by a tiny Spanish-oriented elite. Brazil is emerging as a key player in world politics; Mexico and Venezuela are major oil producers, but Bolivia flounders in poverty, bankruptcy, and political frustration. Traditionally included in "Latin" America has been the French-speaking black-populated Haiti, but the neighboring English-speaking Caribbean islands of Jamaica and Trinidad-Tobago are not so clearly included. Although geographically part of the hemisphere, the insular ministates of Barbados, Dominica, Grenada, and St. Kitts-Nevis are not regarded as culturally, historically, or even racially part of the hemisphere; nor are the Dutch- and French-speaking populations of Aruba and Martinique. In fact, only three of the English-speaking Caribbean states are members of the OAS: Barbados, Jamaica, and Trinidad-Tobago. It is important to keep the distinctions in mind when comparing the political and revolutionary processes in a place like Grenada to those in El Salvador or Nicaragua.

As the Falklands/Malvinas episode demonstrated, foreign policy interests may differ as well. Argentina and Chile have typically engaged in a mini–arms race with each other. Peru, too, watches Chile's arms levels; Brazil watches Argentina's. Honduras and El Salvador have a long history of conflict, including a brief war fought in 1969—a war sparked by a soccer match between the countries' national teams. Additionally, there have been disagreements in the hemisphere over relations with revolutionary states. Mexico in the 1960s, for example, insisted on maintaining ties with Cuba, while most of the region joined the U.S. attempt to isolate the Castro regime.

In conclusion, the concept of a distinctive, common mission among the states of the hemisphere remains a persistent and important symbol. However, the diversity of the region, the disparities in power and wealth, and the disputes over foreign policy undermine the reality of the concept. The symbol has created illusions, especially in the United States, about the unity of the hemisphere, and it has come to be viewed by some as a cloak of dubious legitimacy for U.S. intervention. The Western Hemisphere Idea, in short, does not explain U.S. foreign policy.

NOTES

1. For the best review of this concept, see Arthur P. Whitaker, *The Western Hemisphere Idea: Its Rise and Decline* (Ithaca: N.Y.: Cornell University Press, 1954).

2. This pattern is clearly spelled out in Norman Graebner, ed., *Manifest Destiny* (Indianapolis: Bobbs-Merrill, 1968), and in Richard W. Van Alstyne, *The Rising American Empire* (New York: Oxford University Press, 1960).

3. The text can be found in James D. Richardson, ed., *Compilation of the Messages and Papers of the Presidents, 1787–1897* (Washington, D.C.: Government Printing Office [GPO], 1897), 776–789.

4. U.S. Department of State, *Tenth Inter-American Conference, Caracas, Venezuela, March 1–28, 1954*, Publication 5692 (Washington, D.C.: 1955), 8.

5. Ernest R. May, *The Making of the Monroe Doctrine* (Cambridge, Mass.: Harvard University Press, 1975).

6. Harold E. Davis, John J. Finan, and Taylor F. Peck, *Latin American Diplomatic History* (Baton Rouge: Louisiana State University Press, 1977).

7. M. C. Meyer and W. L. Sherman, *The Course of Mexican History* (New York: Oxford University Press, 1979).

8. Gordon Connell-Smith, *The Inter-American System* (New York: Oxford University Press, 1966), 54.

9. Thomas G. Paterson et al., *American Foreign Policy: A History* (Lexington, Mass.: D. C. Heath, 1977), 183–184.

10. Whitaker, *The Western Hemisphere Idea*, 41.

11. Quoted by Arthur P. Whitaker, *The United States and the Independence of Latin America* (Baltimore: Johns Hopkins University Press, 1941), 43.

12. Allison W. Bunkley, ed., *A Sarmiento Anthology* (Princeton, N.J.: Princeton University Press, 1941).

13. Whitaker, *The Western Hemisphere Idea*, 4.

14. U.S. Department of State, *Report of the Delegates of the United States to the Seventh International Conference of American States*, Conference Series 19 (Washington, D.C.: 1934).

15. U.S. Department of State, *Report of the Delegates of the United States to the Inter-American Conference for the Maintenance of Peace* (Washington, D.C.: 1937).

16. For a thorough study of the Good Neighbor Policy, see Bryce Wood, *The Making of the Good Neighbor Policy* (New York: Columbia University Press, 1961).

17. U.S. Department of State, *Foreign Relations of the United States, 1933*, vol. 5 (Washington, D.C.: 1952), 358–359.

18. *Roosevelt's Foreign Policy, 1933–41: Roosevelt's Unedited Speeches and Messages* (New York: Wilfred Funk, 1942), 25.

19. Wood, *The Making of the Good Neighbor Policy*, 77–78.

20. Graham Stuart, *Latin America and the United States* (New York: Appleton-Century-Crofts, 1955), 244.

21. For the text of the treaty, see U.S. Department of State, *Inter-American Treaty for Reciprocal Assistance*, Publication 3390 (Washington, D.C.: 1949). By 1984, there were twenty-two parties to the Rio Pact: Argentina, Bolivia, Brazil, Chile, Colombia, Costa Rica, Cuba (suspended), the Dominican Republic, Ecuador, El Salvador, Guatemala, Haiti, Honduras, Mexico, Nicaragua, Panama, Paraguay, Peru, Trinidad-Tobago, the United States, Uruguay, and Venezuela. Also see J. Lloyd Mecham, *The United States and Inter-American Security, 1889–1960* (Austin: University of Texas Press, 1961).

22. For the text of the charter, see "Report on the Ninth International Conference of American States," *Annals of the OAS*, vol. 1 (Washington, D.C.: 1949), 76–86. The original members were Argentina, Bolivia, Brazil, Chile, Colombia, Costa Rica, Cuba (now in suspension), the Dominican Republic, Ecuador, El Salvador, Guatemala, Haiti, Honduras, Mexico, Nicaragua, Panama, Paraguay, Peru, the United States, Uruguay, and Venezuela. Later members included: the Bahamas, Barbados, Dominica, Grenada, Jamaica, Santa Lucia, St. Kitts-Nevis, St. Vincent and the Grenadines, Surinam, and Trinidad-Tobago. Also see Connell-Smith, *The Inter-American System*.

23. Agency for International Development, "President Kennedy Speaks on the Alliance for Progress," mimeographed (Washington, D.C.: n.d.), 3–4.

24. Agency for International Development, *U.S. Overseas Loans and Grants, July 1, 1945–June 30, 1975* (Washington, D.C.: 1976), 33.

25. Text from *New York Times*, February 25, 1982, 8.

26. For a critique of the notion of shared values, see Edward J. Williams, *The Political Themes of Inter-American Relations* (Belmont, Calif.: Duxbury Press, 1971), 15–21. Also see Lewis Hanke, ed., *Do the Americas Have a Common History?* (New York: Alfred Knopf, 1964).

27. *New York Times*, May 30, 1982, 1.

28. Howard J. Wiarda, "Toward a Framework for the Study of Political Change in the Iberic-Latin Tradition: The Corporative Model," *World Politics* 25 (January 1973), 206–235.

2
THE SPHERE
OF INFLUENCE

The Western Hemisphere Idea has served to justify U.S. policy in Latin America as an endeavor consistent with cooperation and community, but it has also contributed to popular illusions in the United States about shared interests and Latin support for the U.S. view of the world. Some analysts discount the Western Hemisphere Idea as mere rhetorical frosting for the exercise of pure power politics. They explain U.S. policy using a different concept: the *sphere of influence*.[1]

THE CONCEPT

Traditionally, areas adjacent to major powers have been characterized as zones—or spheres—of influence, and Latin America may well fit this description because of its sharing of the Western Hemisphere with the United States. A standard definition is that a sphere of influence is an area "in which one Great Power assumes exclusive responsibility for maintenance of peace . . . it denotes a situation in which one power has acquired a monopoly or near monopoly for its services to that area."[2] A sphere of influence is a region in which a major power has hegemony or preeminence, and from which other major powers are excluded. A common form of control in a sphere is major power intervention, especially when a small country shows signs of independence and of developing ties with another major power.[3]

The concept of sphere of influence is most often associated with the "realist" approach to international relations. This approach contends that all nations pursue power and that relations between nations are based almost entirely on power considerations. Since the pursuit of power is always in the national interest, states constantly seek to promote and protect their strength and influence. National self-interest is all that matters. Adherence to community values, ideology, and moral factors—or even to peace—are possible only when these ideals are congruent with the national interest; they are not pursued for their own sake.[4]

Thus, a U.S. realist would evaluate events in Latin America only in terms of how they affect the United States, not in terms of how they affect the Latin Americans. The realist's approach is not meant to be cynical, but rather to reflect the same reality that the national leadership faces when it assumes responsibility for the security of the nation. What counts in U.S. policy, therefore, is how developments in Latin America contribute to or erode the political, military, and economic interests of the United States. The criterion for judging a policy is how well it promotes the power of the United States, not necessarily how well it promotes other values such as the level of democracy, economic development, or human rights. These factors may at times have an impact on the U.S. national interest, but they take second place to security, exclusive military access, political influence, and stability. Support for a dictator, for example, may not be conducive to democracy, but it may provide for stability and thus an avenue for the exercise of U.S. influence.

A typical means by which a major nation enhances its power, according to the realist conception, is to guarantee that adjacent areas are under its dominance. It can be argued that the establishment of a sphere of influence is an inevitable consequence of great-power status. Great powers have always asserted hegemony over smaller neighbors, and they still do so; we should not expect anything different. Exercising power in a sphere of influence need not require the stationing of troops but may mean armed intervention at times. The great power need not have exclusive control over the adjacent area but tends to have certain rights and privileges recognized by the rest of the world. This status is recognized not because it is "right" or "good," but because it is a predictable and usually unstoppable outgrowth of national power. This status also implies that other major powers will not attempt to intrude or exert unusual influence in the zone.

That Latin America is a sphere of influence for the United States is suggested by the extensive involvement of the United States in the politics and economics of the region and by its proclivity for direct and indirect intervention. The sphere is a frequently used basis for explaining U.S.-Latin American relations, in spite of the impression that the United States does not always *behave* as though it has hegemony. Latin Americans, it has been argued, have sensed that they are in a U.S. sphere, although the actual conduct of U.S. policy has not always conformed to that role.[5]

The Concept Applied to Latin America

Does Latin America qualify as a genuine sphere of U.S. influence? If, as is often done, the region is compared to the Soviet Union's sphere in Eastern Europe,[6] then the concept does not, on the surface, apply very well. For instance, in the past there have been few cases of U.S. troops being permanently stationed in the countries of the region. The clear exceptions are the U.S. naval base at Guantánamo in Cuba and the extensive bases and training facilities in Panama. The air and naval installations in Puerto Rico are also important. In recent times, the continued presence of several thousand U.S. forces in Honduras can no longer be attributed to temporary maneuvers. Clearly, the United States has a considerable capacity for rapid projection of power in the Caribbean area, as President Reagan demonstrated in the October 1983 invasion of Grenada. Perhaps these cases of presence are sufficient to qualify as evidence of a sphere of influence, but they are not comparable to the Soviet military presence in Eastern Europe.

The Latin American states are not truly integrated into a military alliance such as the Warsaw Pact, and the direct control of economics and politics in Latin America by the dominant power is much less evident than in Eastern Europe. Moreover, the case of Fidel Castro's Cuba stands out. How could any self-respecting hegemonial power allow such a deviant in its immediate neighborhood?

There are additional difficulties in applying this concept to Latin America. It may be that the Latin Caribbean and Central America have been a U.S. sphere of influence—the United States has intervened so often there. Nevertheless, assuming that military intervention is a key indicator of dominance, South America would not qualify as a sphere. It could also be argued, however, that U.S. control is so effective, through the use of more subtle, covert, and indirect means, that direct military presence or intervention is not necessary to maintain hegemony. In any event, if the sphere concept is employed, it is important that it be precisely defined and that the criteria for classification be identified. Geographic proximity and historical ties are insufficient by themselves to place Latin America in the same category as Eastern Europe or even Finland.

The behavior of the United States has not always followed a consistent pattern. Occasionally the nation acts as a sphere-of-influence power, as it did in the Dominican Republic intervention of 1965 or in the destabilization of Allende's Chile in the 1970s, but it also defers from operating in that manner when it tolerates Castro's Cuba or seems unwilling to take direct military action against the Sandinistas in Nicaragua. Arming exiles to harass or subvert hostile governments has proved, in these two cases, an inadequate method for maintaining a sphere. Officials may at times act as though the United States intends to maintain control of the region—and most Latin Americans are suspicious enough of U.S. motives to expect the worst—but more often the reality is that Washington has not established the hegemony requisite for a proper sphere of influence.

Abraham Lowenthal's contention is that the "hegemonic presumption" may no longer apply. Because the erosion of U.S. dominance has not been fully acknowledged by Washington, the application of U.S. power, he claims, continues to be insufficient and inappropriate for handling problems in the area. According to Lowenthal:

> The fundamental flaw of U.S. policy toward Latin America and the Caribbean during the past 20 years is not the failure to implement proposed new policies, but the failure to deal with the overriding fact of contemporary inter-American relations: the re-distribution of power. Since the early 1960s, U.S. policy has failed to cope with hegemony in decline.[7]

And still, there is enough U.S. interference in Latin America to rule out a claim that the special relationship has completely vanished. The direct U.S. involvement in El Salvador's domestic politics in the 1980s, the critical U.S. economic ties, and the continued exclusion of serious threats to the region from other major powers all point to some preeminent role for the United States. Again, although U.S. policymakers at times behave as though Latin America is a sphere, paradoxically they do not reconcile such selfish, traditional superpower behavior with U.S. liberal and anti-imperialist values. Because of the tendency in the United States to view the nation's role in the world as unique, as a defender of democracy and independence, it is virtually impossible for policymakers to invoke the more narrow, self-serving image required for a sphere-of-influence policy. As a consequence, policymakers resort to the cold war rationalizations that place the United States in the more acceptable role as leader of the free world. Such a stance relieves the United States of guilt for behaving as a traditional major power interested in controlling its borders and enables its citizens to distinguish between their country and the Soviet Union— a ruthless enforcer that shows no restraint in intervening in Czechoslovakia or Afghanistan.

The next two chapters will review several incidents in which the United States appears to have acted as a sphere-of-influence power. The sphere concept may not always fit, but it can prove to be a useful beginning for understanding the U.S. relationship with Latin America.

THE ROOSEVELT COROLLARY

Nothing better illustrates the sphere-of-influence attitude toward Latin America that emerged in Washington at the turn of the century than President Theodore Roosevelt's Corollary to the Monroe Doctrine. Faced with the possibility of European intervention to collect debts from bankrupt Caribbean countries such as the Dominican Republic, in 1904 Roosevelt drew upon the exclusionary provisions of the Monroe Doctrine to formulate a policy that more appropriately reflected both the new realities of U.S. power and the president's own assertion of the "big stick" in foreign policy. He declared that irresponsibility and instability in the Americas could "ultimately require intervention by some civilized nations, and in the Western Hemisphere the adherence of the United States to the Monroe Doctrine may force the United States, however reluctantly, in flagrant cases of such wrongdoing or impotence, to the exercise of an international police power."[8]

The meaning was unmistakable: Roosevelt was extending the Monroe Doctrine to justify U.S. intervention to prevent European intervention. This ultimatum clearly defined, for Europe and for Latin America, U.S. hegemony in the region. It was an assertion of the United States as both a patron and a policeman. In Roosevelt's eyes, however, it was an inevitable consequence of U.S. responsibility for maintaining order in the Caribbean: "If the Monroe Doctrine did not already exist," he said, "it would be necessary forthwith to create it." U.S. action, he claimed, was "not a matter of law at all [but] a matter of policy."[9]

The words were backed up by a show of naval force off the Dominican Republic's coast, and in 1905, U.S. officials stepped in to take over the country's customs collections in order to guarantee the repayment of debts to both U.S. and European banks.

The precedent of the corollary is far-reaching. It has helped shape U.S. attitudes toward the hemisphere over the past eighty years. The proposition that the United States, in its role as regional policeman, has the right to intervene to prevent intervention has influenced Washington's responses to such modern events as the Guatemalan revolution, Castro's assumption of power in Cuba, and the Nicaraguan revolution. Persuasive as it may be to Washington, to Latin Americans the corollary is a perversion of the Monroe Doctrine and an arrogant presumption of authority by the United States. The corollary continues in force, however, not because it is right or lawful, but because, as Roosevelt himself implied, it is a necessary extension of U.S. power.

CUBA AND THE SPANISH-AMERICAN WAR

Although Roosevelt best articulated the U.S. sphere of influence concept, it originated in the nineteenth century in relation to the island that has come to play such a central role in U.S. policy in the hemisphere: Cuba. It is easy to focus only on Castro's Cuba and to overlook the tangled web of relations preceding Fidel's arrival and binding that island's fate so closely to the United States. I have already mentioned Franklin Roosevelt's repeal of the Platt Amendment and his effort to place U.S. ties with Cuba on a more reasonable and less paternal basis, but to grasp fully the origins of U.S. difficulties with Cuba we need to go back to the early years of the nineteenth century.

A Special Relationship

The special status of this island on the U.S. back doorstep was first acknowledged by Thomas Jefferson, who in 1808 openly opposed a rumored attempt by Spain to transfer the colony to British or French control. Later, as a result of the Mexican War and U.S. acquisition of California in 1848, Cuba's harbors became important for U.S. commercial interests desirous of shipping routes across the Central American isthmus.

But it was the slavery issue that almost brought Cuba into the United States itself. As the South sought to protect its power in the U.S. Congress, the addition of one or two slave states to the Union could have proven to be a vital asset. The outstanding candidate for admission was Cuba, and in 1848 the Polk administration even went as far as to open negotiations with Spain on possible purchase of the island. Although rebuffed by the Spanish, the Cuban annexation issue did not go away: First, adventurers from the United States attempted to "liberate" Cuba, and then, in 1854, the Spanish seized a U.S. ship, the *Black Warrior*, in Cuban waters. In the infamous, but unofficial, Ostend Manifesto of 1854, U.S. diplomats threatened Spain with liberation of the island if Spain refused to sell it. When this threat became public, President Franklin Pierce was compelled to back down, and the effort to negotiate Cuban freedom from Spain faded with the emergence of pre–Civil War tensions.[10]

Impact of the Spanish-American War

The Spanish-American War in 1898 marked the rise of the United States as a major world power. As a result of the war, the United States obtained Puerto Rico, established a protectorate over Cuba, and acquired a colony in the Pacific: the Philippines. Although ostensibly fought to liberate Cuba from Spain, the war was essentially a means by which the United States could gain a foothold in the Pacific. The vision of the nation's new realists was important. Theodore Roosevelt (then assistant secretary of the navy), navy Captain Alfred T. Mahan (who outlined the naval requirements for U.S. entry into world politics), and Admiral George Dewey (commander of the U.S. Pacific fleet) did not see Cuba as the main issue but rather as the catalyst for the war, or perhaps an excuse to build an empire.[11] Nonetheless, in a brief, uncoordinated war, with a poorly equipped army, the United States found itself occupying Cuba.

In accord with the terms of President William McKinley's Declaration of War, which had denied any intention to annex Cuba, Washington did grant the island its independence—but with the restrictive Platt Amendment added to Cuba's constitution. The amendment made it clear that Cuba was not truly sovereign. The government was forbidden to incur a debt beyond its means; it could not allow a foreign power to establish control over any part of the island, but it would agree to lease sites for U.S. naval bases. Furthermore, it allowed the United States the "liberty to intervene for the purpose of preserving order and maintaining Cuban independence."[12]

Not unexpectedly, it was President Theodore Roosevelt who took advantage of the amendment to send troops to Cuba in 1906 to restore order. They were withdrawn in 1909. Roosevelt's comments on Cuba are a useful illustration of an attitude that, in less pejorative words, may well prevail today in Washington:

> I am so angry with that infernal little Cuban republic that I would like to wipe its people off the face of the earth. All that we wanted from them was that they would behave themselves and be prosperous and happy so that we would not have to interfere. And now, lo and behold, they have started an utterly unjustifiable and pointless revolution and may get things into such a snarl that we have no alternative save to intervene—which will at once convince the suspicious idiots in South America that we do wish to interfere after all.[13]

THE PANAMA CANAL

The U.S. acquisition of the Panama Canal Zone and the building of the canal epitomize the U.S. rise to power and the assertion of quasi-imperialism in Latin America.[14] The canal also became a flash point in U.S. diplomacy, an interest that, when threatened even indirectly, has provoked forceful U.S. pressures and interference. In addition, the canal took on such emotional importance that when the decision was eventually made in 1977 to return it to Panama, the act was viewed by some in the United States as tantamount to treason. President Carter had "given our canal away."[15] The obsession with the canal and the consequences of operating it had a number of dimensions: commercial, strategic, symbolic, and political and helped to justify and define a U.S. sphere of influence in the Central American and Caribbean area.

U.S. interest in a canal across the isthmus had originated with the annexation of California in 1848. Once the United States became a two-ocean nation, it was crucial to find a way to connect the two coasts. A connection was particularly important to commercial interests in the eastern states who were seeking to take advantage of the new opportunities for trade with China. China had just been opened to Western commerce by virtue of its defeat by the British in the Opium War of 1839–1842. The discovery of gold in California in 1849 and the length and danger of the sailing voyage to the west coast via Cape Horn intensified interest in an isthmian route. It would be much more expedient to cut across the narrow Central American isthmus. Some goods were shipped overland across Panama and Nicaragua, but this was a difficult and time-consuming route. A canal made better sense. The main factors in the canal history are the rapid identification of the isthmus as vital to the United States, the pattern of intervention and sharp practice that gave the United States control of the canal, and most importantly, the consequences of that behavior for more recent U.S. problems in Latin America.

In 1846, in keeping with the principles of the Monroe Doctrine, the United States signed a treaty with New Granada (an early name for Colombia, which controlled the area known as Panama). By this accord, Washington agreed to help maintain the neutrality of the isthmus, particularly in face of British or other European threats to interrupt free transit of the region. In return, New Granada granted the United States special rights to use the area. Subsequently, U.S. companies constructed the Panama Railway in 1855 to carry freight across the isthmus.

T. Roosevelt and the Canal

The events of 1901–1903 brought the United States the long-sought canal.[16] By that time, U.S. attitudes and interests were clear. Originally, President Roosevelt and Congress had preferred a Nicaraguan route because it was likely to be cheaper and also because a French company, which had been granted a concession by Colombia to build a canal, was asking an exhorbitant price from the United States for the company's rights in Panama. However, intense lobbying by the French company's representative in Washington, Philippe Bunau-Varilla, and the unfortunate—for Nicaragua—eruption of a volcano in Nicaragua convinced Washington to go with the Panamanian route. Negotiations then commenced with Colombia for permission to build and operate a canal.

Colombia demanded more money than the Roosevelt administration was willing to pay. The United States had offered, in March 1903, $10 million plus $250,000 per year for a six-mile wide zone through Panama. Colombia indicated it wanted about $25 million. There was also the prospect that when the French rights expired in 1904, Colombia could sell the United States the French equipment and holdings for $40 million. Impatient with the delays and concerned about his chances in the 1904 election, Roosevelt preferred a more immediate solution.

The U.S. ability to capitalize on Panamanian resentment of the Colombian government turned the tide for Washington. Residents of the isthmus had periodically revolted against Bogotá, and the prospect of losing the canal prompted them to join the United States in the planning of another revolt. The Panamanians, with the help of Frenchman Bunau-Varilla, devised their plot for secession from Colombia in Room 1162 of the Waldorf Astoria Hotel in New York City.[17] There is no evidence of direct U.S. complicity in the affair, although the White House indicated that it would not oppose the independence of Panama. Conveniently, a U.S. warship, the *Nashville,* arrived in Colón, Panama, on November 2, 1903. On November 3, a makeshift army of patriots seized control of the province with almost no bloodshed. Colombian attempts to send in troops to quell the revolt were halted by the U.S. Navy, which was merely carrying out its duties under the 1846 treaty to guarantee Panamanian neutrality. Independence was declared November 4; the new country was immediately recognized by Roosevelt. By November 18, the United States signed a treaty with the government of Panama for the construction of a canal. The treaty provided for the same $10 million payment and $250,000-a-year rent that had been offered to Colombia. The zone, however, was widened to ten miles and the United States was granted virtual sovereignty over the canal.

Did the United States "steal" the canal from Colombia? Was it guilty of excessive intervention because of domestic pressures on the president to get results? Was the episode a reflection of a growing world power asserting its muscle in an area it was determined to dominate? Although the answer to these questions is probably "yes," the fact remains that the canal became a symbol in Latin America of U.S. imperialism. The method by which the canal was obtained and the nature of absolute U.S. control over the zone proved to be a constant source of friction and resentment in the hemisphere. It was not until 1964 that the United States began negotiations to revise the unequal treaty and not until 1977 that the new treaty, ceding the canal back to Panama, was approved by the Senate.

DOLLAR DIPLOMACY

Intervention in Latin America continued after Theodore Roosevelt's "big stick," but under William Howard Taft (1909–1913) and the administrations of fellow Republicans Warren Harding, Calvin Coolidge, and Herbert Hoover in the 1920s, as well as that of Democrat Woodrow Wilson, the motives were more consistent with the creation of an economic zone of influence than with power politics.[18] To Taft and his secretary of state, former corporate lawyer Philander C. Knox, the major purpose of U.S. foreign policy was to protect and promote U.S. business interests abroad. Labeled *dollar diplomacy*, the foreign policy of Taft and Knox treated investments as a key instrument of U.S. influence in the world; Latin America was not alone in being viewed as an area for economic exploitation. However, because it was consistent with their views to use U.S. armed forces to protect U.S. property and commercial interests abroad, the small, neighboring states to the south became vulnerable to military intervention.

The Dominican Republic

In 1912, 750 U.S. Marines were sent to the Dominican Republic to bring enough order for Santo Domingo's international debts to be paid. U.S. officials also arranged for the country's president to resign so that the Dominican congress could elect a man deemed by Washington to be more popular.[19] Over the next four years, the United States supervised a number of elections, but even the Wilson administration in 1916 saw fit to send in marines to keep order.

Wilson, outwardly antibusiness, was caught up in the same syndrome as his Republican predecessors and proved just as aggressive in using force to compel the reimbursement of U.S. banks and investors. In fact, there were more instances of intervention in the Wilson administration than in Roosevelt's and Taft's combined. Wilson was also noted for his intervention in Mexico, but given the ethical nature of that case, it will be discussed in Chapter 6.

In November 1916, the Dominican Republic was declared under U.S. military command, and a U.S. admiral took over as "governor general," dismissed the Dominican congress, and appointed U.S. naval officers to fill cabinet positions.[20] The United States finally withdrew in 1924. Left behind was a history of erratic elections and a well-trained army headed by General Rafael Trujillo. Elected to the presidency in 1930, Trujillo remained in control of the Dominican Republic until his assassination in 1961.

Although the Dominican intervention is but a footnote in the history of U.S. foreign relations, it stands as a major episode in Caribbean history. Intervening in that country, primarily to collect debts, may have been in keeping with the precepts of dollar diplomacy, but it constituted another piece of evidence for those Latin Americans convinced that their nations were at the mercy of the U.S. Marines. Historical experiences such as these can often be magnified as symbols for mobilizing nationalist and anti-U.S. movements.

Haiti

The Dominican Republic's neighbor on Hispaniola, Haiti, was subjected to U.S. intervention by the Wilson administration in 1915. The marines remained until 1934 to oversee payment of debts, to establish a sanitation system, and to instruct the Haitians on democracy. The marines succeeded in the first two goals.[21] The lesson in democracy, however, was forgotten by François "Papa Doc" Duvalier, who, having been elected in 1957, decided in 1964 to proclaim himself "President for Life." Upon his death in 1971, Duvalier's son, Jean-Claude ("Baby Doc"), assumed control of the country without benefit of election.

Nicaragua

Nicaragua was a favorite target for the Taft-Knox dollar diplomacy, in part because of Knox's connection with U.S. mining interests there, but also because of the still-attractive canal route. Eventually Nicaragua became a major concern of U.S. policymakers in the 1920s, and of course, those U.S.-Nicaraguan dealings have helped to shape the reaction of the Sandinistas in the Nicaragua of the 1980s. Because of the importance of Nicaragua today, more detailed discussion of its relations with the United States will follow in Chapter 8.

Subjected to both U.S. dollar diplomacy and sphere-of-influence politics, Nicaragua can serve as a model of how the population of one country can be alienated by a major power. The Taft administration had a difficult time adjusting to the independent, nationalistic, and often authoritarian policies of Nicaraguan dictator, José Santos Zelaya, a Liberal, who had resisted Washington's attempts to control a canal route through his country and who, in 1909, was thought to be negotiating a secret agreement with the British and Japanese to build a canal. Zelaya also sought tighter control over U.S. investors in Nicaragua and arranged to refinance his country's debt through European banks.[22]

The U.S. reaction in 1909 was first to issue a set of guidelines for proper Nicaraguan behavior. These included demands that Nicaragua depend on U.S.—not British—banks. The United States also demanded control, via a U.S. agent, over the Nicaraguan customs house.[23] Zelaya's refusal to accede prompted Washington to encourage the Conservative party opposition to overthrow his government.

In the subsequent civil war, U.S. troops intervened, ostensibly to protect U.S. lives and property, but in reality to help depose Zelaya. By August 1910, the Conservatives, under Adolfo Díaz, took control of the government, and U.S. officials immediately began to supervise the repayment of Nicaragua's foreign debt. When the confused political and economic situation in Nicaragua threatened to undermine U.S. interests, Taft again, in 1912, ordered the marines into the country. For the next thirteen years U.S. armed forces kept the Liberals at bay and propped up a government friendly to U.S. businessmen.[24]

In 1916, the Wilson administration, in an effort to find a way to withdraw the remaining one hundred marines from Nicaragua, managed to obtain Senate approval of the one-sided Bryan-Chamorro Treaty. Among the provisions of this accord, the United States was granted the exclusive right "in perpetuity" and "free from taxation" to build a canal through Nicaragua and the right to build a naval base on the Gulf of Fonseca. In return, the United States would pay Nicaragua $3 million in gold.[25] Wilson could not pass up this opportunity to extend U.S. hegemony in Central America.

The marines were eventually withdrawn in August 1925, but within a month the political system, which had been supervised by the United States since 1912, began to come apart. When the Conservative president, Carlos Solorzano, was deposed, the Liberal vice president, Juan Sacasa, claimed the presidency. Such a development was unacceptable to the Coolidge administration, which immediately turned to America's old Conservative friend, Adolfo Díaz. To guarantee his success, the marines were returned to Nicaragua in December 1926. President Coolidge claimed their presence was to protect U.S. property and business interests.[26] By this time though, Nicaragua was becoming a virtual U.S. colony, a country unable to determine its own political and economic life.

At Coolidge's request, Henry L. Stimson (later Herbert Hoover's secretary of state) headed a mission to try to resolve the Nicaraguan problems. Stimson's report outlined a policy that would be followed over the next four years: U.S.-supervised elections in 1928 and in subsequent years as necessary, the organization of a National Guard, and the retention of a marine presence to keep order. Stimson's attitude was one of a benevolent overseer when he commented on U.S. aid to the Nicaraguans: "For a century we have been the scrupulous protector of their independence, not only against Europe, but sometimes against themselves."[27]

Most of the efforts of the marines went into the futile pursuit of rebel leader Augusto César Sandino. Sandino's forces insisted that they were not opposed to elections but that if Nicaraguans were going to decide their own political future, they should do it without the interference of the U.S. Marines. To assure the world that free elections were possible, Sandino proposed that Latin American observers would be welcome.[28] Nonetheless, the marines stayed. They could not, however, capture Sandino nor completely quell the popular support for his movement. Faced with a frustrating guerrilla-style resistance in Nicaragua and growing criticism at home, U.S. troops began a phased withdrawal in 1929. It was hoped that the U.S.-trained National Guard would be able to maintain order. As for Sandino, he agreed to a conciliation with the government in 1933, but was ultimately betrayed, hunted down, and shot by the *Guardia* in 1934.[29]

Upon finally leaving Nicaragua in 1933, the marines turned over command of the *Guardia* to General Anastasio Somoza García. In three years, Somoza overthrew the government and with the backing of his ruthless National Guard, he, and later his sons, established total control over the country until the revolution of 1979—conducted in the name of Sandino.

CONCLUSIONS

The systematic pattern of U.S. intervention in the Caribbean and Central America from 1898 to 1933 (see Table 2.1) had two major consequences. First, it established a habit of treating the region as an arena where there were no restraints on U.S. power, and where, by virtue of superior military force and economic leverage, the United States could presume the right to control the internal developments of those states. And second, it sowed the seeds for future revolutions.

TABLE 2.1
U.S. Armed Intervention in the Caribbean Area, 1898-1933

Cuba	1898-1902, 1906-1909, 1912, 1917-1922
Dominican Republic	1912, 1916-1924
Haiti	1915-1934
Mexico	1914, 1916-1917
Nicaragua	1909-1910, 1912-1925, 1926-1933
Panama	1903

Intrusions that to North Americans may have been minor—and even beneficial in terms of restoring order—became critical and humiliating events in the minds of Cubans, Nicaraguans, and others.

Latin Americans resent, moreover, not only the interventions themselves but also their political and economic effects. U.S. military forces guaranteed a free hand for U.S. business interests. No government could realistically contemplate controlling, much less nationalizing, U.S.-owned property, or even imposing fair taxes, or attempting to relate private investment to national development. The sense of becoming an economic appendage of the United States through no choice of their own did little to promote the Latin Americans' admiration of U.S. business.

To compound the difficulties, U.S. intervention usually left behind powerful and ruthless dictators, in spite of the proclaimed effort of the marines to promote democracy. The following were part of the legacy of U.S. troops: in the Dominican Republic, Rafael Trujillo; in Nicaragua, Anastasio Somoza; in Cuba, Fulgencio Batista; and in Haiti, François Duvalier. The nondemocratic results of U.S. intervention are made worse by the friendly dealings between the dictators on the one hand and the U.S. armed forces and U.S. business on the other. Thus, the United States has been viewed as responsible not only for bringing some rather brutal characters to power but also for helping to keep them there.

An additional sore point was the means by which the United States gained control of the Panama Canal and its authoritarian rule over the zone. The taking of the canal was an action based not on negotiation and fair dealing, but on power. Power is a key currency in international politics, but if its use is abused, the consequences can be costly. In the case of Panama, the United States eventually did decide to alter the status of the canal and recognize Panamanian sovereignty over it.

U.S. activities in the Caribbean constitute a history of which too few U.S. citizens, including policymakers, are aware, but it is one they should learn. Though the Good Neighbor Policy of the 1930s implied that things had changed, the dictators remained. After World War II the euphoria of inter-American cooperation was soon taking second place to U.S. security interests. Only with Cuba's successful challenge to U.S. hegemony have Latin Americans seen a prospect for modifying their relations with Washington. And yet, the Cuban model has many risks, from a strong U.S. reaction on the one hand, to Soviet dependency on the other. In the final analysis, however, the turmoil in the 1980s in Latin America may well be a case of inevitable historical dynamics, or as the saying goes, a case of the chickens coming home to roost.[30]

NOTES

1. For example, see Samuel Flagg Bemis, *The Latin American Policy of the United States* (New York: Harcourt, Brace, 1943), and Edy Kaufman, *The Superpowers and Their Spheres of Influence* (New York: St. Martin's Press, 1976).

2. George Modelski, *Principles of World Politics* (New York: Free Press, 1972), 156.

3. Kaufman, *The Superpowers and Their Spheres.*

4. The realist doctrine is spelled out in Hans Morgenthau, *Politics Among Nations* (New York: Alfred A. Knopf, 1976).

5. Trygve Mathisen, "Factors Promoting Spheres of Influence," *Cooperation and Conflict* 8 (April 1973), 160.

6. Charles Goochman and James Lee Ray, "Structural Disparities in Latin America and Eastern Europe, 1950–1970," *Journal of Peace Research* 16:3 (1979), 231–254.

7. Abraham Lowenthal, "Change the Agenda," *Foreign Policy* 52 (Fall 1983), 64–77; also see Lowenthal, "The United States and Latin America: Ending the Hegemonic Presumption," *Foreign Affairs* 55 (October 1976), 199–213. Another author claims that the decline in U.S. influence undermines any attempt today to label U.S. policy in the region as "imperialist." See Tony Smith, *The Pattern of Imperialism* (Cambridge: Cambridge University Press, 1981), 211–214.

8. *Congressional Record,* 58th Cong., 3d Sess. (December 6, 1904), 19.

9. Roosevelt's statements are quoted in Howard K. Beale, *Theodore Roosevelt and the Rise of America to World Power* (New York: Collier Books, 1956), 368–369.

10. Norman Graebner, ed., *Manifest Destiny* (Indianapolis: Bobbs-Merrill, 1968), 285–293.

11. For an overview of these events and ideas see Beale, *Theodore Roosevelt.*

12. *Foreign Relations of the United States, 1904,* vol. 1 (House Document), 58th Cong. 3d Sess. (Washington, D.C.: 1905), 243–246.

13. Quoted by Thomas A. Bailey, *A Diplomatic History of the American People* (New York: Appleton-Century-Crofts, 1964), 500.

14. For a survey of U.S. involvement in the canal, see David McCullough, *The Path Between the Seas: The Creation of the Panama Canal, 1870–1914* (New York: Simon and Schuster, 1977).

15. Indicative of this attitude is Representative Philip Crane's treatment of the canal issue in *Surrender in Panama* (New York: Dale Books, 1978).

16. McCullough, *The Path Between the Seas.*

17. Ibid., 352, 357.

18. Dana Munro, *Intervention and Dollar Diplomacy in the Caribbean, 1900–1921* (Princeton, N.J.: Princeton University Press, 1964). For a broader overview, see Lester D. Langley, *The Banana Wars: An Inner History of American Empire, 1900–1934* (Lexington: University of Kentucky Press, 1983).

19. *Foreign Relations of the United States, 1912* (House Document), 62d Cong. 2d Sess. (Washington, D.C.: 1919), 366; *Foreign Relations of the United States, 1913* (House Document), 62d Cong. 2d Sess. (Washington, D.C.: 1920), 425, 449.

20. Senate Select Committee on Haiti and Santo Domingo. *Hearings,* pt 1, 67th Cong., 1st Sess. (Washington, D.C.: 1921), 90–94.

21. *Report of the President's Commission for the Study of Conditions in the Republic of Haiti* (Washington, D.C.: 1930).

22. For a review of this period, see Thomas W. Walker, *Nicaragua: The Land of Sandino* (Boulder, Colo.: Westview Press, 1981), 15–20. Also see Bemis, *The Latin American Policy.*

23. *Foreign Relations of the United States, 1911* (House Document) 62d Cong. 1st Sess. (Washington, D.C.: 1918), 661–662.

24. *Foreign Relations, 1912,* 1032, 1043. Also see Edwin Lieuwen, *U.S. Policy in Latin America* (New York: Praeger, 1965), 44–46; and Walker, *Nicaragua,* 18–20.

25. Thomas A. Bailey, "Interest in a Nicaraguan Canal, 1903–1931," *Hispanic American Historical Review* 16 (Fall 1936), 2–28.

26. James W. Gantenbein, ed., *The Evolution of Our Latin American Policy: A Documentary Record* (New York: Columbia University Press, 1950), 626; also see William Kammen, *A Search for Stability: United States Diplomacy Toward Nicaragua, 1925–1933* (Notre Dame, Ind.: University of Notre Dame Press, 1968).

27. Henry L. Stimson, *American Policy in Nicaragua* (New York: Charles Scribner's Sons, 1927), 94.

28. U.S. Department of State, *Foreign Relations of the United States, 1928,* vol. 3 (Washington, D.C.: 1943), 569.

29. Walker, *Nicaragua,* pp. 20–23; and Neill Macaulay, *The Sandino Affair* (Chicago: Quadrangle Books, 1927).

30. For a forceful statement on this theme, see Walter LaFeber, *Inevitable Revolutions: The United States in Central America* (New York: W. W. Norton, 1983).

3
THE SPHERE
OF INFLUENCE
IN THE COLD WAR

THE CARIBBEAN ZONE

Using the sphere-of-influence approach is worthwhile, as we have seen, to explain U.S. policy in Latin America in the 1898–1933 era. It may also be a useful method of analyzing three recent cases of U.S. intervention: Guatemala in 1954, Cuba in 1961, and the Dominican Republic in 1965. Because U.S. action in each of these incidents became wrapped up in the goals and rhetoric of the cold war contest with communism, the application of the sphere approach takes on a different character.

In Latin America, direct U.S. military intervention has occurred only in the Caribbean area, i.e., the region composed of the island nations in the Caribbean Sea and the bordering states of Central America. Although U.S. naval forces have exerted pressure in Venezuela and Chile—both outside of the Caribbean zone—U.S. ground forces have not been sent into any nation south of Panama. This suggests that it is the Caribbean that constitutes a sphere of influence, not necessarily all of Latin America.

It is odd that scholars and policymakers seldom make the distinction between the Caribbean area and the rest of the hemisphere. One who did, in the 1940s, was Samuel Flagg Bemis, who explicitly identified the region as vital to U.S. protection of the Panama Canal and as an area where intervention could be strongly justified.[1] Another analyst, J. Lloyd Mecham, identified a "Caribbean consciousness" in the United States that has emerged as a result of years of political and economic interests in the region.[2] These views, however, are not typical of most scholarship on Latin America, which tends to classify the entire hemisphere as being within the U.S. sphere. Even among policymakers the tendency is to make no distinction. When crises in the Caribbean arose, for example, during the cold war, there was virtually no public attempt to articulate a Caribbean policy. Instead, events were treated as broadly Latin American in nature or simply placed in the context of the cold war without reference to geography.[3]

It is evident that although U.S. behavior in the Caribbean has been consistent with action toward a sphere of influence, there is little acknowledgment of this phenomenon. In part the acknowledgment may be lacking because of certain perceptions: U.S. interests are hemisphere-wide, and it is merely coincidental that military interventions have occurred exclusively in the Caribbean. Or if U.S. leaders were to speak of the Caribbean as a zone of special influence, this would suggest a selfish, power-politics role that is out of keeping with the myths of U.S. policy and the prevailing attitudes of the public. It is more acceptable to characterize the relationships as those of a good neighbor or as a hemispheric partner in the struggle against communism.

Although the Caribbean/Central American region may retain the characteristics of a sphere of influence, global strategic and ideological considerations are what have generated U.S. intervention in the post-1945 period. The sphere approach by itself, therefore, is probably inadequate to explain fully U.S. actions. What made the problems in Guatemala, Cuba, and the Dominican Republic so threatening to Washington was not simply their destabilizing potential, but the perceived link of the problems to the USSR.

Implications for Today

For students of U.S. involvement in Central America and the Caribbean, the cases of Guatemala, Cuba, and the Dominican Republic provide a basis for analyzing contemporary policies. It is clear that U.S. reactions to problems in Grenada, El Salvador, and Nicaragua share many characteristics with the responses to the three interventions in the 1950s and 1960s. Moreover, these cases of U.S. policy toward revolutions may help one to understand the recent suspicions—even the paranoia toward the United States—in Managua. The examples are important, therefore, and may well point to a pattern that continues in U.S. policy and may help explain Latin perceptions of it.

A comparison of the results of these incidents is also instructive: In each case the outcome is different and the impact on U.S. interests is not entirely negative. In fact, not every action of the United States in Latin America results in an undermining of U.S. influence or in a repudiation of democratic principles. The lessons learned about revolutions from the experiences in Guatemala, Cuba, and the Dominican

Republic, however, may not have always contributed to U.S. policy wisdom. These three cases are still significant factors in shaping U.S.–Latin American relations.[4]

GUATEMALA

The case of U.S. covert intervention in Guatemala in 1954 was the first genuine test of the U.S. effort to keep communism out of the Americas.[5] Besides the fear of communism, an instinctive desire to protect U.S. economic interests motivated U.S. action. Moreover, Guatemala's strategic location: bordering Mexico and near the sea routes to the Panama Canal, made it too close to allow even the semblance of communism to emerge—especially when U.S. property was being threatened by nationalization. Although the United States is likely to oppose leftist governments and their economic systems anywhere in the world, it is not likely to intervene unless the problems occur in areas deemed vital to U.S. security.

What makes the Guatemalan case interesting, aside from the covert machinations involved, is how the problem came to be perceived as so threatening when the events leading up to the "crisis" appear to have been so inauspicious. In retrospect, the "threat" seems to have been simply a result of the democratic process working its difficult way through Guatemalan politics and culture. For thirty years after the U.S. repression of the threat in 1954, Guatemala experienced no democracy.

The Prelude

This story has a modest beginning, one that does not foretell the ultimate outcome. Following the bloodless revolution of 1944, Guatemala adopted a democratic constitution. it marked the coming to power, for the first time, of the new Guatemalan middle class of teachers, doctors, lawyers, small-business people, and mestizos (those of mixed Spanish and Indian blood). The revolution was a repudiation of over a century of rule by a series of right-wing strongmen who governed on behalf of a landed elite directly descendant from Spaniards. In December 1945 in Guatemala's first democratic election, a former teacher, Juan José Arévalo, was chosen as president, with more than 85 percent of the vote.

Arévalo's program of reform was based on broad social democratic principles. The program included competition among political parties, free speech and press, labor union organization, land reform, and control of foreign investment. The major obstacle to the last two points was the United Fruit Company, a U.S.-owned corporation whose impact on the Guatemalan economy was immense. It controlled large tracts of usable agricultural land for its banana plantations; it was the major source of revenue and foreign exchange for the government; it was the country's largest single employer; and the country's only railway system was a company network used primarily for hauling bananas.[6] For the Guatemalan government to gain any influence over this enterprise meant a head-on confrontation with a powerful company backed by the U.S. government.

Arévalo's attempt to break up some of the huge coffee plantations and to distribute land to small farmers led him to a clash with the country's landed aristocracy, and in turn, with its allies in the United States. As sympathetic to the democratic reforms as Washington appeared to be, an attack on private property and foreign investment was bound to arouse concern. A complicating factor was Arévalo's attempt to gain protection for labor, including agricultural workers, most of whom were Indians. The United States became more wary when Arévalo took his ideas to inter-American conferences: In Mexico City in 1945, he urged the states of the Americas to join in isolating the nondemocratic regimes in the hemisphere. He repeated this theme in Bogotá in 1946. Neither the United States nor the rest of Latin America rallied to Arévalo's cause.[7]

Internal opposition to Arévalo's reforms began to crystallize by 1948; for example, rebels found it possible to obtain arms from such sources as the United Fruit Company.[8] The government, however, survived, and Guatemala's second election was successfully carried out on November 30, 1950. One of the leaders of the 1944 revolution, the former army captain Jacobo Arbenz Guzmán was elected president. Carrying out Arévalo's reforms was Arbenz's major goal, and in his inaugural address, in March 1951, he promised "to convert our country from a dependent nation with a semi-colonial economy to an economically independent country." He reiterated the need for control of foreign investment and for the redistribution of land.[9]

It was the agrarian reform bill of 1952 that may have marked the turning point for the Arbenz administration. On the one hand, the reform promised to provide land and work for much of Guatemala's rural population. It held out hope that some uncultivated lands held by huge companies would be used to produce food for local consumption rather than coffee and bananas for export. In its first eighteen months, the program distributed 1.5 million acres to more than 100,000 families. The land had not been nationalized but purchased with government bonds.[10]

On the other hand, the land reform's impact on United Fruit provoked a sudden effort to suppress the Arbenz program. In 1953, the government had seized 210,000 acres of uncultivated plantation land and had compensated United Fruit with US$672,572 in bonds, based on the company's own assessment of the land's tax value. United Fruit's protests that the compensation was $15 million short received little sympathy from the Guatemalan government. The company had been victimized by its own practice of deliberately undervaluing its property. The government was paying United Fruit $2.99 per acre; the company had originally paid $1.48 per acre and now wanted $75.00 per acre. Failing that, United Fruit took its case to Washington.[11]

The United Fruit Company's intensified efforts to halt the Guatemalan land reform, as well as the passage of additional labor and tax laws, escalated into a major showdown with what was perceived as communism in Central America. The company may have been concerned only about its investments, but the U.S. government, persuaded that more was at stake, undertook a major covert operation to overthrow the government. Its success would have a continuing influence on U.S. policy in Latin America.

Covert Action

It was not difficult to convince Washington of a communist threat in Guatemala. The antics of United Fruit's public relations man, Edward Bernays, coupled with Secretary of State John Foster Dulles' anticommunism, practically guaranteed U.S. intervention. To Washington officials, leftist-inspired instability so close to Mexico and the canal could not be tolerated.

The seeds of intervention were first sown by Bernays as early as 1950 when he warned United Fruit of the growing communist threat to its properties in Guatemala. Bernays then set about to convince not only his company, but the press and the U.S. government as well, that the Arévalo/Arbenz policies were a menace to capitalism.[12] It took Arbenz's land expropriations in 1953 to give credibility to Bernays' cause. Assisting Bernays in Washington was a former aid to Franklin D. Roosevelt, Thomas B. Corcoran, a lobbyist with close ties to all levels of government, including the Central Intelligence Agency (CIA). With someone of Corcoran's impressive credentials on the United Fruit team, its case gained an unparalleled reception in Washington— and a cover of respectability.

While the lobbying and public relations campaign was building, the CIA and the Department of State were also contemplating action in Guatemala, not necessarily to save United Fruit, but to contain the apparent spread of communism. In fact, there had been misgivings in Washington about the course of events in Guatemala from the days of the 1944 revolution. As early as 1948, the State Department had produced a report entitled "Communism in Guatemala." Richard Immerman's summary of that confidential document provides a revealing insight into the perceptions of U.S. policymakers in the early days of the cold war when communism was seen as being capable of threatening the United States anywhere in the world. The report assumed that the reforms introduced by Arévalo were evidence of Marxist ideology and communist infiltration. It was taken for granted that the Guatemalan labor movement was led by Communists.[13]

The threat was not sufficient to persuade Harry Truman to intervene, though. There is evidence that the president cancelled a CIA plan in 1952 to overthrow Arbenz with the help of Nicaragua's Anastasio Somoza—who had apparently been the first to propose the scheme.[14]

With the arrival of the Eisenhower administration in 1953, United Fruit and the anti-Arbenz forces were able to put their schemes into action. Secretary John Foster Dulles and Allen Dulles, his brother, director of the CIA, both had personal and family ties to companies doing business in Latin America, including United Fruit. In fact, United Fruit's connections with the Eisenhower administration went quite deep.[15] For these people, committed to a hard-line position on the containment of communism, the formulation and implementation of an intervention was virtually preordained.

The plan to depose Arbenz got under way in the summer of 1953. Cloaked in extensive secrecy, the CIA began the process of assembling Guatemalan exiles and mercenaries in Florida and the Canal Zone, and later in Nicaragua and Honduras. Every attempt was made to minimize the participation of the United States. This was to be a "liberation" of Guatemala by Guatemalan "patriots." Among those running the show from the CIA were Director Dulles, Deputy Director for Covert Action Richard Bissell, Tracy Barnes, Rip Robertson, and Howard Hunt—all of whom would be playing similar roles in the ill-fated 1961 Bay of Pigs invasion of Cuba.

Accompanying the covert operation was a widespread propaganda campaign in the United States to discredit the Arbenz government and to link it to international communism. Latin opposition was rallied at the 1954 Caracas inter-American conference. The final resolution adopted there classified communism as a threat to the hemisphere, although Guatemala itself was not singled out.[16] The selling of the communist threat was so effective that even scholarly works written soon after the intervention echoed the official line.[17] There is little evidence of public or even private dissent among the press and scholars or in the executive branch and Congress. As secret as the operation was, Washington was acting in a permissive environment, one that implicitly sanctioned any action necessary to remove Arbenz.[18]

Giving some credibility to administration claims of a communist beachhead on the American continents was the arrival in Guatemala, on May 15, 1954, of a shipment of arms from Czechoslovakia. Arbenz's purchase of arms from Eastern Europe could have been justified by the 1948 U.S. suspension of arms sales to Guatemala and Washington's successful effort in closing the door to other Western arms sources. Moreover, arming Guatemala's forces seemed a logical step for Arbenz in light of the growing hostility to his government from groups both within and outside of the country. The arms shipment, however, gave Washington the grounds for an intervention, and both the president and the secretary of state made strong public statements accusing Arbenz of paving the way for a "communist dictatorship" in the middle of the hemisphere and within sight of the Panama Canal.[19]

The Invasion

Selected to lead the intervention force training in Nicaragua and Honduras was Carlos Enrique Castillo Armas, a former Guatemalan army colonel who had plotted a coup in 1949 and had fled Guatemala in 1951. As the date for the invasion approached, fighter aircraft, some flown by CIA pilots from the United States, buzzed Guatemala City; others dropped propaganda leaflets warning of a revolution, and radio broadcasts bombarded the country with rumors of a patriotic liberation. Every attempt was made to give the impression that the liberation force possessed considerable military might and numbers. This image building worked. In both Guatemala and the United States, press reports and popular impressions had Castillo Armas leading thousands. In fact, there were never more than four hundred men in the invasion force.[20]

A key element in the U.S. strategy was to undermine the Arbenz government psychologically. Economic pressures, propaganda, military threats—including arms shipments to Honduras—and internal agitation were designed to weaken support for the government so much that the intervention would be only the final blow. The strategy largely succeeded. Confusion and paranoia in Guatemala was rampant; the military was increasingly backing away from Arbenz.

The invasion began on June 18, 1954. The liberation forces were met by unexpected resistance from Guatemalan troops and the anticipated popular uprising did not welcome them. When the forces crossed the border, CIA aircraft with U.S. pilots provided only modest help, and in the first three days the operation fared poorly. Its amateurism was showing. Eisenhower, however, approved sending in additional aircraft, and the invasion was saved. Convinced (to a great extent by CIA propaganda) that a massive attack on the capital was imminent, the army and the people lost the will to resist, and Arbenz stepped down on June 27.[21] In ten days, Castillo Armas's forces never penetrated more than a few miles into the country.

Conclusions

Castillo Armas was immediately selected as president and recognized in Washington. Guatemala's next free election was not until 1985. However, in sphere-of-influence politics, what counts is the protection of U.S. interests, not whether elections are held. In the short term, the United States achieved its goals. United Fruit could return to Guatemala with relative freedom to conduct its business as usual. Washington had a friendly government in power, one willing to keep tight control over presumed communist threats. The friendship was so close that in 1961 Guatemala allowed its territory to be used to train Cuban exiles for the invasion of their homeland.

Although U.S. complicity was not admitted, most Latin Americans had no difficulty drawing the conclusion that the United States had been behind the invasion. In the game of power politics such messages, even when implicit, are quite valuable. The Guatemalan action was a demonstration that the United States would tolerate neither leftist regimes nor an economic nationalism that threatened U.S. security interests or U.S.-owned companies. Presumably, by dampening the prospects for a revolutionary victory in Latin America, the United States had quashed the hope upon which revolutions depend.

Another consequence of the intervention was to elevate Guatemala into an instructional model on how to control or overthrow "communist" governments. The same strategy and tactics, the same plans and words, and even the same people reappeared in 1961 in the effort to depose Fidel Castro. Not having learned from that failure, Washington resurrected the same model for use against the Sandinistas in Nicaragua in 1981.

There were other effects, too. The model's influence on Castro and the Cubans was to suggest that U.S. intervention is inevitable, and it convinced the Nicaraguans that the United States would attempt to overthrow the Sandinistas. Thus, the impact of Guatemala cut two ways. It did restore a pro-U.S. regime, but it kindled a fear and resentment that undermined U.S. credibility throughout the region. It certainly enabled threatened governments to justify large expenditures for arms.

The decisive action against Arbenz also demonstrated that the United States was unwilling to give revolution a chance in Latin America. Rather than work with the process and try to ameliorate its negative effects through negotiations and patience, the United States preferred to take no chances. The cost of living with the Guatemalan revolution was perceived as higher than the cost of halting it.

In terms of explanatory approaches, the Guatemalan case is so overwhelmed by global ideological and economic interests that it is inadequate to rely solely on the sphere-of-influence perspective. The proximity of Guatemala was certainly a critical factor in moving the United States to action, but other nonregional concerns were just as important in determining policy.

THE BAY OF PIGS

The euphoria and self-confidence that followed the triumph in Guatemala led the United States into a humiliating defeat seven years later on the beaches of Cuba's Bay of Pigs. U.S. relations with Fidel Castro's Cuba have been stormy, contentious, and emotional. Castro's continued presence ninety miles off the coast has become an obsession with the United States, a bête noire that has plagued U.S. politics and presidents since Castro took power on January 1, 1959.

Background

As we saw in Chapter 2, Cuba had long been treated as a virtual satellite of the United States. A protectorate of the United States from 1898 to 1933, Cuba even with full independence was not immune from U.S. influence. Washington meddled in Cuban politics, openly supported Batista, and promoted U.S. business interests in the country. Cuba was a star attraction for conventioneers in Miami, who could spend evenings in Havana taking advantage of the city's widespread prostitution and gambling. A corrupt and dictatorial regime benefited from extensive U.S. investments, especially in sugar plantations. In 1958 U.S. companies owned 37 percent of Cuba's sugar production (Cubans owned 62 percent) and therefore controlled the North American market. U.S. private investment in Cuba was worth $955 million in 1959. In 1955, 40 percent of Cuba's banks were foreign owned.[22]

Cuba's economic condition in the mid-1950s was extremely fragile. An unstable economy, tied to volatile sugar prices—over which the

Cubans had no control—was the breeding ground for revolutionary sentiment. The gap between upper and lower classes widened in spite of heavy North American investments in manufacturing enterprises. The upper classes exported much of their profits and wealth (an amount estimated at $312 million in 1955) rather than investing it at home. Little concern was shown by large landowners in using land for food production. Thus, only 22 percent of the arable land was being cultivated.[23] The poverty and unemployment, the lack of Cuban control of land and industries, the rampant crime and vice in Havana, and political repression by the Batista regime were increasingly being blamed on the United States. The history of U.S. involvement in Cuba and the prominent visibility of the U.S. presence lent a high degree of credibility to that perception.

Much has been written about Castro's revolution.[24] In those accounts, there are a number of persistent questions that are directly related to the United States. First, was Fidel a Communist when his movement began on July 26, 1953? If not, when did he decide to become one and thereby link his revolution's future to the USSR? Did the United States drive Castro into the arms of the Soviets? Was Castro a threat to the United States, and was there ever an opportunity to negotiate a settlement with him? Did the United States genuinely try to work out a mutually acceptable coexistence pact with Cuba? Absolute answers to these questions are not available. The way in which Washington, however, chose to confront these issues helped propel the United States into an irreconcilable conflict with Cuba.

Central to understanding the attitudes contributing to the Bay of Pigs is the nature of the threat posed by Castro. Most sources seem to agree that when Castro's guerrilla operation began, he was not a Communist. Although he had Communist associates such as Ché Guevara and his brother Raul, there is no evidence that Fidel himself was a party member or that he had even made a decision to align with the Communists in Cuba. He may have been a Marxist-Leninist in his interpretation of history and of the role economic imperialism played in Cuba's past, but that would have been typical of many Latin American intellectuals and activists who would not wish to be part of a rigidly disciplined party. Fidel's earliest writings and speeches indicated a goal of restoring the democratic constitution of 1940, with its provisions for elections, to its rightful place in Cuba.[25]

In general, Castro's statements of 1956 to 1958 were moderate pleas for all dissenting forces in Cuba to join together against Batista. (Castro's group of guerrillas was only one of several factions opposing Batista.) The primary goal of the Fidelistas was to depose Batista and disband the army. Little was mentioned about expelling U.S. businesses, but the economic nationalism of the movement was not hard to detect.

U.S. officials knew little of Castro's movement in its early days, and there was considerable debate about its direction and the appropriate U.S. response. The Department of State apparently was willing to accept the inevitability of the revolution and to pull away from identification with Batista. The prospect of a dictator being replaced by a "democrat" offered an unusual opportunity for the United States to be on the side of the masses. Eisenhower's "wait and see" policy took the atypical step in early 1958 of cutting off all U.S. arms shipments to the Batista regime. This was the turning point for the Cuban army; its support for Batista dissipated rapidly. By its brutal efforts to control the guerrillas, the army had already alienated the population; now there remained little will for the soldiers to continue the fight.

When Castro came to power, it was with the backing of a wide variety of groups representing all those who had suffered at the hands of Batista or who had been alienated from the established order by economic poverty and political repression. It was not a communist revolution, although Fidel had, in mid-1958, apparently come to terms with the Cuban Communist party on its joining in the revolution. Even as late as November 1959, the CIA did not classify Castro as a Communist; however, it did point to the party's pleasure about Fidel's willingness to let the Communists operate freely.[26]

Jousting with Castro

The debate over policy toward Castro picked up steam in Washington in spite of the quick recognition bestowed on his government. Ambassador Earl Smith claimed that he recommended against any toleration of Castro. In his memoirs, Smith asserted that in 1959 he urged that action be taken against Castro out of fear that Cuba would become a Soviet base and that the Caribbean would grow into a "Communist lake." The United States, he argued, had "a duty and obligation" to intervene if necessary to prevent a communist takeover.[27]

The Eisenhower administration was openly wary of Castro's anticapitalist, nationalistic rhetoric. The United States is not very comfortable with revolutionary enthusiasm, especially when it is so close to home and aimed at so many North American companies. The U.S. response was clumsy. Initially, there were official statements of support and appreciation and even a recognition of Cuba's right to expropriate property with fair and prompt compensation. However, Castro's hostility and suspicions toward the United States and its companies, combined with doubts in Washington about Fidel's commitment to democracy, made it very difficult for the Eisenhower administration to develop any consensus for accommodation.

At the invitation of some U.S. newspaper editors, an outwardly friendly Castro visited New York and Washington in April 1959. Although a popular success, the visit marked the onset of a deterioration in official relations. Castro was applauded by crowds on the streets; he charmed members of Congress, and in interviews on national television, he indicated that he was a noncommunist nationalist and that he had no plans to expropriate U.S. property. All was not rosy, however. Castro was publicly criticized by some members of Congress for his communist affiliation and he had a testy confrontation with Vice President Richard M. Nixon.[28] Nixon, who had built his reputation on anticommunist campaigns, was substituting for the president who was golfing in Georgia when Castro arrived in Washington. Nixon met the fatigue-clad Cuban in a private session about which there is little firsthand knowledge. Apparently, the vice president lectured Castro on the evils of communism and quizzed him about free elections and fair trials for his opponents. Fidel, it has been suggested, tried to explain about poverty and land reform. Afterward, Nixon concluded that every attempt should be made to remove him from power.[29]

Much has been made of this visit as a turning point. On the one hand, it is treated as a missed opportunity to seek accommodation with Fidel and to extend support and aid for his reforms.[30] The contention is that if Nixon and others had been more forthcoming and less condescending toward the revolution, Fidel's fears and suspicions about the United States would have been allayed. On the other hand, the fact that Castro did not ask for money was significant. To receive aid from Washington was to run the risk either of re-creating those ties of dependence the revolution was rejecting or of corrupting the revolution. Moreover, Castro was probably aware that Congress and the State Department would not support an aid program to any country taking over U.S. businesses. Fidel's message seemed to be that the Cubans would handle their own affairs, without U.S. help.

Much of the impulse behind the revolution, of course, was to wipe out U.S. dominance over Cuban life. Revolutions are not compromises; they seek to overturn the old order completely and to purge the country of all vestiges of former repression. The United States was closely identified with the old order; thus Cuba's relationship with Washington could not be collaborative, at least not in 1959. Not long after the revolution, the United States had embarked on an operation that would drive Castro even further from rapprochement. By mid-1959, Cuba's nationalism and socialism, along with CIA plots for overthrowing Castro, had put into motion a series of rapidly escalating tensions from which there would be no recovery.

No doubt aware of the U.S. action in Guatemala, Castro appeared to be attempting to minimize direct confrontation with the United States. Castro *expected* a move against his revolution; it was an inevitability for which Cuba would have to prepare.[31]

To make matters worse, eighty Cubans were intercepted in Panama, in April 1959, in an apparent attempt to export the revolution. In June, a similar adventure against the Trujillo regime in the Dominican Republic was defeated in about two days.[32] Not to be outdone, Trujillo launched an abortive attack on Cuba in August 1959. In addition, Radio Havana began broadcasting revolutionary and anti-imperialist propaganda to Latin America. Fidel had become a heroic figure throughout the region.

The Anti-Castro Campaign

Cuba's revolutionary program remained vague throughout 1959 perhaps because Castro himself was uncertain about its precise shape. By early 1960, however, a series of attacks on U.S. economic interests began. These interests were easy targets because they were concrete symbols of dependency. Cuba's economy was dependent on the sale of nearly all its sugar to the United States, which often purchased it at prices above the world market. Sugar sales to the United States were estimated at $153 million in 1959. Moreover, 70 percent of Cuba's imports were from the United States.[33] Some U.S. property had been seized in 1959, but it was Castro's takeover of the U.S.-operated hotels and a mining company that seemed to intensify U.S. protests about the lack of adequate compensation. The right to expropriate was not explicitly challenged.

Stronger reaction, however, was provoked by Castro's signing, in February and March 1960, trade agreements with the Soviet Union. Moscow agreed to buy most of Cuba's sugar, at the world price, and the Soviets and East Europeans would provide Cuba industrial goods, oil, and arms. An arms buildup began in June. The United States had not lifted the 1958 arms embargo against Cuba, and it had pressured its West European allies not to sell arms to Castro.[34] Castro also proceeded to denounce the Rio Pact of 1947 and he entered into diplomatic relations with the Soviet Union in May 1960.

Clearly, Castro was attempting to establish alternatives to reliance on the United States for all of Cuba's trade and to arm his new, untrained military forces as quickly as possible for the expected intervention from the North. Seeking to enhance a country's independence and its ability to stave off an attack can be seen, on the surface, as perfectly reasonable behavior, but it shocked Washington. Cuba's opening of ties to the Soviet Union was more of a challenge to U.S. interests and hegemony than was the seizure of U.S. businesses. The diplomatic relations may not have constituted a substantive threat to the United States, but the act as a symbol of defiance was beyond the threshold of U.S. tolerance.

In its first harsh response to Castro, the Eisenhower administration suspended all imports of Cuban sugar in July 1960. Castro then quickly negotiated a deal with the People's Republic of China to sell additional Cuban sugar. As Castro's relations with the USSR expanded and as more Communists were brought into his government, the U.S. attack intensified. In response to assertions by Soviet Party Chairman Nikita Khrushchev's claim that the Monroe Doctrine was dead and that Soviet rockets would protect Cuba against U.S. intervention, the Department of State proclaimed the doctrine's principles "as valid today as they were in 1823."[35] Eisenhower joined in with the declaration that the United States would never "permit the establishment of a regime dominated by international communism in the Western Hemisphere."[36]

The theme that Castro was a hemispheric problem was repeated by Secretary of State Christian A. Herter at the inter-American meeting of foreign ministers in San José, Costa Rica, in August. Herter described the Cuban government as an agency of "Sino-Soviet imperialism" in defiance of the principles of the inter-American system. The conference did adopt a resolution condemning intervention "by an extracontinental power in the affairs of the American Republics," but made no explicit mention of Cuba. Nevertheless, the Cuban delegation got the message and walked out of the meeting.[37]

Prior to these events, on March 17, 1960, Eisenhower had approved the CIA's latest plan for the overthrow of Castro. The agency had been working on such a scheme since at least December 1959.[38] In November 1960, Assistant Secretary of State Thomas Mann began to plant publicly the idea of intervention when he advocated "collective intervention" to restore democracy to Cuba.[39]

The Cuban situation was moving from a minor disturbance to a cold war crisis. As could be expected, Cuba had become a campaign issue between Nixon and Senator John F. Kennedy. Domestic politics can persuade presidential candidates to try to "out-tough" each other and Kennedy, in August 1960, claimed that "For the first time in the history of the United States, an enemy stands poised at the throat of the United States." Later he said, "We must let Khrushchev know that we are permitting no expansion of his foothold in our hemisphere." As president-elect, he declared, "We will not permit or commit aggression in the Caribbean."[40]

In spite of the official and superficial U.S. tolerance of Fidel in 1959 and 1960, the mood in Washington was one of growing anxiety— and of a willingness to consider intervention seriously. On Capitol Hill, a senate subcommittee on internal security, chaired by conservative James Eastland conducted hearings in an open effort to indict Castro as a threat to the United States. Castro's promiscuity with the Communists was taken as evidence of a threat "only 90 miles from our shores." The hearings, lasting more than two years, provided a platform for the anti-Castro coalition, thus helping to keep the Cuban issue alive and contributing to the legitimization of some kind of interference.[41]

U.S. pressure continued to build. On October 19, 1960, nearly all U.S. exports to Cuba were banned. On January 2, 1961, no doubt worried about U.S. intentions, Castro ordered the U.S. embassy staff in Havana reduced to eleven—to match the number of Cubans in the Washington embassy. On the following day, Eisenhower took the drastic step of breaking diplomatic relations with the Cuban government. No event seemed by itself sufficient to justify the action, but given the attitude in Washington that U.S.-Cuban relations were beyond repair and that only Castro's removal would restore them, the decision, in hindsight, was not so surprising.

The idea that ideological and strategic factors were driving U.S. policy more strongly than was a concern for stability in the U.S. sphere was echoed by Kennedy adviser Arthur M. Schlesinger, Jr., who served as White House liaison on Latin America. Schlesinger noted that it was not the Cuban revolution that bothered the new administration, but rather Castro's turning his country "over to the Communists." To the White House, the prospect of a communist victory was undesirable in any country, but it was intolerable *where* it was occurring. Even Schlesinger implicitly acknowledged the sphere-of-influence factor when he suggested that this particular case had a special meaning for the United States just as Poland had a special meaning for the USSR.[42]

As in the earlier Guatemalan case and the later campaign against the Sandinistas in Nicaragua, U.S. policy seems to have been activated by ideological antipathy coupled with the cold war power struggle. What provoked the more extreme move to intervention was the perception of a threat in a zone of U.S. hegemony. However, even in its own sphere, the United States could not use force with impunity.

Previous pledges of nonintervention and the high political cost, at home and abroad, of intervention discouraged Washington from direct, overt action. As Guatemala had shown, covert action enabled the United States to protect its interests without the high risk of a direct invasion with U.S. troops. Although the U.S. role had been widely suspected, there was sufficient "plausible deniability" in the Guatemalan episode to encourage a repeat performance in 1961. However, the determination to keep the risks low by minimizing the U.S. involvement—and at the same time to depose Castro—proved to be the undoing of the operation. The latter could not be accomplished under the conditions of the former.

Planning the Invasion

By the time Kennedy arrived at the White House, plans for a covert operation against Castro were well under way. The CIA had already moved beyond the original idea of a small-scale guerrilla infiltration to plans for a larger direct attack by Cuban exiles. Under the leadership of Richard Bissell, the CIA's deputy director for plans, the agency had begun recruiting Cuban refugees in the Miami area and had established training camps in Nicaragua and Guatemala. Pilots, primarily from the Alabama Air National Guard, were being assembled for instruction and, potentially, for combat missions. A small CIA "navy" was also being rounded up to provide transportation for the invasion forces.

The objective of the invasion was clear—to overthrow the Castro government—but specific steps and means were left rather vague. There was hope that word of the arrival of a liberation force would spark a popular rebellion, or failing that, that the exiles could establish a beachhead and set up a provisional government. Such a government could then call on the United States for aid and thereby provide a base for conducting a civil war. The CIA did organize a coalition of Cuban political leaders into a government-in-exile that planned to land in Cuba once the brigade of invaders had control of a small area. This coalition was also intended to provide a symbol of political unity for both the refugees in the United States and the dissidents in Cuba, but the distinct factions and strong, conflicting personalities involved could not agree beyond the goal of deposing Castro.

Throughout this planning and preparation, there was minimal consultation with the Pentagon or Department of State. Obsessed with secrecy and confident of their capabilities, the CIA planners saw little need to brief even the highest ranking U.S. military body, the Joint Chiefs of Staff, with anything but the sketchiest outline of the operation. To outsiders, the CIA's anti-Castro activities appeared to be aimed merely at harassment and the infiltration of agents, rather than at a military invasion. The lack of wider discussion meant an inadequate consideration of the political consequences of the action and a poorly coordinated, insufficient military effort.

The invasion plans were based on a number of dubious assumptions: (1) that Castro's position was weak and that he did not have sufficient military or popular support to resist a direct challenge; (2) that there was such popular discontent in Cuba that the arrival of liberators would spark a mass uprising throughout the country; (3) that an effective, but small, force of Cubans could be successfully trained and landed in Cuba with adequate equipment to launch Castro's removal; (4) that estimates based on intelligence provided by Cuban exiles could be taken as accurate; (5) that minimal air and naval support would be sufficient; (6) that secrecy could be maintained; (7) that U.S. involvement could remain invisible and deniable; and (8) that if the invasion did run into trouble, U.S. forces would intervene to guarantee success.

Probably, the assumptions about Castro's weakness and popular uprisings were based as much on wishful thinking as on faulty, biased intelligence from the exile community. Exiles and refugees are notoriously unreliable sources of information, but combined with Washington's quick judgments about Fidel's lack of popularity and naïveté about revolutions, the CIA's plot was being built on precarious grounds.

The tendency to take for granted that a military invasion could be launched with so little U.S. military advice and support was, of course, another fatal flaw. Training even a small force of 1,500 soldiers and pilots in the middle of Central America, then moving them secretly across the Caribbean, and landing them with adequate supplies and equipment required more attention to intelligence, logistics, and protection than the CIA planners were able to give. Moreover, because it had been made clear from the beginning by both Eisenhower and Kennedy that U.S. forces would not be allowed to participate, it is curious that the planners, and especially the Cuban exiles, never seemed to take that condition seriously. Throughout, a firmly held belief appeared to be that Washington would not allow the invasion to fail.

And finally, the invasion was not "secret." It was widely known in the Cuban community in Miami and by the Miami press that the CIA was recruiting a force to liberate Cuba. The details of date and place were not known, but the essential facts were no secret—not even to Castro. Ignorance of the details of the invasion was highest where it might have mattered most: in Washington. Key personnel in the departments of state and defense and among the Joint Chiefs and White House staff were poorly informed. Those who did become aware of the plans and raised questions found their protests shunted aside.[43]

Almost immediately after his inauguration, Kennedy was advised by the CIA director, Allen Dulles, of the plans to invade Cuba. Assured of the CIA's expertise and of the political necessity to get rid of Castro, Kennedy approved the plan but repeated the warning about no direct U.S. involvement. The CIA had already been plotting for some time to assassinate Castro and Kennedy's willingness to continue those plans reflected his general disposition toward the Cuban leader.[44]

As newspaper reports of a pending action against Castro became more widespread, Kennedy took great pains to play down U.S. participation. In a press conference five days before the invasion, Kennedy made clear his position on the use of U.S. troops: "I want to say that there will not be, under any conditions, an intervention in Cuba by the United States armed forces."[45]

The Invasion

The culmination of two years of anti-Castro planning came on April 17, 1961, when an armed force of 1,443 Cuban refugees, calling themselves Brigade 2506, landed on the southern coast of Cuba at a place with the unappealing name of "Bahia de Cochinos," or Bay of Pigs.[46] From the moment the first shot was fired, the invasion, despite the bravery of the attackers, began to turn sour. First, the attempt to eliminate the Cuban Air Force fell short. Attacking at dawn on April 16 from its base in Nicaragua, the brigade air force of old B-26s was unable to trap all of Castro's planes on the ground. This was a critical mistake since the invasion's success was premised on no threat from the air.

To the CIA, the need for a second air strike to finish off the Cuban aircraft appeared obvious, but with considerable public attention already generated by the first attack, the president and his advisers refused to authorize such a strike. Kennedy's decision was consistent with the restrictions designed to minimize any impression of U.S. involvement and to keep the mission as limited as possible. And yet, to the agency and to the brigade, the refusal loomed as a serious betrayal. Although a second air strike might have given the invaders more time, such a strike would not, in retrospect, have been adequate to save the operation.

News of the bombing raids provoked an immediate mobilization of the Cuban armed forces and militia. Castro was not surprised;

however, the rapid Cuban response to the attack was not anticipated by U.S. planners.

Off the invasion beaches of Playa Giron and Playa Larga, the brigade prepared for its Sunday night assault—and suddenly the costs of faulty intelligence became apparent. The landing craft ran aground on an underwater coral reef 50 yards offshore. The presumably deserted beach areas were full of Cuban construction workers, families, and a few militia personnel, who were quickly alerted by the lights and noise accompanying the struggling invasion. When gunfire broke out, the entire Bay of Pigs area was awakened, and word of the attack was telephoned to Havana, 120 miles away. The hope for a swift, silent, surprise landing had vanished.

At daylight, while the brigade troops and supply ships were still unloading ammunition and equipment, the makeshift and wounded Cuban Air Force attacked, sinking two of the five ships at Playa Giron. The exhausted Cuban pilots in the brigade air force gave way to U.S. civilian (CIA) pilots, who tried to provide air cover at the beaches, but even that effort could not rescue the developing disaster. (Four U.S. pilots were killed.) Short of ammunition and under attack from the air, the brigade soon ran into Castro's militia.

In an informal and ad hoc style, Fidel Castro himself took charge of the Cuban retaliation.[47] Without elaborate communications capability, Fidel ran the counterattack by telephoning from various mills and shops along the roads leading to the Bay of Pigs. In addition, Castro knew the region very well; he had often fished in the area and had surveyed it for the construction of a resort. The invaders could not have selected a less appropriate site.

Moreover, the location had other problems besides the reef, the number of inhabitants, and Castro's intimate knowledge of it. Because the beaches were bordered by swamps, it was almost impossible for the brigade to move inland without running into Cuban troops coming down the few roads. Actually, the Bay of Pigs had not been the original site selected by the CIA. Initially, the landing was to have been made at beaches 100 miles to the east, near Cienfuegos and Trinidad, in part so that if trouble occurred, the brigade could escape into the nearby Escambray Mountains where they could conduct guerrilla operations. When the CIA concluded that the large population in the area made a covert landing more difficult and that the guerrilla option was too problematical, the site was moved to the "deserted" Bay of Pigs.

The possibility of the exiles melting into the mountains and engineering a guerrilla effort from there, although reminiscent of Castro's success three years earlier, was at best a pipe dream. And yet it was considered by some CIA operatives a viable option even after the landing site had been moved. The agency's misunderstanding of the sources of Castro's movement, of the widespread support for Fidel, and of the lack of political credibility of the exiled Cubans are revealed in the CIA's giving this plan any credence at all. The success of a guerrilla movement requires, if nothing else, popular disaffection from the existing government, and in the Cuba of 1961 this condition did not exist. The unquestioned assumption that a guerrilla option was possible reflected the kind of fundamental misunderstanding of revolutions that doomed the Bay of Pigs from the outset.

The invaders held out until April 20, but brave as they may have been, they were no match for Castro's well-trained and equipped army. In the end, 1,189 brigade members were captured; 114 died. About 150 either escaped or never made it to the beaches. The captured invaders were returned to the United States in 1962 after a mass trial, in exchange for $53 million worth of food and drugs.

Consequences

The propaganda victory for Fidel was, of course, tremendous. Now his warnings that the United States would do anything to overthrow him were believable; his concerns for security and military power appeared justified. The episode certainly gave credibility to his pleas for arms from the Soviet Union—a development that would eventually lead to the missile crisis. Moreover, Cuba had become the first Latin American country to defy successfully—even defeat—the United States. The prestige and legitimacy bestowed on Castro so strengthened his hold on Cuba that he became virtually immune from opposition.

In private, Kennedy was moved to ask, "How could I have been so stupid to let them go ahead?"[48] In a major address, the president assumed full responsibility for the failure, but at the same time he warned Castro that although direct intervention against his regime was not now called for, continued misbehavior on his part could justify such action:

Any unilateral intervention, in the absence of an external attack upon ourselves or an ally, would have been contrary to our traditions and to our international obligations, But let the record show that our restraint is not inexhaustable. Should it ever appear that the inter-American doctrine of non-interference merely conceals or excuses inaction . . . then I want it clearly understood that this government will not hesitate in meeting its primary obligations, which are to the security of our nation.[49]

Department of State pronouncements on Castro now placed the Cuban problem in the context of the global struggle between freedom and tyranny and pictured Castro as a willing ally of the Soviet Union as well as the vanguard of "communist imperialism in the hemisphere."[50] There was considerable outcry in the United States for direct action against Castro. Senator Barry Goldwater urged the United States not to be "blinded into inaction" by the principle of nonintervention. Because a "communist bastion on our Southern doorstep" could not be tolerated, Castro, he said, "must be eliminated."[51]

The United States had had an opportunity in 1959 and 1960 to work out a relationship with the Castro government. The Eisenhower administration did not immediately sever relations or cut trade, but its suspicions toward the revolution left the Cubans little room for compromise. Alternatively, Fidel's movement had been so highly motivated by hostility toward the U.S. government that a cordial arrangement was probably beyond a reasonable expectation. Thus, in spite of initial flexibility, the Eisenhower administration began to plan Castro's removal, perhaps without serious consideration of the requirements and results. Once the CIA had the operation in gear, bureaucratic inertia linked with an ideological fixation almost guaranteed the plan's execution. Kennedy, who felt bound by Eisenhower's commitments, awed by the confidence of the CIA, and convinced of the political liabilities if Castro survived, authorized the mission with scarcely a second thought.

Again, trouble in the U.S. sphere of influence took on an elevated importance because of the ties to the USSR and the ideological issues involved. The United States seemed to misunderstand the history of U.S.-Cuban relations and the dynamics of revolution, and undertook the operation as though it were engaged in a vital showdown with communism, and one, because of its proximity, that would be easy to win. In the end, of course, the United States showed no sign of being closer to understanding revolutions, and Castro's subsequent alliance with Moscow only served to confirm Washington's worst expectations about what happens when leftist revolutionaries are allowed to stay in power.

Although Washington, after April 1961, suggested that it could live with a revolutionary next door, it would not tolerate a direct challenge to U.S. security. (That challenge arose in October 1962 when the Soviet Union attempted to install offensive nuclear missiles in Cuba.) Another message from the Bay of Pigs, however, was that the United States might have bungled the intervention and waited too long to crush a revolution, but next time, its threshold of tolerance would be much lower. The U.S. intervention in the Dominican Republic (ostensibly to prevent another Cuba) demonstrated how low that threshold had become.

THE DOMINICAN REPUBLIC, 1965

A third case illustrating the convergence of sphere-of-influence interests and the demands of the cold war is the 1965 U.S. intervention in the Dominican Republic. As noted in Chapter 2, the United States had a long record of interfering in this small Caribbean country and had supported for twenty-five years the authoritarian rule of General Rafael Trujillo. Although elections had been held in the Dominican Republic from time to time after the departure of the U.S. Marines in 1924, Trujillo remained the central figure in the country. He and his family controlled nearly all the country's sugar industry and much of the country's agricultural land, in addition to the nation's army. As in Nicaragua and Cuba, the United States showed few misgivings about collaborating with a strong dictator who supported the U.S. stance against communism in the hemisphere. Reliable friends like this were willing to accept the dominant role of the United States in the region in exchange for their regimes' survival.

Trujillo was frequently praised by the U.S. government for his leadership. When the United States installed a missile-tracking station in the Dominican Republic in 1952, the U.S. ambassador there declared: "Governments are taking an interest in the welfare of peoples. . . . Your own illustrious president . . . Trujillo . . ." has committed himself to this goal.[52]

Embracing Dictators

Oblivious to anything except stability and the communist threat, the United States consistently put these short-term interests ahead of the long-term consequences of appearing always to side against the masses. Even outside the Caribbean, the United States maintained close relationships with dictators. In 1954, the Eisenhower administration gave the U.S. Legion of Merit to two of Latin America's most ruthless military rulers, Perez Jiménez of Venezuela and Manuel Odría of Peru.

Even when these two regimes fell, the association of the U.S. government with dictators was so widely resented that Vice President Richard Nixon, on a tour of Latin America in 1958, was greeted with open hostility. In Lima, student demonstrations blocked his route to a university speaking engagement; his car was pelted with rocks, and he was spit on as he entered his hotel. In Caracas, the hatred took a more ominous turn. Nixon's arrival in the Venezuelan capital was marked first by angry crowds of workers, then by a blocked highway that brought his limousines to a halt. The vice president's car was assaulted with pipes and rocks by an angry mob of students and workers. Just before the car doors could be forced open, Nixon's driver was able to race to an escape.[53]

Nixon was treated to a hero's welcome on his return to Washington; the meaning of his violent reception in Venezuela received little attention, except as an example of a communist-inspired conspiracy to intimidate the United States. There was no sense of an urgent need to reevaluate policy or to confront the sources of Latin discontent.

All this is prelude to an examination of the Dominican case, for it demonstrates the priority the United States put on having reliable friends, such as Trujillo, in its sphere of influence. The policy works best, however, when one can be sure of full control; in the revolutionary ferment of the 1960s, the Cuban case indicates that this was not always possible. But, Washington was determined not to allow U.S. power to deteriorate much further.

The End of Trujillo

U.S. policy toward the Dominican Republic from 1960 to 1965 is an excellent example of the tensions between tradition and change in U.S. foreign policy and between the demands of short-term stability and long-term solutions to political problems. The period begins with a politics-as-usual attitude, goes through a stage of active support for democratic forces, and ends with a major military intervention.

In an atypical departure from previous practice, the Eisenhower administration in early 1960 began to move from treating Trujillo as an ally to viewing him as a pariah. Perhaps fearful that the brutality of the Dominican regime could lead to another Cuba, Eisenhower, in February 1960, began plans to aid opposition groups in the Dominican Republic secretly. By April, the president approved a plan for "political action to remove Trujillo from the Dominican Republic."[54] The White House also approved a request to supply the opposition sniper rifles, but apparently the rifles were not delivered.

The United States also stepped up diplomatic pressure on Trujillo in an effort to persuade him to resign, especially after the June revelation that Trujillo's agents had attempted to assassinate the newly elected president of Venezuela, Rómulo Betancourt. The Eisenhower administration broke diplomatic relations with Santo Domingo (then called Ciudad Trujillo) and intensified its ties to the dissidents through the CIA station chief who remained behind in the country. By

September it had become clear to U.S. officials that Trujillo would have to be killed in order to be "removed." Moreover, they thought there would be a constant threat that an exiled Trujillo would return to his country and even in exile be a continuing embarrassment to the United States. In the words of the station chief, "If you recall Dracula, you will remember it was necessary to drive a stake through his heart to prevent a continuation of his crimes."[55]

Active collaboration with Dominican opposition forces continued into the Kennedy administration, but the United States had still not delivered the requested grenades, pistols, and rifles. This delay prompted the station chief to complain in a memo that came to be known as the "picnic letter": "The members of our club are now prepared in their minds to have a picnic, but do not have the ingredients for the salad. . . . Last week we were asked to furnish three or four pineapples for a party in the near future, but I could remember nothing in my instructions that would allow me to contribute this ingredient."[56]

In the wake of the Bay of Pigs fiasco, however, the Kennedy White House began to have second thoughts about the risk of being identified with an assassination, and thus the president appeared to be trying to disassociate himself from the attempt to kill Trujillo. Nonetheless, the White House did want it known that it sympathized with the rebels and if they did succeed in coming to power, they would have the backing of the United States. In any event, the momentum in the Dominican Republic had gone too far to be halted. On May 30, Trujillo was assassinated by a group that had collaborated with the U.S. officials, to which the United States had supplied some weapons, and in an ambush plan closely resembling one proposed by the CIA. There was no evidence of direct U.S. participation in the killing.[57]

Supporting Democracy

The removal of Trujillo gave the Kennedy administration an opportunity to achieve stability in the Dominican Republic through democratic means. The White House made a determined effort to prevent a return to the conditions in that country that might have sparked a Castro-style revolution. The step away from support for a dictator was a novel departure in U.S. foreign policy. Could it succeed without jeopardizing national security interests?

To accomplish this goal, the first task was to prevent the Trujillo clan from seizing power, and this led to a U.S. show of force on the side of democracy. In November 1961, when two Trujillo brothers appeared to be poised to lead a coup, Kennedy sent a navy task force to patrol just off the Dominican coast, in an area clearly visible from Santo Domingo. He also threatened to send in the marines if the efforts to hold elections were stymied. Thwarted in their comeback, the Trujillos understood this message from their former patron and fled the country.

Elections were held in December 1962 under the supervision of the OAS and the U.S. embassy. The new president was a Social Democrat, Juan Bosch, a writer and former professor, who had been in exile since 1937 because of his anti-Trujillo activities. He was elected with 60 percent of the vote. The return of democracy to the Dominican Republic was enthusiastically endorsed by the United States, and Bosch was warmly greeted by Kennedy on a visit to Washington. It was a far cry from the visits of Jiménez and Odría.

Inaugurated on February 27, 1963, Bosch undertook a series of economic and social reforms, attempted to gain control of the military, and set out to establish his independence from the United States. Bosch's program proved to be his undoing. His administration was regarded in Washington as inefficient and slow in carrying out reforms. He alienated the Kennedy administration and his own military with a clumsy attempt to invade neighboring Haiti in the name of democracy.

The U.S. ambassador, John Bartlow Martin, quickly became dis-illusioned with this particular experiment in democracy. In his own account,[58] Martin criticized Bosch for his inattention to detail and for his lax attitude toward Communists—although there was actually little evidence of communist activity in the country. When the United States refused to provide sufficient economic backing for Bosch's reforms, in spite of their correspondence to Alliance for Progress guidelines, it was clear to dissident Dominican business and military interests that the United States had no stake in seeing Bosch serve out his term. Martin claims that he did not support a military coup, but his open frustration with Bosch communicated a different impression. On September 25, seven months after coming to power, Bosch was thrown out by a group of military officers led by Colonel Elias Wessin y Wessin.

Bosch's threatened reforms frightened the established interests in the Dominican Republic. His often poetic, whimsical approach to politics so discouraged U.S. officials that no effort was made to save him, even though Ambassador Martin did make some last-minute appeals for U.S. military intervention to prevent the coup. Rather than condemn the military for the takeover or insist on democratic procedures, the Department of State and the U.S. press blamed Bosch himself. One commentator summed it up this way, "Juan Bosch's personality, more than his actions or inactions, led to his overthrow."[59]

The prospect of instability and the perception of leftist influence caused the United States to waver; predictable, orderly rule by the military was more in line with the interest in preventing another Cuba. Washington was reluctant to jettison all of the progress that had been made toward democracy. It did break diplomatic relations with the military junta in the hope of encouraging some commitments to pluralism, but beyond the junta's vague promise to hold elections in the future, nothing was accomplished by this act. Diplomatic relations were restored in December.

Intervention

U.S. policy toward the new government was controlled largely by the Department of State's assistant secretary for Latin American affairs, Thomas Mann, who had been involved in the planning of both the Guatemalan intervention in 1954 and the Bay of Pigs in 1961. Bosch has described Mann as "a Southern aristocrat who can't abide any faction that isn't 'his kind of people.'"[60]

The new Dominican leader was a wealthy car salesman, Donald Reid Cabral, who had a reputation for being close to the U.S. embassy. Cabral tried to stabilize the nation's economy and to control the military but failed to achieve sufficient popular support to counter military resentment. He also raised eyebrows in the country with hints that he might cancel the elections scheduled for late 1965. Reformist army officers, dissatisfied with the inability of Cabral to clean up the military, joined with members of Bosch's Democratic Revolutionary party (PRD), seized a radio station on April 24, 1965, and announced their intention to return Bosch to power. At this time it appeared to be simply an attempt at an army coup, but upon Cabral's resignation on April 25, thousands of Dominicans filled the streets, took up arms, and declared a victory for Bosch and "constitutionalism." The air force, however, led by Wessin y Wessin (who had become a general), quickly regrouped and established order over much of Santo Domingo. By April 27, the minirevolution was pronounced dead.[61]

But April 27 was a critical day; the revolt had not actually died. The rebels, led by José Raphael Molina Ureña of the PRD, appealed to U.S. Ambassador W. Tapley Bennett to use his influence to stop the continuing air attacks on rebel-held areas and to mediate a settlement. Bennett refused, saying that to mediate would be to intervene and, instead, urged the rebels to accept a military junta as a provisional government. Molina Ureña reluctantly agreed, but his followers did not, and the fighting continued. Bennett ordered the evacuation of all U.S. citizens. On April 28, with bullets ricocheting around the embassy, the ambassador asked President Johnson for marines to protect U.S. lives. On television that night, the president said that 450 marines had been landed in Santo Domingo to save lives, not to become involved in the conflict.

At this point there was no official mention of a communist problem, but in the press there were leaks from both the CIA and the Defense Department that extremists were involved in the revolt and that there was a real danger that "Communists were ascendent."[62] The next day, April 29, 4,000 U.S. troops were in the Dominican Republic, officially to protect U.S. citizens. It was not until April 30 that the Johnson administration asserted that people trained outside the Dominican Republic were about to take control and that additional U.S. troops might be needed to protect the Dominicans from an "international conspiracy."[63]

The State Department followed this with an announcement that fifty-eight Communists, eighteen of whom had been trained in Cuba, were participating in the revolt. A revised list of fifty-four Communists was released four days later. The list proved to be of generally known Dominican Communists, some of whom were shown to be nowhere near the Dominican Republic at the time of the fighting.[64] The United States had now defined the situation in such a manner that its response was predetermined: the Communist-led rebels, in collaboration with the untrustworthy Bosch, who had been known to visit Cuba since his exile in 1963, were attempting to stage another Cuba. Bosch, who remained in Puerto Rico during the rebellion, claimed that the Communists did not control the revolt. This was confirmed by reports that the rebels consisted of "radicals of every stripe," moderates, nationalists, social Christians, generals and privates, lawyers, students, workers and "plain people."[65] The junta was clearly composed of senior air force officers and supported by privileged sectors of Dominican society.

In its determination to prevent any possibility of a communist victory, the United States had landed 22,000 troops in the country by May 10. The response had been immediate and overwhelming. The president had made it clear that the United States "cannot, must not, and will not permit the establishment of another communist government in the Western Hemisphere." And furthermore, he said, "We are not the aggressors in the Dominican Republic. Forces came in there with evil persons who had been trained in the overthrowing of governments and in seizing governments and establishing communist control."[66]

Thomas Mann claimed that the United States was sympathetic to the aspirations of Latin Americans but warned them "not to taint democratic reform movements by participation with Communists." The possibility of a communist takeover anywhere in the hemisphere, he said, would warrant U.S. intervention.[67]

Even former ambassador John Bartlow Martin, who at one point had tried to support the democratic process in the Dominican Republic, conceded that the president "had no choice but to send troops" when there appeared to be a danger of a communist takeover. Suggesting that domestic politics may have also shaped the U.S. response, Martin claimed that it was "politically impossible in the United States to accept a revolutionary communist regime in the Dominican Republic; it might not be impossible to accept one farther away."[68] The interesting point in Martin's statement was that the Dominican Republic's location gave the revolution a special impact. The cost of a hostile government so close to the United States was too much to risk.

The Johnson administration did make an effort to legitimize its intervention by giving it the stamp of an international peacekeeping force. On April 29, an emergency session of the OAS Council met in Washington and agreed to send a five-man peace commission to the Dominican Republic to investigate the problem. The OAS had not been consulted prior to the arrival of the first 4,000 U.S. soldiers. Under Secretary of State George Ball asserted that the U.S. action was consistent with a 1962 OAS resolution declaring that the "extension of Marxist-Leninist power into the hemisphere is incompatible with the inter-American system."[69] Article 15 of the OAS Charter, which prohibits intervention into the internal affairs of other countries, was not mentioned by Ball.

By the end of May the United States succeeded, by a slim margin, in getting the necessary votes for the establishment of an inter-American peace force. Such democratic states as Chile, Mexico, Uruguay, and Venezuela did not support this idea of multilateral intervention. Nonetheless, a force was created under a Brazilian commander, with troops from Brazil, Costa Rica, Honduras, Nicaragua, Paraguay, and the United States. Indications are that the OAS presence, although rather modest, did restrain the aggressiveness of U.S. forces in Santo Domingo and did establish workable conditions for negotiations. Thus, with criticism of Washington's unilateral interference muted by the OAS role, more than just a cloak of legitimacy for the intervention resulted. The diplomatic efforts of various Latin Americans, plus the 2,000 non-U.S. troops helped buffer the combatants. The eventual settlement was made possible largely because the OAS mediators recognized the grievances of the rebels and guaranteed their participation in any agreement.[70]

Aftermath

In any event, U.S. intervention had accomplished its goals. Juan Bosch was not returned to power and stability was brought to the country. In August a provisional government acceptable to both sides was established and elections set for June 1, 1966. Fearing for his personal safety, Bosch refused to campaign in public. The winner was U.S. favorite Joaquín Balaguer, once Trujillo's vice president, but a person instrumental in the transition to democracy after 1961. The last of the OAS and U.S. troops left the country in September 1966.

The issue of the degree of communist influence is still debated. While there is evidence that some Communists (probably not fifty-eight) were involved in the revolution, they were not the leaders. What seemed to concern President Johnson was the prospect that once the revolt got going, the situation would be so fluid that the Communists could seize control and lead the way to another Cuba. It was a chance on which the Department of State and the White House—remembering Castro in 1959—were not willing to gamble. Moreover, intervention was easy. The site was nearby, the rebels were still few in number and centered in the capital, and in the wake of the Cuban missile crisis, the U.S. public was unlikely to castigate a president for preventing what appeared to be a potential communist victory.

Even though the intervention did result in stability and elections (which, in fact, have continued into the 1980s), the fact of U.S. intervention with so overwhelming a force did little to reassure the Latin Americans that the United States would refrain from sending in the marines in the future. The intervention reaffirmed U.S. hegemony in the Caribbean; it reestablished a low level of tolerance for revolutionary behavior in the region. It also made a mockery of U.S. pledges not to intervene and weakened the credibility of an OAS that so readily came to Washington's aid. Whatever one's evaluation of the outcome, the specter of an interventionist United States looming on the horizon was a clear reminder to Latin Americans of their place in the U.S. sphere. According to the realists in Washington, such a reminder was healthy because it might discourage other revolutionaries. For those who had looked to the Alliance for Progress as the path for solving hemispheric problems, the intervention demonstrated that the traditional ways of doing business had not really changed. The Alliance's commitment to reform was taking second place to security and stability.

It is useful to note that in 1965, the Dominican intervention was not out of step with the prevailing trends in U.S. policy around the world. U.S. involvement in Vietnam was under way, and there was no sign of restraint in the global use of U.S. power. It was the age of the U.S. "empire," and the use of force to protect U.S. security against even a hint of a communist threat was consistent with the cold war fixation that had governed U.S. policy since 1947. The intervention, then, was not generally treated as unusual behavior nor as a departure from standard U.S. values. Nonetheless, the action did provoke a number of questions about the role of U.S. power and about the United States as the global policeman. The questions intensified, of course, as the Vietnam War progressed, but in the Dominican intervention some early hints that the cold war consensus was crumbling did emerge.

NOTES

1. Samuel Flagg Bemis, *The Latin American Policy of the United States* (New York: Harcourt, Brace, 1943), 143.

2. J. Lloyd Mecham, *A Survey of U.S.–Latin American Relations* (Boston: Houghton Mifflin, 1965), 239–241.

3. For a review of this problem, see Harold Molineu, "The Concept of the Caribbean in the Latin American Policy of the United States," *Journal of Inter-American Studies and World Affairs* 15 (August 1973), 285–307.

4. For the best analytical study of U.S. policy in these three cases, see Cole Blaiser, *The Hovering Giant: U.S. Responses to Revolutionary Change in Latin America* (Pittsburgh: University of Pittsburgh Press, 1976).

5. Objective surveys of this period in Guatemalan history are in short supply. Two volumes that deal reliably with the U.S. role are Richard H. Immerman, *The CIA in Guatemala* (Austin: University of Texas Press, 1982) and Stephen Schlesinger and Stephen Kinzer, *Bitter Fruit: The Untold Story of the American Coup in Guatemala* (Garden City, N.Y.: Doubleday, 1982). Also see Philip B. Taylor, "The Guatemalan Revolution: A Critique of United States Foreign Policy," *American Political Science Review* 50 (September 1956), 787–806.

6. A detailed study of United Fruit's economic role in Guatemala and a defense of the company was done by Stacy May and Galo Plaza, *The United Fruit Company in Latin America* (Washington, D.C.: National Planning Association, 1958).

7. Immerman, *The CIA in Guatemala*, 49–50.

8. Schlesinger and Kinzer, *Bitter Fruit*, 42.

9. Quoted in Susanne Jonas, "Guatemala: Land of Eternal Struggle," in Ronald Chilcote and Joel C. Edelstein, eds., *Latin America: The Struggle with Dependency and Beyond* (New York: Schenkman, 1974), 156; also *New York*

Times, March 16, 1951, 17; and *Christian Science Monitor,* March 13, 1951, 9.

10. Jonas, "Guatemala," 159.

11. Thomas and Marjorie Melville, *Guatemala: The Politics of Land Ownership* (New York: Free Press, 1971), 61–65; also see Jonas, "Guatemala," 160; and Schlesinger and Kinzer, *Bitter Fruit,* 75–76.

12. Edward Bernays, *Biography of an Idea* (New York: Simon and Schuster, 1965).

13. Immerman, *The CIA in Guatemala,* 89–90.

14. Ibid., 89. In his memoirs of this period, Truman's secretary of state, Dean Acheson, does not mention Guatemala. See: *Present at the Creation* (New York: Norton, 1969).

15. Frederick S. Cook, "The CIA," *Nation* 192 (June 24, 1961), 537–541; also Immerman, *The CIA in Guatemala,* 82.

16. U.S. Department of State, *Tenth Inter-American Conference, Caracas, Venezuela, March 1–28, 1954,* Publication 5692 (Washington, D.C.: 1955).

17. Among those works that reflected the government's viewpoint were Ronald Schneider, *Communism in Guatemala, 1944–1954* (New York: Praeger, 1958); Richard Stebbins, *The U.S. in World Affairs, 1954* (New York: Harper Bros., 1956), 367–372; and Frederick Pike, "Guatemala, the U.S. and Communism in the Americas," *Review of Politics* 17 (April 1955), 233–245.

18. For the government's case against Arbenz, see U.S. Department of State, *Intervention of International Communism in Guatemala,* Inter-American Series 48 (Washington, D.C.: 1954); and U.S. Department of State, *A Case History of Communist Penetration of Guatemala,* Inter-American Series 52 (Washington, D.C.: 1957).

19. *New York Times,* May 18, 20, 26, 1954.

20. Schlesinger and Kinzer, *Bitter Fruit,* 185.

21. Present that fateful week in Guatemala City was an Argentine doctor, Ernesto (Ché) Guevara, who later fled to Mexico and teamed up with Fidel Castro to lead the revolution in Cuba. See Andrew Sinclair, *Ché Guevara* (New York: Viking, 1970), 10.

22. Henry Wriston, "A Historical Perspective," in John Plank, ed., *Cuba and the United States* (Washington, D.C.: The Brookings Institution, 1967), 29.

23. Robert E. Smith, "Castro's Revolution: Domestic Sources and Consequences," in Plank, *Cuba and the United States,* 49–51.

24. For example, see Philip Bonsal, *Cuba, Castro and the United States* (Pittsburgh: University of Pittsburgh Press, 1971); Herbert L. Matthews, *The Cuban Story* (New York: Braziller, 1961); and Andres Suarez, *Cuba: Castroism and Communism, 1959–1966* (Cambridge, Mass.: MIT Press, 1967).

25. Theodore Draper, *Castroism: Theory and Practice* (New York: Praeger, 1965).

26. See the CIA testimony in Senate Committee on the Judiciary, Subcommittee on Internal Security, *Communist Threat to the U.S. through the Caribbean,* Hearings, 86th Cong., 1st Sess., Pt 3 (Washington, D.C.: 1959), 163–164.

27. Earl E. T. Smith, *The Fourth Floor* (New York: Random House, 1962), 224, 232.

28. *New York Times*, April 17, 18, 19, 1959; and *Newsweek*, April 27, 1959, 34–35.

29. Peter Wyden, *The Bay of Pigs* (New York: Simon and Schuster, 1981), 28.

30. Javier Pazos, "Cuba: Was a Deal Possible in '59?" *New Republic*, January 12, 1963, 10–11.

31. Tad Szulc and Karl Meyer, *The Cuban Invasion* (New York: Ballantine, 1962), 22.

32. Tad Szulc, *The Winds of Revolution* (New York: Praeger, 1963), 121–128.

33. Blaiser, *The Hovering Giant,*, 183–184.

34. U.S. Department of State, *Cuba* (A White Paper) Inter-American Series 66 (Washington, D.C.: 1961); and *Bulletin* 41 (November 16, 1959), 715–718.

35. U.S. Department of State, "U.S. Reaffirms Principles of Monroe Doctrine," *Bulletin* 43 (August 1, 1960), 170–171.

36. U.S. Department of State, *Bulletin* 43 (July 25, 1960), 139–140.

37. U.S. Department of State, *Bulletin* 43 (September 12, 1960), 395–406. Also see Margaret Ball, *The OAS in Transition* (Durham, N.C.: Duke University Press, 1969), 460.

38. Wyden, *The Bay of Pigs*, 19, 24–25.

39. "The Democratic Ideal in the Latin American Policy of the U.S.," U.S. Department of State,, *Bulletin* 43 (November 28, 1960), 811–814.

40. "Senator John F. Kennedy on the Cuban Situation, 1960," *Inter-American Economic Affairs* 15 (Winter 1961), 79–95. Also see *New York Times*, October 16, 21, 1960, and November 21, 1960.

41. Senate Committee on the Judiciary, 86th Cong., 1st Sess.; and 86th Cong., 2d Sess. (Washington, D.C.: 1960), and 87th Cong., 1st Sess. (Washington, D.C.: 1961).

42. Arthur M. Schlesinger, Jr., *A Thousand Days* (Boston: Houghton Mifflin, 1965), 245, 263.

43. For a review of the restricted policy process, see Irving Janis, *Groupthink* (Boston: Houghton Mifflin, 1982), 14–47.

44. For an account of the plots against Castro, see Senate Select Committee to Study Government Operations, *Alleged Assassination Plots Involving Foreign Leaders* (An Interim Report), 94th Cong., 1st Sess. (Washington, D.C.: 1975), 71–189.

45. *Public Papers of the Presidents of the United States, John F. Kennedy, 1961* (Washington, D.C.: GPO, 1960–1963), 877.

46. The best sources for an account of the invasion are: Wyden, *The Bay of Pigs*; Szulc and Meyer, *The Cuban Invasion*; and *Operation Zapata: The Ultrasensitive Report and Testimony of the Board of Inquiry on the Bay of Pigs* (Frederick, Md.: University Publications of America, 1981).

47. Wyden, *The Bay of Pigs*, 248–264.

48. Quoted by Theodore Sorensen, *Kennedy* (New York: Harper & Row, 1965), 309.

49. U.S. Department of State, *Bulletin* 44 (May 8, 1961), 659.

50. U.S. Department of State, *Inter-American Efforts to Relieve Tension in the Western Hemisphere*, Inter-American Series 79 (Washington, D.C.: 1962), 48–85, and "The Castro Regime," mimeographed (Washington, D.C. August 1961).

51. *Congressional Record*, 87th Cong., 1st Sess. (April 19, 1961), 6219.

52. U.S. Department of State, *Bulletin* 27 (July 14, 1952), 51–53.

53. Richard M. Nixon, *Six Crises* (Garden City, N.Y.: Doubleday, 1962), 182–234; also see Szulc, *The Winds of Revolution*, 108–114.

54. Senate, *Alleged Assassination Plots*, 192.

55. Ibid., 194–195.

56. Ibid., 199.

57. Ibid., 211, 213–215.

58. John Bartlow Martin, *Overtaken by Events* (Garden City, N.Y.: Doubleday, 1966).

59. Selden Rodman, "A Close View of Santo Domingo," *Reporter*, July 15, 1965, 24.

60. Ibid.

61. For this review, see Senate Committee on Foreign Relations, *Background Information Relating to the Dominican Republic*, 89th Cong., 1st Sess. (Washington, D.C.: 1965), and Jerome Slater, *Intervention and Negotiation: The United States and the Dominican Revolution* (New York: Harper & Row, 1970).

62. *New York Times*, April 29, 30, 1965; and *Newsweek*, May 10, 1965, 35–38.

63. U.S. Department of State, *Bulletin* 52 (May 17, 1965), 743.

64. *New York Times*, May 2–9, 1965.

65. Slater, *Intervention and Negotiation*, 39–44, and *New York Times*, May 16, 1965.

66. U.S. Department of State, *Bulletin* 52 (May 17, 1965), 746–747, and *Bulletin* 52 (May 24, 1965), 822.

67. U.S. Department of State, *Bulletin* 53 (November 8, 1965), 730–738.

68. Martin, *Overtaken by Events*, 661, 705–707, 739.

69. U.S. Department of State, *Bulletin* 52 (June 28, 1965), 1046.

70. Slater, *Intervention and Negotiation*, 73–75.

4
REGIONAL ECONOMIC INFLUENCE

Up to this point U.S. relations with Latin America have been discussed primarily in the context of regional political, military, and strategic factors. We have generally dealt with U.S. policy as a product of government decisions; for example, in explaining the reaction to Castro in Cuba we focused on what officials of the U.S. government sought and how that influenced the outcome of events. Relationships between political agencies (governments) were assumed to be critical elements in understanding the reality of the U.S.-Cuban connection. This is the typical approach for examining relations between nations.

However, there are alternative viewpoints, and one set of them revolves around economic factors rather than strategic or political ones. In this chapter, we will examine the proposition that U.S. policy has been driven primarily by the economic interests of private companies supported by the government. We will also examine specific economic issues confronting U.S. policymakers in Latin America: the foreign debt problem and the expropriation of property.

U.S. ECONOMIC INTERESTS

The Link to Foreign Policy

It can be argued that the extensive economic stakes of the United States in Latin America are major determinants of its foreign policy. The need to protect investments, gain access to raw materials, and market manufactured goods is so important to the economic health of the United States that the government has little choice but to team up with private business and financial interests in formulating and implementing policy in Latin America.

It is, nonetheless, difficult to demonstrate convincingly the direct linkage between economic interests and foreign policy actions. In part, this is because of the informal and often unseen relationships that exist between private corporations and the U.S. government. It is also due to the tendency of political and strategic interests to become meshed with economic concerns during the implementation of policy.

Two cases discussed earlier can be cited as examples of economic interests exercising considerable, perhaps decisive, influence over policy. The rationale for the Guatemalan intervention of 1954 was clearly shaped by the United Fruit Company's potential loss of valuable property. Fidel Castro's expropriation of U.S. businesses in Cuba in 1960 and 1961 helped to convince Washington that his revolution was not conducive to U.S. interests in the region. Chapter 3 pointed out that in these cases economic, strategic, and ideological interests often became entwined, with the last typically serving as the public justification of action. This complicates the task of identifying the critical determinant of policy.

An essential contention of the economic dominance perspective, however, is that the pervasive U.S. corporate involvement in Latin America has made it impossible for the United States to tolerate political developments that threaten those interests. Thus, although it might be difficult to insist that economic forces determined U.S. policy, it can be inferred that economic values and pressure groups influenced and shaped the general U.S. commitment to maintaining its preeminence in a stable hemisphere. Preserving an atmosphere in the region supportive of U.S. economic interests has been a consistent policy of the U.S. government and helps explain the recurring resistance to revolutionary and nationalistic regimes in Latin America.

A prerequisite for understanding the economic dimensions of U.S. policy in Latin America is a recognition of the extent of U.S. economic involvement in the region. With so much at stake, is it any wonder that economic interests exercise an influence over policy?

Raw Materials

From Latin America, the United States imports a number of important natural resources. Most noticeable is the oil from Mexico, Venezuela, Peru, and Ecuador, suppliers that are generally more reliable than those from the politically unstable Middle East. Mexico, for instance, accounts for over 20 percent of the total oil imported into the United States; Venezuela accounts for about 5 percent.[1] In 1981, the value of Mexican and Venezuelan oil purchased by U.S. companies exceeded $10 billion. Not only is this oil important for the United States, the U.S. market is crucial for Mexico and Venezuela.

TABLE 4.1
Value of Latin American Exports to the United States, 1980
(in thousands of dollars)

Country	Value of Exports
Mexico	12,519,567
Venezuela	5,297,082
Brazil	3,714,630
Trinidad/Tobago	2,378,279
Peru	1,386,203
Colombia	1,240,464
Other Latin American Countries	5,074,546
Total	31,610,771

Source: U.S. Department of Commerce, U.S. General Imports/
World Areas by Commodity Groupings, 1980, Washington, D.C.
1981.

Especially noteworthy is the considerable value generated by
Trinidad and Tobago's export of petroleum products, both crude and
refined, which makes it the fourth-ranking exporter in Latin America
to the United States (see Table 4.1).

Oil producers in today's energy-dependent world, of course, may
well have the upper hand, but producers of other raw materials do
not. Bauxite, the source of aluminum, is the major export of such
countries as Jamaica and Surinam, but their attempts to control prices
in the fashion of oil producers have usually failed. (Jamaica supplies
48 percent of U.S. bauxite purchases; 18 percent comes from Surinam.)
U.S. companies are the key figures in bauxite production and export
and in aluminum smelting in the region.

Chile's copper suffers a similar fate: No producer cartels—or
monopolies—are possible because of abundant or alternative supplies,
and U.S. companies typically own, or at least control, the critical
elements in the mining, processing, transportation, and marketing of
these raw materials.

The United States depends on Latin America also for other "critical"
minerals. Among these are columbium (83 percent of U.S. imports
from Brazil); strontium (85 percent, from Mexico); and manganese
(37 percent, from Brazil).[2]

As Table 4.2 indicates, in 1980 the United States imported $1
billion worth of raw materials from Latin America, plus over $15 billion

TABLE 4.2
U.S. Imports from Latin America, 1980 (in thousands of dollars)

Nonmanufactured Materials		Manufactured Products	
Foods	7,532,757	Major Goods	2,433,051
Raw Materials	1,573,914	Transport and	
Mineral Fuels	15,118,170	Machinery	2,666,810
Chemicals	593,198	Miscellaneous	
		Goods	1,692,871
	Total 24,818,039		Total 6,792,732

Source: U.S. Department of Commerce, U.S. General Imports/
World Areas by Commodity Groupings, Washington, D.C., 1981.

worth of petroleum and other fuels. In addition, imports of food products (grains, fruit, sugar, and livestock) came to over $7.5 billion. These and other nonmanufactured imports from Latin America had risen to a total of over $31 billion in 1982. Total imports from the hemisphere in 1982 came to $38 billion or 19 percent of the total value of all U.S. imports.[3]

Manufactured Goods

By comparison with nonmanufactured products, in 1980 the United States imported only $6.79 billion worth of manufactured goods from Latin America, and a large proportion of that can be traced to automobile manufacturing operations in Mexico.

One of the major points of economic disagreement between Latin America and the United States is the lack of access to U.S. markets for manufactured products. If economic development is linked to industrialization and jobs, then the manufacturing sectors of the economy, the Latins contend, must be expanded, and this requires improved participation in the U.S. market. To remain dependent on the export of raw materials and foodstuffs, it is argued, is not the best path to development.

The markets for Latin American exports are diversifying, through openings to Western Europe and Japan, but the United States is still the largest single customer for Latin America, and this situation shows no signs of changing. For example, in 1965, 33 percent of Latin American exports went to the United States; in 1980, the percentage had risen to 35.5.[4]

Some countries in Latin America, of course, are more dependent on the U.S. market than others. Sixty-five percent of Mexico's exports go to the United States; 66 percent of the Dominican Republic's and 57 percent of Honduras's. In contrast, Argentina sends only 9 percent of its exports to the United States; Chile, only 13 percent.[5]

Latin American Imports

Continuing with this statistical survey, we turn now to the import side of the picture (see Table 4.3). Not only is the United States the predominant customer for Latin America as a whole, it is also the number one seller. About 30 percent of Latin America's imports (in 1980) were from the United States, down from 36 percent in 1965.[6] For U.S. companies Latin America is a major market, with U.S. exports to the region reaching a total of $32.1 billion in 1982. This was 20 percent of the value of all U.S. exports.[7]

The major importers of U.S.-produced goods, as measured by percent of total imports, tend to be the same as those who also sell a large proportion of their exports to the United States. Mexico buys 60 percent of its imports from its northern neighbor; the Dominican Republic, 40 percent, and Honduras, 42 percent (see Table 4.4). Those least likely to import U.S. products are Uruguay (10 percent of its total imports), Paraguay (11 percent), Argentina (18 percent), and Brazil (21 percent).[8]

Investments

Another indicator of the U.S. stake in economic stability in Latin America is the level of private capital investment. Although most U.S. investment goes to Canada and the industrialized countries of Western Europe, the value of Latin America remains important. In 1981, for example, direct U.S. investment in the region came to $38.9 billion, with nearly 40 percent of that ($15.7 billion) in manufacturing enterprises (see Table 4.5). About $4.5 billion was invested in petroleum operations. Brazil, Mexico, Venezuela, and Panama have been the most favored targets for U.S. investors; least favored have been Paraguay and Bolivia.[9]

The impact of foreign investment in a developing country can be both positive and negative. It can provide needed capital for building an industrial base and for developments in areas unattractive to local investors or beyond their means. But foreign capital, because of its size, may supplant and discourage local investment. It may go into areas not directly tied to economic development, but instead to quick-profit enterprises. As Table 4.5 shows, U.S. interests have invested

TABLE 4.3
Latin American Imports from the United States, 1980
(in thousands of dollars)

Nonmanufactured Materials		Manufactured Products	
Foods	4,710,451	Major Goods	4,631,722
Raw Materials	1,788,521	Transport and	
Fuels	864,257	Machinery	14,210,608
Chemicals	4,997,740	Miscellaneous	
		Goods	2,450,545
Total	12,360,969	Total	21,292,875

Source: U.S. Department of Commerce, U.S. Exports/World Areas by Commodity Groupings, 1980, Washington, D.C., 1981.

TABLE 4.4
Value of Latin American Imports from the United States, 1980
(in thousands of dollars)

Country	Value of Imports
Mexico	14,884,768
Venezuela	4,512,760
Brazil	4,306,372
Argentina	2,452,488
Colombia	1,708,376
Chile	1,338,696
Peru	1,160,584
Other Latin American Countries	3,289,800
Total	33,653,844

Source: U.S. Department of Commerce, U.S. Exports/World Areas by Commodity Groupings, 1980, Washington, D.C., 1981.

heavily in Latin American manufacturing enterprises, an area where local investment is perhaps at a disadvantage when competing with foreign capital.

U.S. POLICY INSTRUMENTS

The promotion of economic development in Latin America has been a regularly stated goal of the U.S. government. Government-

TABLE 4.5
U.S. Direct Investments in Latin America, 1981
(in millions of dollars)

Petroleum	4,499
Manufacturing	15,762
Other	18,622
Total	38,883

Source: U.S. Department of Commerce, Survey of Current Business 62. Washington, D.C., August, 1982, p. 13.

to-government assistance and private capital are both used in pursuit of that goal.

In light of the private enterprise orientation of the United States, it is reasonable to expect any administration in Washington to treat private capital as an important component of economic policy for Latin America. Development may depend as much on the growth of private industry as on government funding for nonprofit infrastructure projects such as schools and public health facilities. Thus, the U.S. government, has, over the years, devised a number of plans to encourage private capital to invest in Latin America and other Third World regions. The Alliance for Progress, for example, envisioned more than $1 billion a year in private investment to supplement foreign aid projects, and Reagan's Caribbean Basin Initiative called for a major contribution from private capital.

OPIC and the Eximbank

In 1969, Congress created the Overseas Private Investment Corporation (OPIC) to insure corporate investments in the Third World. In Latin America, as in other developing regions, private investment was considered to be at risk from revolution, expropriation, and sudden shifts in currency values. Through OPIC, for a modest fee (about 1 percent of valuation) companies could purchase insurance against these political risks.

The idea of a government insurance agency for private corporations has generated considerable debate in Congress, especially when it was revealed in 1973 that much of OPIC's support went to projects such as resorts and rent-a-car services that had little to do with development. Moreover, OPIC-insured activities tended to be located in wealthy developing countries where the risk appeared minimal, such as in Brazil, and not in the poorest countries most in need of capital. Between 1974 and 1976, for example, Brazil alone accounted for 21 percent of OPIC's total insurance. In addition, there seemed to be little relationship between insurance and support for democratic regimes.[10]

Nevertheless, OPIC continues as a representative of the government's commitment to private enterprise's role in economic development. By the end of the Reagan administration's first year (1981), OPIC-supported investment had grown by 600 percent from its 1978 levels (from $665 million to $4.5 billion).[11] Thirty-three percent of OPIC's insurance projects in 1981 were in Latin America. These ranged from a $69,000 wood products industry in Honduras to a $83 million hydrocarbon project in the Dominican Republic. A total of twenty-seven Latin American and Caribbean nations had OPIC-backed projects, with major ones in Brazil, Costa Rica, and Haiti.[12]

The major agency available to the U.S. government for promoting private investment and trade is the Export-Import Bank (Eximbank), established in 1934. The bank's primary role is to help finance U.S. exports; for developing countries that often means an extension of credit so that they may buy U.S.-made products. This is not a uniquely U.S. device; other industrialized countries have similar banking services. The bank generally tries to stay aloof from partisan political debates, but it did become involved in human rights issues during the Carter administration. Overall though, the Eximbank is an additional reminder of the close ties between government and business and thus a demonstration of the opportunities for the U.S. government to influence economic and political development in Latin America.

Eximbank loans over a twenty-year period (1962–1982) have tended to go to the wealthiest and largest Latin American countries, with the surprising exceptions of Venezuela and Chile (see Table 4.6). Argentina, Brazil, and Mexico continued to receive Exim credits, and it is noteworthy that a small country, Paraguay, which had received only $3 million in credits from 1962 to 1981, received a whopping $64 million in 1982 alone. In 1982, eight countries plus the Caribbean Region were recipients of Exim loans.

Economic Assistance

The most prominent economic instrument of U.S. policy is government-to-government foreign aid. The extension of economic assistance tends to reflect the particular interests and priorities of the various administrations, and it often entails lengthy debates in Congress

TABLE 4.6
Export-Import Bank Loans to Latin America, 1962-1982
(in millions of dollars)

Country	1962-1982	1982
Argentina	1193.1	551.0
Bolivia	44.6	0.0
Brazil	2051.3	91.0
Chile	381.5	0.0
Columbia	828.1	540.3
Costa Rica	42.7	0.0
Dominican Republic	111.3	0.0
Eçuador	64.6	0.0
El Salvador	18.7	0.0
Guatemala	100.3	0.0
Haiti	3.1	0.0
Honduras	34.0	0.3
Jamaica	95.8	0.0
Mexico	3123.6	293.4
Nicaragua	28.3	0.0
Panama	139.1	0.0
Paraguay	66.9	63.9
Peru	226.8	0.0
Trinidad/Tobago	336.3	35.8
Uruguay	22.3	0.0
Venezuela	589.2	26.0
Caribbean region	75.2	18.8
Total	9576.8	1620.5

Source: Agency for International Development, U.S. Overseas
Loans and Grants, July 1, 1945-September 30, 1982, Washington
D.C., 1983, pp. 33-64.

over both the ends and the means of U.S. policy. Economic aid,
because it has always been closely tied to the political and security
interests of the United States, has often included military assistance
and the sale of arms to Latin American governments. In this chapter,
however, we are concerned with aid as a manifestation of U.S. economic
influence in the Western Hemisphere.

Economic assistance provides a means not only for supporting
friendly governments; more importantly, it is a mechanism by which
Latin America's economic future can be tied to U.S. economic interests.
Aid can shape development and investment in directions consistent
with private U.S. business interests. Because aid is typically channeled

through local governments, ruling elites are able to use it to enhance their power, much in the way Nicaragua's Somoza directed U.S. assistance into companies and projects controlled by him, his family, his friends, and his National Guard commanders. Moreover, Congress normally requires that goods and services bought with U.S. aid be purchased in the United States. An estimated 80 to 90 percent of U.S. economic assistance funds are spent in the United States, thus benefiting U.S. companies as much as Latin America.

Critics of U.S. aid claim that because so many Latin American governments are dependent on U.S. assistance assertions of their political independence are a sham. Although aid can be used to influence political developments, evidence that direct manipulation of aid is an effective tool of policy remains in doubt. Too often governments have defied the United States when unpleasant strings have been attached to economic or military aid. Kennedy had no success in using the Alliance for Progress in 1962 to affect politics in Argentina and Peru, Carter and Reagan had little success in using an aid embargo to change Guatemala's internal policies.

Frustrating for economists in both the United States and Latin America is the political nature of bilateral assistance. When the executive branch or Congress evaluates the effectiveness of aid, it will generally apply political criteria. Aid is "effective" when it supports U.S. security and strategic interests, when it enables a friendly government to survive, and when it facilitates U.S. access to a country's political and economic machinery. Effectiveness is not necessarily measured by the advancement of economic development, the growth in per capita income, or the improvement in health and education. An examination of the past two decades of U.S. assistance reveals this concern for political and security priorities, not economic development.

An analysis of the aid summaries in Table 4.7 shows the relatively low priority accorded to Latin America compared to other regions of the world. The region, despite its poverty, its proximity, and its 300 million people, received only 12 percent of U.S. economic assistance over the twenty-year period surveyed. Compared to Israel, Egypt, South Korea, South Vietnam, and Turkey, the countries of Latin America must be considered less critical to the security and strategic interests of the United States, or, perhaps, the threats to U.S. interests from Latin America have been less urgent. By comparison, the Latin American claim on overall U.S. aid is not significant, but for certain governments (such as those in Brazil, the Dominican Republic, and El Salvador), the aid can be crucial.

TABLE 4.7
U.S. Loans and Grants to Latin America, 1962-1982
(in millions of dollars)

Country	Economic	Military	Total
Argentina	186.5	261.5	448.0
Barbados	3.7	0.2	3.9
Belize	11.2	0.0	11.2
Bolivia	717.0	79.9	796.9
Brazil	2230.3	413.9	2644.2
Chile	1060.5	145.9	1206.4
Colombia	1384.1	199.0	1583.1
Costa Rica	281.8	9.0	290.8
Cuba	0.0	0.0	0.0
Dominican Republic	795.4	47.4	842.8
Ecuador	333.6	87.0	420.6
El Salvador	539.8	140.1	679.9
Guatemala	341.6	40.2	381.8
Guyana	133.8	0.1	133.9
Haiti	297.8	3.2	301.0
Honduras	418.9	71.5	490.4
Jamaica	404.3	4.8	409.1
Mexico	227.8	11.3	239.1
Nicaragua	374.8	30.6	405.4
Panama	407.1	20.7	427.8
Paraguay	157.6	30.0	187.6
Peru	722.7	175.5	898.2
Suriname	3.6	0.1	3.7
Trinidad/Tobago	35.9	0.0	35.9
Uruguay	138.5	57.6	196.1
Venezuela	185.2	121.5	306.7
Regional Central America	309.1	0.0	309.1
Regional Caribbean	281.9	1.0	282.9
Regional Latin America	703.7	0.1	703.8
Total [a]	12,688	1,952	14,640
U.S. loans and grants worldwide	105,566	65,236	170,802
Latin American percent of world total	12.0	3.0	8.5

[a] Total is not exact due to rounding.
Source: Agency for International Development, U.S. Overseas Loa and Grants, July 1, 1945-September 30, 1982, Washington, 1983, pp. 33-64.

What also can be important is the impact of even minimal amounts of economic and military assistance on governments of small countries. It is not necessarily the amount of aid, but its capacity for keeping friendly forces in power in countries whose economic bases are vulnerable to outside capital or whose armies are dependent on U.S. weapons.

In summary, economic assistance provides an instrument for the U.S. government to protect its various interests in Latin America. However, because these interests are not necessarily economic, aid by itself is not a useful means of explaining U.S. economic objectives in the region. Aid does, nevertheless, represent the importance attached to certain countries in the area and can therefore indicate, from year to year, where U.S. priorities lie. The large amounts of economic assistance to El Salvador, for instance, compared to other Central American states, highlights that country's important place in recent U.S. policy. El Salvador, in fact, has received more military aid over the past twenty years than all but five of the largest countries in the hemisphere.

THE DEBT PROBLEM

An increasingly important symbol of Latin American economic dependence on the United States is the growing problem of national indebtedness to U.S. and West European banks. During the early 1970s, when economic growth seemed inevitable in Latin America, when in fact rapid gains were being made in a number of economies, Latin governments borrowed heavily from foreign banks to finance their new development and social welfare projects. Expecting these debts to be repaid from exports stemming from an expanding economy and from exports of oil and other raw materials, West European and U.S. bankers willingly extended billions of dollars in credit to Latin American governments.

Regrettably for both the governments and the bankers, the predicted growth and prosperity did not occur. Oil prices went down, cutting revenues for the oil producers. Raw materials prices fell, and the cost of manufactured imports rose, resulting in serious imbalances between what was being paid out and the revenues coming in.

In addition, the dramatic rise in the value of the U.S. dollar increased the cost of importing the goods from the United States that were necessary for development and those for which consumers had become expectant. The high price of the dollar relative to local currencies also meant it cost more in 1984 to repay loans arranged in 1974. This problem was compounded by an increase in interest rates in the United States, which raised even further the cost of borrowing and which encouraged local capital to flow to the United States where it could earn a better return than at home.

Consequently, countries such as Mexico, Brazil, and Argentina were suddenly faced with huge debts of billions of dollars, far beyond their current capacities to repay. For example, in 1984 the foreign debt of all the Latin American countries stood at $340 billion. Brazil owed more than $100 billion; Mexico, $90 billion; and Argentina, $45 billion. These amounts are equal to 35 to 40 percent of their gross national products (GNPs) and do not include the large annual interest payments. For 1984 Brazil's interest payment alone came to about $12 billion.

According to the International Monetary Fund (IMF), Argentina must spend 85 percent of its earnings from exports to pay the interest on its foreign debt. The region as a whole was spending 42.7 percent of its export earnings on interest in 1983. This was money that could not be devoted to economic development.[13]

Dealing with the Debt

To cope with such debt problems, default is an option most governments prefer to avoid because it could damage their ability to borrow money in the future. Alternative options are to restrict imports, to impose restrictions on the removal of capital, and to increase exports. The dilemma arises when the expansion of exports requires imported technology that must be paid for in expensive dollars or when the exports confront markets so saturated that there is no room for a profitable expansion.

In seeking a solution, governments have turned to international agencies such as the IMF for emergency credit and for funds to salvage national budgets. This option, however, entails compliance with IMF guidelines such as strict limits on imports, cuts in government spending, and wage freezes to control inflation. Obviously, these are not politically popular steps, and governments interested in remaining in power have been reluctant to take them.

In the Dominican Republic, for example, consumers and workers erupted in protests and strikes in April 1984 when the government began complying with IMF guidelines as part of the process of repaying its $2 billion debt. The IMF had granted Santo Domingo a loan of $40 million but had insisted on a number of austerity measures that increased taxes, devalued the peso (which increased the price of imports such as oil and wheat), and cut government spending. With reduced government subsidies, the price of beans went from $.30 to

$.65 a pound; cooking oil, from $9.75 to $25.00 a gallon. The resulting riots claimed about sixty lives.[14]

For the United States, the Dominican Republic is a close friend and testimony to a generally successful foreign policy, and yet, the Reagan administration refused to grant the country any increase in the $100 million in aid it was to receive in 1984. This rejection came despite a personal visit to Washington by the Dominican president, Salvador Jorge Blanco.

Argentina has taken the lead in attempting to renegotiate its debts. By means of renegotiation, repayment schedules and terms can be altered and outside help (from the IMF and U.S. government, for instance) can be sought. This option provided some short-term breathing space, but the crisis did not end. Political opposition to the newly elected Raul Alfonsín government's efforts to repay debts incurred by the discredited military regime produced pressure for outright default. But unless the Argentine economy can rebound, even renegotiation may not solve the problem.

U.S. Role

The current crisis is of such proportions that it provides an opportunity to examine the degree of Latin America's dependence on the United States. Governments are unable to control their own national economies or to plan development because they have little influence over the cost of credit, the prices of exports and imports, or the value of the U.S. dollar. The political consequences are potentially very serious as governments struggle to keep their economies afloat and still meet the demands of their expectant publics.

Possibilities for the U.S. government to help rescue the region existed, but the Reagan administration, in keeping with U.S. tradition, was reluctant to interfere in the debt issues or help bail out its victims. As the economic instability accelerates, however, Washington may be compelled by events to acknowledge some responsibility for the debt, and step in with the aid. In addition to granting direct financial subsidies, Washington could explore refinancing arrangements with U.S. banks, take steps to reduce U.S. interest rates, and consider preferential treatment for certain Latin American imports.

The chairman of the U.S. Federal Reserve Board, Paul A. Volcker, did suggest that banks limit the rates they charge on loans to developing countries and that they "reward" with extended repayment periods countries that have taken austerity measures. Such a rescheduling of the debt was worked out with Mexico in 1984 so that its debt repayment could be stretched out over fourteen years at lower interest rates. In addition, in mid-1984 the major Latin American debtors came to an agreement on a common strategy for refinancing. In 1985, the Reagan administration did propose a $29 billion plan for debt financing in the Third World, but since it would rely primarily on private banks and appeared linked to "market-oriented economic policies," there was skepticism about its chances for success.[15] Nonetheless, if this pattern is followed elsewhere and if there is some global economic recovery, then a major financial crisis may be averted.

For Raul Alfonsín, president of Argentina, "Latin America cannot take any more. . . . It is like a neutron bomb in which men and women remain alive, but all the generated wealth is destroyed. It is as though madness has taken over the financial centers."[16]

THE EXPROPRIATION PROBLEM: PERU

In this text we have already touched on the consequences of economic nationalism in Latin America. Government expropriation of private U.S. companies and property in Guatemala, Cuba, and Chile have provoked strong interventionary responses from Washington. If there is any one act that seems to signal hostility to Washington, it is the nationalization of private investments, especially when the seizures are not accompanied by what is regarded as fair compensation. Such acts are taken as signs that a government is embarked on a path that will go beyond just economic nationalism and in the direction of challenges to the diplomatic and security interests of the United States.

To review these cases: The Allende government in Chile took over U.S. copper mines without compensation, due to the alleged failure of the companies to pay Chile a fair return for the copper ore. Castro seized U.S. factories and sugar properties with payment of twenty-five–year bonds of dubious reliability. Guatemala attempted to take over United Fruit Company lands with only token compensation, based on the company's own declaration of its tax liabilities. In each instance, the U.S. government sympathized with the grievances of the private corporations and took action to bring down the respective governments.

However dramatic these cases may be, they are not the only incidents of nationalization. The United States has struggled over the years to develop a policy to deal with nationalization, and although such a policy exists on paper, its implementation has been difficult. As a result, Washington today usually ends up reluctantly accepting the fact of expropriation.

The U.S. government has never denied that a sovereign state has the right to nationalize foreign property. But in keeping with international law, Washington has insisted that prompt, adequate, and effective compensation be paid. A major obstacle, of course, is determining just what is "prompt, adequate, and effective" compensation. Recognition of the right of nationalization notwithstanding, the U.S. generally has opposed the action and has sought to punish governments that have insisted on it.[17]

The Hickenlooper Amendment

Representative of U.S. policy toward expropriation is the Hickenlooper Amendment adopted by Congress in 1962. This legislation provided that economic assistance would be cut off to any government that failed to take steps (within six months) to compensate fairly for the expropriation of U.S.-owned property.

As Lars Schoultz notes, this amendment and ones like it have been products of effective and continuous corporate lobbying efforts in Washington to marshal the power of the U.S. government to resist expropriation attempts. In fact, the Hickenlooper legislation was drawn up by an attorney attempting to discourage the Honduran government from seizing United Fruit Company property.[18]

The IPC Takeover

The most notable application of the amendment came in retaliation for the Peruvian government's 1964 seizure of the International Petroleum Corporation (IPC), a subsidiary of Exxon. Not only was no compensation paid, but IPC was presented a bill for $690 million for its years of illegal drilling and tax evasion. The company claimed its property in Peru was worth only $120 million.

IPC had been a target of criticism for some years in Peru, in part because it happened to be so large and so dominant in the country's oil industry. Its owner (Standard Oil of New Jersey) had annual revenues three times greater than Peru's gross national product. Exxon's 1969 payroll was 25 percent larger than the Peruvian government's budget. However, the takeover may have had more to do with Peruvian politics than with a concerted effort to place Peru's oil industry under government ownership or to drive Exxon completely out of the country. IPC's involvement in supporting President Belaúnde Terry helped precipitate the 1968 military coup that turned against all U.S. companies in Peru for their presumed meddling in domestic politics.[19]

The Department of State began immediately to phase out aid to Peru because of this case and other takeovers of U.S.-owned property.

By 1970, nearly all U.S. aid had been suspended, and the Nixon administration was acting to freeze Peru's access to credit from the international banking system. There was, however, little indication of Peru's willingness to settle. The Hickenlooper approach was not accomplishing its purpose.[20]

In 1974, a compensation agreement with Peru was finally worked out. It was a scheme, however, funded primarily by the U.S. Export-Import Bank, the World Bank, the Inter-American Development Bank, and private U.S. banks, not by Peru itself. The settlement provided for reimbursement of a number of U.S. companies, such as W. R. Grace and H. J. Heinz, and an amount for the U.S. government to distribute to other aggrieved parties. Peru had not conceded a debt directly to IPC, but IPC did receive $22 million from the compensation funds.[21] With Peru's credit worthiness restored, U.S. assistance and loans from U.S. banks resumed.

A Changing Policy

By the mid-1970s, Congress had ceased to include the Hickenlooper Amendment in foreign assistance legislation. The statement had generally proven ineffective and stood as a symbol of old-fashioned dollar diplomacy and an arrogant challenge to the sovereign right to nationalize foreign-owned property. Rather than automatic punishment of a nation by cutting off assistance, bilateral diplomacy was proving to be a more appropriate approach.

In light of the changing political context in the United States, we are unlikely to see similar ultimata attached so readily to congressional acts. Although the opposition to expropriation will continue, corporate interest groups are no longer guaranteed exclusive access and influence on foreign assistance legislation. They must now compete with changing times and values that have given increased status to groups representing other interests such as human rights.[22] As a result, U.S.–Latin American economic relations may become more pragmatic.

Nonetheless, as Latin American governments seek to gain control over their economies, recurring steps toward expropriation of key industries—especially those that are foreign owned—should be anticipated. In response, we can expect U.S. insistence on adherence to the international legal principle that expropriation requires fair compensation. The United States is also likely to continue advising Latin Americans that a government-run economy is not the way to achieve economic development. U.S. policymakers will probably continue to follow the practical course of arranging compromises, such as in the Peruvian case and in earlier ones in Mexico and Bolivia, rather than attempting to enforce rigidly the Hickenlooper concept.

THE EXPROPRIATION PROBLEM: VENEZUELA

Perhaps indicative of a change in the U.S. approach to nationalization is the reaction to Venezuela's expropriation of its oil industry in the mid-1970s. As explained by Paul Sigmund, the moderate response of the U.S. government in the case was considerably different from its reactions to expropriations in Cuba, Chile, and Peru.[23]

Background

In the years immediately preceding the 1976 nationalization, the Venezuelan government had been systematically increasing its regulation of the country's extensive oil industry and had begun gradually to take control of portions of the production and refining operations. Venezuela has been a major world oil producer since the 1920s, and nearly the entire industry had come to be dominated by foreign companies such as Esso and Shell.[24] By 1970, Venezuela was among the top five oil exporters in the world and by far the largest Latin American producer.

Oil meant a sustained economic boom for Venezuela, particularly because of the precedent-setting arrangement in 1948, whereby the oil companies were required to pay 50 percent of their profits and income to the Venezuelan government. From the early years, the government's control over oil had been established. Additional regulations were added, following the installation of a democratic government in 1958.

The Nationalization

When the nationalization process started in earnest in 1974, the government proceeded with careful attention to educating both the companies and the public. The politics of the process were not easy, but the experience provides a lesson on alternative strategies for a country seeking ways to gain control over natural resources.[25] By October 1975, most of the compensation arrangements were worked out, with payments ranging up to $512 million to Exxon (formerly Esso). The U.S. government was not an active participant in the negotiations nor did it protest the settlement.

Implications

The rather smooth nationalization process in Venezuela may be explained by several factors:

1. Venezuela was a functioning, stable democracy with cordial ties to the United States.
2. The nationalization was not part of a systematic attack on all foreign or U.S. investment.
3. The government had a long-established habit of responsible regulation of and participation in the oil industry.
4. The context of the times (1974–1975) was conducive to bargaining on oil, due to the global oil shortages and the demonstrated strength of the Organization of Petroleum Exporting Countries (OPEC).
5. The U.S. government did not see the developments as a threat to its security interests or political influence in the region.

Whether or not the Venezuelan model, and the flexible U.S. reaction to it, represents a new pattern for U.S.–Latin American relations remains to be seen, but the precedence for pragmatism has been set.

CONCLUSIONS

On the basis of the topics discussed in this chapter, we can draw a number of conclusions about the economic dimensions of U.S. relations with Latin America.

1. U.S. economic interests in Latin America are important but not vital. Moreover, these important interests are scattered throughout the region, from oil in Mexico to copper in Chile, and from sugar in the Dominican Republic to banking in Brazil. No one product, no one country is essential for U.S. prosperity and security.

2. These interests are largely private. That is, the major beneficiaries and promoters of U.S. investment in mining, agriculture, and manufacturing are private U.S. corporations, banks, and multinational firms. These special interests may lobby the U.S. government for help in the region, but they also engage in their own bargaining with governments in Latin America. These companies are not instruments of U.S. policy, although they may at times act in concert with the U.S. government. They may, of course, also act contrary to the interests of the U.S. government.

3. Because the U.S. government does see the welfare of U.S. corporations and U.S. access to raw materials in Latin America as being in the national interest, there is an inevitable support for private enterprise in the region. The Export-Import Bank and OPIC are two agencies created to help U.S. commerce, and legislation like the Hickenlooper Amendment also tries to protect private U.S. property.

The frequent cases of U.S. government actions against economic nationalism demonstrate the intensity of Washington's concern.

4. U.S. economic and military assistance to Latin America has not kept pace with assistance elsewhere in the world where security interests are seen as more seriously threatened. This disproportion reflects the relatively low priority of the Western Hemisphere on the U.S. foreign policy agenda. The aid that is sent to Latin America tends to be a response to security problems and revolutions. Primacy in aid is usually granted to friendly governments standing firm against communism. As we have seen, however, aid is no guarantee that anti-U.S. revolutions will not occur.

5. Trade and investment patterns reveal the importance of the United States as a market for Latin American products and as a source of capital investment. The United States is also the predominant provider of manufactured goods to Latin America. Economic relations with the United States can be critically important for any given country in the region. The reverse is not true: The United States is not dependent on economic ties to any single Latin American state.

6. The contemporary problem of Latin America's foreign debt may be seen as an illustration of dependence on foreign capital. The foreign debt threatens the economic and political health of several large and small countries. The U.S. government's tendency to disregard the seriousness of this problem could well create a backlash in the region against the U.S. and international banking community.

7. A major cause of friction in U.S.–Latin American relations has been the battle over nationalization of private U.S. property. The U.S. response to this action appears to be moderating, but the ideology and symbolism that expropriation entails are still capable of producing misunderstandings and conflict.

8. The primary driving force behind U.S. actions in Latin America tends to be those interests associated with security and political influence. The cases of Guatemala in 1954 and Allende's Chile reveal the involvement of economic interests, but as the reaction to the Peruvian and Venezuelan nationalizations indicates, economics alone has not been sufficient cause for intervention.

NOTES

1. Central Intelligence Agency, *Estimated Energy Statistical Review* (Washington, D.C.: October 25, 1983), 4.

2. A thorough study of U.S. dependence on raw materials is in Margaret Daly Hayes, *Latin America and the U.S. National Interest* (Boulder, Colo.: Westview Press, 1984), 59–62.

3. U.S. Department of Commerce, *U.S. General Imports/World Areas by Commodity Groupings, 1980* (Washington, D.C.: 1981). Also see *Trade: U.S. Policy Since 1945* (Washington, D.C.: Congressional Quarterly, 1984), 9.

4. United Nations, *Handbook of International Trade and Development Statistics* (New York, 1983), 114-115.

5. United Nations, *1979/80 Statistical Yearbook* (New York, 1981), 502-510.

6. United Nations, *Handbook of International Trade*, 116-117.

7. U.S. Department of Commerce, *Survey of Current Business* 62 (August 1982), 66-67. Also see *Trade: US Policy Since 1945*.

8. United Nations, *1979/80 Statistical Yearbook*.

9. U.S. Department of Commerce, *Survey of Current Business*, 13. Also see U.S. Department of Commerce, *U.S. Direct Investment Abroad* (Washington, D.C.: annually).

10. Senate Committee on Foreign Relations, *OPIC Authorization* (Hearings), 95th Cong., 1st Sess. (Washington, D.C.: July-August 1977). Also see Lars Schoultz, *Human Rights and United States Policy Toward Latin America* (Princeton, N.J.: Princeton University Press, 1981), 312-321.

11. "Development Report," *Topics* (an OPIC publication) 11 (May/June 1982), 15.

12. Overseas Private Investment Corporation, *1981 Annual Report* (Washington, D.C.: 1982), 11, 46, 53-56.

13. Reported in *New York Times*, May 14, 1984, 37 and June, 17, 1984, E2. For a discussion of the political impact of the debt, see Riordan Roett, "Democracy and Debt in South America: A Continent's Dilemma," in William P. Bundy, ed., *America and the World, 1983* (New York: Pergamon Press, 1984), 695-720.

14. *New York Times*, April 29, 1984, 11, and May 1, 1984, 24. For a summary of the criticism against the IMF, see *Financial Times*, September 16, 1985, 1, 16.

15. *New York Times*, August 28, 1984, 31, and *International Herald Tribune*, October 9, 1985, 1. Peru's president, Alan García, announced in 1985 that his government would pay only 10 percent of its export earnings to service the country's debt of $14 billion. "Banking on South America," *Economist*, August 17, 1985, 13.

16. Quoted in *New York Times*, May 11, 1984, 6.

17. For an authoritative account of this problem, see Paul E. Sigmund, *Multinationals in Latin America: The Politics of Nationalization* (Madison: University of Wisconsin Press, 1980). Also see Cole Blaiser, *The Hovering Giant: U.S. Responses to Revolutionary Change in Latin America* (Pittsburgh: University of Pittsburgh Press, 1976), ch. 4.

18. Schoultz, *Human Rights*, 98-99.

19. Sigmund, *Multinationals in Latin America*. Also see Adalento I. Pinelo, *The Multinational Corporation in Latin American Politics: A Case Study of the International Petroleum Company in Peru* (New York: Praeger, 1973). The military junta's nationalistic economic policies are subjected to a radical

critique by Aníbal Quijano Obregón, *Nationalism and Capitalism in Peru: A Study in Neo-Imperialism* (New York: Monthly Review Press, 1971).

20. Sigmund, *Multinationals in Latin America,* 179–224. For a critique of this episode by a U.S. senator, see Frank Church, "Toward a New Policy for Latin America," in Richard B. Gray, ed., *Latin America and the United States in the 1970's* (Itasca, Ill.: Peacock Publishers, 1971), 344–345. Also see Richard N. Goodwin, "Letter from Peru," *New Yorker* 45, May 17, 1969, 41–67.

21. Blaiser, *The Hovering Giant,* 260–262.

22. Schoultz, *Human Rights,* 364, 373–374.

23. Sigmund, *Multinationals in Latin America,* 226–228.

24. Edwin Lieuwen, *Petroleum in Venezuela: A History* (Berkeley: University of California Press, 1954); and Wayne E. Taylor and John Lindeman, *The Creole Petroleum Corporation in Venezuela* (Washington, D.C.: National Planning Association, 1955).

25. Franklin Tugwell, *The Politics of Oil in Venezuela* (Stanford, Calif.: Stanford University of Press, 1975).

PART 2
GLOBAL PERSPECTIVES

Latin America may at times have been treated by the United States as a region deserving special, often paternal, attention. Especially in the last two decades, there has been a tendency to perceive of Latin America's importance primarily as part of U.S. global responsibilities. Thus, events in the hemisphere—revolutions, economic development, military rule—have no particular priority for U.S. policymakers until the events become identified with broader, worldwide security and ideological interests of the United States. Recognition of the dependent role Latin America plays in U.S. foreign policy may help one to understand why Washington's responses so often appear to be out of step with the historical, cultural, and political dynamics of Latin America itself.

There are three main kinds of global perspectives. One relates to the concept of dependency: The regions' role resides primarily in its dependent economic status in the world capitalist system. In this view, Latin America's plight is no different from that of other Third World states seeking economic independence. According to this concept, U.S. policy perpetuates dependence.

Second is the ideological perspective, the democratic mission; Latin America becomes involved in the U.S. effort to promote democracy and halt communism. Concern for democratic procedures and human rights, for example, are universal interests, not specifically intended for Latin America, and yet, when carried to the region without full cognizance of their applicability, they often create more problems for the United States than they solve. On the one hand, the United States stands for democracy; on the other, it is concerned for security. Although these two interests need not compete, policymakers often choose between them. The sense of adhering to a democratic mission has been a strong influence on U.S. policy and it may help us to understand some actions in Latin America. It has, however, also demonstrated the dilemmas of trying to fit regional developments and patterns into a global ideological framework.

The third global perspective is the strategic, which views Latin America as important when it becomes enveloped in the strategic struggle with the Soviet Union. Latin America has, in the cold war era, generally been accorded low priority in U.S. policy considerations, and senior policymakers seem to have preferred it that way. It follows then that the task of U.S. diplomats is to keep Latin America off the desk of the secretary of state or the president by preventing local problems from escalating into strategic importance. Once revolutions or conflicts are linked to the USSR or communism, the United States is compelled to act because of the negative strategic consequences of failing to act. This perspective contends that although a problem may appear local, if there are signs of an outcome favorable to the USSR, Washington must respond or find its global position weakened.

The next four chapters explore this broad approach to U.S.-Latin American relations. Chapter 5 examines the dependency relationship and Chapter 6, the democratic mission. Chapters 7 and 8 consider the strategic interests that also direct U.S. policy.

5
DEPENDENCY

THE CONCEPT

To treat U.S.-Latin American relations in the context of "dependency" is to depart from the usual perspective of governmental or even national relationships. This approach looks beyond the nation-state paradigm to a broader explanation for Latin America's political and economic underdevelopment. It focuses on patterns that have created the Latin American dependency on the economic forces of capitalism emanating primarily from the United States.

Definition

A standard definition of dependency, or *dependencia*, is offered by Theotonio dos Santos, "By dependence we mean a situation in which the economy of certain countries is conditioned by the development and expansion of another economy to which the former is subjected."[1]

Thus, the development of Latin America's economies is a direct reflection of the growth—or decline—of the self-sustaining economies of the capitalist countries. Moreover, the political consequences of this economic relationship tend to be dependent as well. Those elites in Latin America that benefit from the dependent connection invariably gain political control and maintain it through the manipulation of both economic and military instruments.[2]

Dependency is closely related to theories of imperialism and to Marxist analyses of underdevelopment,[3] but some analysts have made a conscious effort to present this framework without relying entirely on those traditional concepts. Of particular utility in this respect is Johann Galtung's "A Structural Theory of Imperialism." Although not explicitly developed for Latin America, his concept helps to illustrate the nature and the scope of a dependent relationship.[4]

Characteristics

Using Galtung's terminology, it is possible to describe U.S.-Latin American relations as controlled by interlocking elites whose power constitutes the "center" of each country. These elites may be large in number and have a variety of differentiated powers, such as in the United States, or they may be small in number with overlapping and duplicate powers. In the United States, elites tend to be specialized and differentiated from each other; for example, the political, military, business, and communications elites are each distinct groups. In Latin America, ruling elites are more likely to have multiple functions; economic elites and military elites may also have positions of political authority. In addition, the highly structured class system in much of Latin America, handed down from the colonial era, contributes to the consolidation of power by the narrow elites in the region.

These "centers" have more in common with each other, whether they be North American or Latin American, than they have with their own mass populations (or "peripheries"). The elite groups share a common interest in capitalism, tend to have an international perspective, which, for example, leads them to send their children abroad for education, and they tend to aspire to values that enhance elite power rather than national development. The national interest, then, becomes synonymous with the elite's interest. The Peruvian center, therefore, is oriented to the U.S. center and the perpetuation of the world capitalist system that has enabled both centers to gain and hold power.

As a result of this link among centers and the lack of influence by peripheries, according to Galtung's theory, economic development will follow capitalist models and be shaped by the interests of the "center country," the United States. Whether it is industrialization, communications, or agriculture, the U.S. private enterprise and market-oriented model will predominate, thereby creating a dependent relationship that deprives the people of Latin America from control over their economic lives. It is not that Peru, for example, is dependent as a nation, but rather that the masses of Peru, along with the masses elsewhere in the region, cannot shape their own destinies. The struggle, for them, is not Peru against the United States, it is the people—regardless of nationality—against the international capitalist system to which the Peruvian elites belong and of which the United States elites are the leaders.

The theory states that radical change is required to alter this structure. It is not enough that national economies prosper, for that guarantees only that the "center" gains, not the people. Moderate change that aims at reform and development within the Western capitalist mode will not, it is argued, seriously affect the prevailing pattern of dependency. Liberation requires radical change, perhaps revolution according to the Cuban model.

However, as recent history has shown, the capitalist elites are committed to preventing revolution or suppressing it whenever it threatens the system. Pressure from the United States has forced Cuba, the argument goes, to depend on the Soviet Union, but Cuba's revolution stands as a symbol for those who strive for liberation. Nonetheless, the intensity of the capitalists' successful purging of Allende's moderate Marxism from Chile is testimony to their determination and power. A similar threat has emerged in the case of Nicaragua: Radical success there could begin to erode the legitimacy and dominance of the ruling elites elsewhere in Central America.

Relationship to U.S. Policy

Viewing U.S. policy through the dependency prism shows how the policy is often perceived in many parts of Latin America, especially among university students and intellectuals. For these groups, the solution to underdevelopment and suppression lies in ridding their countries of ruling classes more attuned to U.S. capitalist interests than to their own people's welfare.

Actions by the U.S. government, therefore, are seen as steps taken to enhance control of local elites so that capitalist exploitation of the region can continue. It is assumed that economic growth and the resulting political stability in the United States is a result of the exploitation of Latin America. The development and prosperity of the United States, accordingly, is directly proportional to the underdevelopment and poverty of Latin America. Military intervention, trade, aid programs, and even cultural and educational exchanges all contribute to strengthening the integration of the capitalist centers, not necessarily to improving the lives of the masses.[5]

A Critique

The difficulties in relying on dependency theory to explain U.S. policy lie in the theory's assumption that economics is the key factor in international relations and that national political and strategic interests are subordinate to class interests. Critics contend that the theory neither accounts fully for nationalism that is not linked to Marxist revolutions nor deals adequately with the Cuban experience of apparently replacing one mode of dependency with another.[6]

However, it is not the purpose of this chapter to offer a complete critique of *dependencia,* but rather to present its basic outline in order to illustrate an alternative, economically based perspective for analyzing the globalist dynamics of U.S. relations with Latin America. The central role of dependency theory in Latin American understanding of U.S. policy cannot be underestimated, making this theory a vital component of any discussion of the sources of the problems facing the United States in the region today.

THE NORTH-SOUTH AXIS

A related theme emerging in inter-American relations is the identification of Latin America as part of the Third World, the grouping of poor, developing states that have suffered common ills at the hands of imperialism and colonialism. According to this view, Latin America is more appropriately dealt with along a North-South axis in which the contest is one of rich versus poor, developed versus undeveloped, instead of along the strategic/political East-West axis favored by the United States. The issues dividing the United States and Latin America are, therefore, primarily economic, not those of the Soviet-American cold war.

As the Latin American countries join the poorer states of Africa and Asia in their common struggle against the northern industrialized states, the implications for U.S. policy are clear. The Latin American agenda, that is, the set of issues given top priority in their discussions with U.S. officials, is increasingly focused on the economic issues of aid, trade, and debts. The United States, over the years, has discouraged Latin American collaboration with such southern coalitions as the "Group of 77" and the Neutral/Non-Aligned Movement and has preferred instead to work with the region directly. Even Latin American participation in the United Nations Conference on Trade and Development (UNCTAD) has not been seen by Washington as necessary for development.

A New International Economic Order

The Group of 77, UNCTAD, and others have called for a New International Economic Order (NIEO), a major revision of the international economic policies of the northern states. In Washington's view these demands were tantamount to overturning the system established after World War II, a system that has brought prosperity and growth to the industrialized countries. Therefore, any thought of agreeing to a new order was invariably rejected.[7] The Carter administration outlined some modest concessions that could be made in the area of tariffs and quotas but argued that the essential characteristics of the global economic system should be maintained. The Reagan administration rejected any notion that the North-South axis could supplant the East-West struggle.

A Latin America united with other Third World states could pose a threat to U.S. access to raw materials and oil, but to date that unity has not developed, and in its absence Washington has not been persuaded to make any concessions. The issues of access to U.S. markets, preferential tariffs, subsidies, and reliable commodity agreements are high priority interests in Latin America; they have received little attention in Washington.

Carter's Efforts

Tentative steps toward accommodation were taken by the Carter administration. Specialists warned of the possibility of debt repudiation by Third World states and the potential for producer cartels on raw materials. Such threats, it was argued, required the United States to make certain conciliatory gestures. These included reduced trade restrictions for the Third World, regional cooperation on managing natural resources, cooperation to prevent dominance by multinational corporations, control of commodity price fluctuation, and long-term efforts to promote nutrition, food supplies, health care, and family planning.[8] In general, though, the United States government has been reluctant to make any major concessions.

The Cancún Meeting

Typical of the prevailing view in the 1980s was President Reagan's approach at the 1981 Cancún (Mexico) meeting on North-South problems.[9] Instead of addressing the specific issues of the NIEO, such as special tariff concessions and preferential trade, the president insisted that the current free trade system was still the best hope for development. He encouraged the developing countries to "get their own houses in order" as a first step toward improving their international economic situation. Poor countries needed to pull themselves up by hard work and discipline; successful development would come from unfettered competition and allegiance to free enterprise. In the eyes of the NIEO advocates, however, the free enterprise system was the problem, not the cure.

The Caribbean Basin Initiative

Reagan's February 1982 announcement of the Caribbean Basin Initiative (CBI) called for a number of steps to promote economic growth and stability in the Central American–Caribbean region.[10] The rather innovative proposals were clearly designed to address the problems likely to contribute to disorder in the area and to respond to critics who had charged that the administration was ignoring the economic difficulties of poor states in the U.S. backyard.

The president identified the troubles arising from high energy prices, inflation, and interest rates, the decline in agricultural productivity, and the failure of manufacturing enterprises. His solution was to give preferential access to U.S. markets for Caribbean products, to provide technical assistance for the development of export industries, and to encourage private investment.[11]

The economic theme of Reagan's statement was the promotion of free enterprise. Private U.S. firms would be encouraged to invest in the region and individual entrepreneurs would be supported by U.S. policies. Private sector participation, then, was seen as more crucial to economic stability than direct government assistance programs. If such a scheme were successful, the Reagan administration might well be credited with a general refocusing of U.S. assistance programs. To date, however, there has been insufficient evidence of major accomplishments. Domestic U.S. politics have caused tariff and quota preferences to be reduced, and the flow of private investment has not increased noticeably, particularly to governments suffering from large outstanding international debts.

The political theme of the CBI, however, was globalist; Reagan did not divorce it from the East-West struggle. Cuba and Nicaragua were not included in the plan and the CBI's ultimate objective was security, not necessarily long-term economic development. Moreover, as Abraham Lowenthal has pointed out, the concept of a "Caribbean Basin" grew out of Washington's geopolitical concept, not out of any inherent sense of community or even common problems that would tie the Central American countries to the variety of island states in the area. The "Basin" may be a convenient strategic reference point, but the result was bilateral aid and trade relations with the United States.[12]

Washington's loyalty to the capitalist model of development was reiterated in August 1984 when U.S. delegates told a conference on population that the problems emanating from population growth could be solved by economic development. If developing countries, they argued, would allow unregulated private competition instead of gov-

ernment-directed development, the resulting economic growth would
take care of overpopulation.[13]

Critics of the Reagan approach contended that what has worked
for the United States may not work in Latin America and that
Washington's inflexible adherence to the capitalist model runs the
risk of making U.S. economic policy and guidance increasingly irrelevant. The disagreement arose out of the conflict between beliefs
deeply held in the United States and the conviction among many in
Latin America that the capitalist model was not appropriate for them.

It is clear that the governing elites in a number of Latin American
countries remain committed to the basic premises of free enterprise,
but even they face the difficulties of dealing with economic pressures
that appear beyond the capacity of the free market system to resolve.
The next few years may see a stronger Latin American alliance with
the South and a more unified, forceful approach to bargaining with
the United States on economic issues.

THE MEXICAN CASE

United States economic relations with Mexico typify the relations
it has with several Latin American countries. These ties are often
characterized by extensive trade and private investment, reliance on
U.S. banks for loans and on U.S. companies for technology. In addition,
the growing economic nationalism and political liabilities of open
accommodation to U.S. interests have created friction in the economic
and diplomatic arenas.

In both small economies, such as Guatemala's or the Dominican
Republic's, and large ones, such as Brazil's or Mexico's, the perception
of dependence on the United States has produced demands for major
alterations in the existing relationships. For Washington—and Wall
Street—the problem lies in how far it is necessary to accommodate
those demands in order to protect U.S. economic interests in the
region. Those who view the issues from a Latin American perspective
tend to use dependency theory; those who approach from a U.S.
point of view tend to accept the givens of the existing system and
seek ways by which U.S. interests can best be served.

A Dependency Analysis

An illustration of the impact of dependency theory on an understanding of U.S. foreign policy was provided in an analysis of
Mexico's political and economic development by James D. Cockcroft.[14]

Cockcroft's account of Mexico's contemporary situation focused on the pervasive role foreign capital has played in the country's history.

During the nineteenth century, Mexico's economy was dominated by foreign ownership of agricultural, mining, and manufacturing enterprises, an ownership that demonstrated no commitment to Mexican industrial development. The objective was to enhance the wealth of foreign companies. The Mexican upper classes were closely linked to foreign capital but unable to influence its use in Mexico. At the time of the Mexican Revolution (1910–1917), according to Cockcroft, "The single most important economic group in Mexico was a *foreign bourgeoisie.*" United States companies, for example, controlled 70 percent of Mexico's oil production, a significant role, considering Mexico provided 24 percent of the world's total oil production.[15]

Moreover, the revolution did not substantially alter this fact of foreign influence. The Wilson administration's intervention was aimed, in Cockcroft's view, more at protecting U.S. investments and property than at guaranteeing democracy. U.S. private and government support of President Venustiano Carranza (1917–1920) smoothed the way for restraining the economic nationalism that threatened to expel foreign capital. This co-optation led to what Cockcroft calls the "misdevelopment" of the Mexican Revolution, a process which enabled the local bourgeoisie "to control, check and throw back the aroused masses."[16]

Today, foreign capital continues to shape the direction of the Mexican economy and, indirectly, the country's political life as well. Even with recent attempts to limit foreign investment to less than 50 percent in certain key industries, multinational and U.S. corporations still control a third of the income of Mexico's top four hundred companies. In addition, Mexico is dependent on U.S. technology and on U.S. banks to support industrial development, and trade with the United States has accounted for more than half of Mexico's foreign trade. Moreover, as in the past, there have been no signs that Mexico's infant industries will be allowed to compete with U.S. and European enterprises. Even new factories near the U.S. border were situated for the convenience of U.S. companies, to be used for their benefit, not for the development of a viable Mexican economy.

Thus, as Cockcroft put it, Mexico's economy is not an autonomous one dealing with the needs of the people, but "one of state capitalism, preponderantly dependent upon a foreign bourgeoisie and conducive to favorable investment conditions for both foreign and national capitalists."[17]

An Alternative View

Although no one can deny the significant role the United States has played in Mexico's economy, another perspective treats the relationship not as a demonstration of dependency, but as a working out of mutual benefits within the existing realities. Typical of this viewpoint is the assertion that it is not dependency or capitalist models with which we should be concerned, but the identification of U.S. economic interests in Mexico and how they might be protected. This view, expressed, for example, in a study by Bruce M. Bagley, is sensitive to Mexico's attempt to control its own economic development but approaches the issue in terms of U.S. foreign policy.[18]

Given the fact that Mexico has been the third largest trading partner of the United States, accounting for 4 percent of total U.S. trade, there is no prospect for the two countries avoiding economic interdependence. The recent development of Mexican oil exports, for instance, has made Mexico the single most important supplier of foreign oil to the United States, a situation that has both generated friction and opened opportunities in relations between the two countries.

Oil provides a means for Mexican movement toward economic stability and development, but only if the export prices remain high and if the revenues are invested in modern industrial activities and infrastructure. Opportunities for expansion of exports depend on technological innovation and on openings in the U.S. market. These achievements are not possible without U.S. cooperation; economic collaboration with Western Europe and Japan have not yet proved to be a sufficient alternative.

And yet, as Bagley pointed out, the political difficulties of U.S.-Mexican cooperation have been made worse by an exaggerated perception in Mexico of U.S. dominance of the Mexican economy. No Mexican government can afford to give the impression of continuously accommodating U.S. interests, especially in sensitive areas such as oil prices. Bagley contended, in contrast to the dependency analysts, that foreign investment in Mexico has been rather closely monitored by the Mexican government and that in recent years only 5 percent of total private investment in Mexico has come from foreign sources.[19]

Summary

The Mexican case can provide both radical and moderate interpretations of U.S. economic policy in Latin America. Radical approaches such as dependency argue that the pervasive, exploitative role of U.S. capital in Mexico co-opted the Mexican ruling classes and paved the way for U.S. control over the economy. For Mexico to achieve an autonomous economy, independent of U.S. government and private interests, and concerned with the welfare of the people, would require a revolutionary change: first, a change in Mexico to expand power to more popular groups and second, a revision of the country's dependent ties to foreign powers.

Although the more moderate analyses acknowledge the influential role of the United States in Mexico, they point to policies that can be carried out within the prevailing system. Thus, although the United States ought to be more sensitive to Mexico's economic plight, there is no need to overturn the private enterprise and market-oriented system to deal with the problem. Adjustments and concessions may be necessary to maintain a collaborative relationship, but these can be made through routine negotiations. From the U.S. point of view, the recent situation may have been troublesome politically, but it was not so serious that major accommodations to radical demands were needed. And further, because large segments of the Mexican population have benefited from and have supported the current status of relations with the United States, it is unreasonable to expect drastic change.

In the final analysis, we can anticipate that U.S. foreign policymakers will respond to cases like Mexico's in terms of what protects and enhances the economic interests of the United States. In Washington's eyes, Mexico's grievances can probably be dealt with by modest adjustments; there is no threat serious enough to warrant a more radical response.

THE BRAZILIAN CASE

Actions of the United States in Brazil over the past twenty years can be cited as examples of the exploitation of a dependent relationship in both the economic and political spheres. U.S. involvement in the 1960s has importance not only because of Brazil's status as Latin America's most populous and wealthiest nation, but also because of the far-reaching impact of U.S. involvement in the overthrow of Brazil's government in 1964. In addition to the economic overtones of U.S. policy, the case also involves strategic and ideological considerations.

The 1964 Upheaval

Briefly, the scene for the 1964 upheaval began with the elevation of Brazil's elected vice president, João Goulart, to the presidency upon the resignation of President Jânio Quadros in 1961. Known for his friendship with organized labor and for his socialist views and not for his strong leadership, Goulart raised doubts throughout the country, but the suspicious military allowed him to take office in September 1961. Although Goulart's early relations with Washington were uneasy, he did properly criticize Castro and speak in moderate terms of his plans for Brazil. Nonetheless, he was clearly committed to moving Brazil toward a more socialist economy.[20]

For example, in 1961 Goulart pushed through legislation regulating the export of corporate profits from the country, an act that produced an immediate decline in foreign investment. The subsequent economic crisis resulted in rapid inflation, labor unrest, and an acceleration of Brazil's foreign debt.

In response to the crisis, Goulart adopted a plan for major changes in Brazil's economy, ranging from land reform to tax reform. His scheme, supported three to one by a popular plebiscite in 1963, did not have the backing of the congress or the middle and upper classes. Moreover, Goulart frequently castigated the foreign corporations that had brought wealth and status to large numbers of Brazilians who now saw their positions threatened. The alienation of the urban bourgeoisie and the landed oligarchy was countered by an increasing mobilization of workers and peasants to whom Goulart had promised a better standard of living and the right to vote.

The resulting polarization compelled Goulart to move to a more radical position, and the congress, backed by the military, shifted to a more conservative stand. Washington was becoming increasingly frustrated with Goulart's apparent inability to control inflation (running at 80 percent) or to cut government spending and his refusal to adopt the strict monetary controls necessary to stabilize the economy. Goulart even indicated that Brazil might have to delay payments on its $350 million international debt. Popular as Goulart was, he seemed unable to cope with Brazil's growing economic problems.

For the Johnson administration, Goulart's radicalism was demonstrated at a mass rally on March 13, 1964, when he announced that he had just signed two decrees: One decree nationalized five private oil refineries, and the other called for the expropriation of idle and "underutilized" land close to federal highways. Amid growing turmoil, a coalition of opposition Brazilian state governors asked the U.S. government for help. Washington let it be known that it would not oppose Goulart's removal and, further, that it might even be willing to send some U.S. troops to Brazil. For the Brazilian army, however, it was not economic nationalism that finally pushed it into action, but Goulart's persistent interference in military affairs.[21]

Washington's Role

When the military leaders did seize power, on April 1, the United States had already been collaborating with them for several weeks on ways to depose Goulart.[22] There was no complaint from Washington; in fact, Secretary of State Dean Rusk called the coup "an expression of support for constitutional government."[23] The military junta and its successors went on to become the final arbiter in Brazil's politics for twenty years.

However, the military has since 1979 slowly been relinquishing power. A congress has been elected, and in 1985 indirect elections for president were held. Despite demonstrations for direct popular elections, Brazil's president was chosen by a 686-member electoral college. It was a gradual step toward democracy, one in keeping with the steps taken in 1984 in neighboring Argentina to dismantle a military regime.[24]

Dependency?

The role of the United States in the 1964 coup and the subsequent domination of the economy by foreign capital have been taken as additional evidence of Brazil's dependent status.[25] Immediately following the coup, the military government lifted restrictions on foreign investors and allowed their profits to be freely exported. In 1984, Brazil was faced with an enormous foreign debt of almost $100 billion and no solution for its long-standing problems of class division, concentrated land ownership, and pervasive foreign economic intervention. What prevails in Brazil, according to a dependency argument, is a state capitalist system where nationalist economic policies have been discredited and where "modernization" has come only to those sectors and elites that collaborate with foreign capital. This modernization has been at the expense of the masses. As a former Brazilian president recently declared, "The Brazilian economy is doing well, but the people are doing badly."[26]

Nevertheless, the economic potential of Brazil is so immense and its resources and technical skills so superior to those of most other countries in Latin America that the prospects for Brazil's defying the dependency syndrome are quite high. The tentative steps toward democracy and the likelihood of an economic recovery would not change Brazil's fundamental "capitalist" orientation, but they would suggest a move toward a more independent economy. U.S. investors and subsidiaries of U.S. companies are not likely to be driven from the country; Brazil's involvement in the international economy is too extensive for that to happen suddenly. It is too early, however, to tell if the masses will benefit from these changes.

CONCLUSIONS

The dependency model argues that it is possible for a country to protect its foreign economic interests without direct intervention. Applying the model to Latin America suggests that the region's underdevelopment is a result of dependency on foreign—primarily U.S.—capital. The evidence and logic of the argument can be persuasive, and there is reason for the U.S. government to be concerned about ignoring the demands for radical change. There does not, however, appear to be much prospect of the United States responding to Latin America as though the dependency relationship actually existed and ought to be corrected.

However, the dependency perspective has increasingly come to shape Latin American perceptions of U.S. policy. In addition, it has contributed to the growing tendency of Latin American governments to identify their interests as better protected by alignment with other Third World states along a North-South axis rather than along the East-West axis preferred by the United States.

The U.S. commitment to capitalist models of development has remained firm. There has been little sympathy for calls for a New International Economic Order and even stronger rejection of dependency and imperialist theories. It is probable, however, that the Latin American economies will continue to depart from the capitalist formula. Whether or not the United States can influence the direction of those forces will depend more on the global economic recovery and positive U.S. policies for the region than on rhetoric and piecemeal solutions such as the Caribbean Basin Initiative.

NOTES

1. Theotonio dos Santos, "The Structure of Dependence," *American Economic Review* 60 (May 1970), 231. Also see Osvaldo Sunkel, "Big Business and 'Dependencia,'" *Foreign Affairs* 50 (April 1972), 517–531; and Raymond Duvall, "Dependence and Dependencia Theory," *International Organization* 32 (May 1978), 51–78.

2. For a thorough survey of how this concept can be applied in Latin America, see Ronald A. Chilcote and Joel C. Edelstein, eds., *Latin America: The Struggle with Dependency and Beyond* (New York: Schenkman Publishing, 1974). Also see Samuel J. Valenzuela and Arturo Valenzuela, "Modernization

and Dependency: Alternative Perspectives in the Study of Latin American Development," *Comparative Politics* 10 (July 1978), 535–557.

3. For example, see Ronald H. Chilcote, ed., *Dependency and Marxism* (Boulder, Colo.: Westview Press, 1982); and F. H. Cardoso, "The Consumption of Dependency Theory in the United States," *Latin American Research Review* 12:3 (1977), 7–24.

4. Johann Galtung, "A Structural Theory of Imperialism," *Journal of Peace Research* 13:2 (1971), 81–118.

5. Susanne Bodenheimer (Jonas), "Dependency and Imperialism: The Roots of Latin American Underdevelopment," *Politics and Society*, May 1971, 327–358.

6. For a critique of dependency theory, see David L. Ray, "The Dependency Model of Latin American Underdevelopment: Three Basic Fallacies," *Journal of Inter-American Studies and World Affairs* 15 (February 1973), 4–20; and R. Kaufman, D. Keller, and H. Chernotsky, "A Preliminary Test of the Theory of Dependency," *Comparative Politics* 7 (April 1975), 303–330.

7. The extensive literature on the NIEO includes: Carol Geldart and Peter Lyon, "The Group of 77: A Perspective View," *International Affairs* 57 (Winter 1980–1981), 79–101; Fehmy Saddy, "A New World Economic Order: The Limits of Accommodation," *International Journal* 34 (Winter 1978–1979), 16–38; and Craig Murphy, "What the Third World Wants: An Interpretation of the Development and Meaning of the NIEO Ideology," *International Studies Quarterly* 27 (March 1983), 55–76.

8. Discussions by two members of the Carter administration are Richard N. Cooper, "A New International Economic Order for Mutual Gain," *Foreign Policy* 26 (Spring 1977), 66–120; and C. Fred Bergsten, "The Threat from the Third World," *Foreign Policy* 11 (Summer 1973), 102–124.

9. A criticism of Reagan's approach is in Thomas Ehrlich and Catherine Gwin, "A Third World Strategy," *Foreign Policy* 44 (Fall 1981), 145–166.

10. The text of Reagan's address is in *New York Times*, February 25, 1982, 8.

11. For an analysis of the CBI, see the discussion by Abraham Lowenthal, et al., "The Caribbean Basin Initiative," *Foreign Policy* 47 (Summer 1982), 114–138.

12. Ibid., p. 116. Also see Margaret Daly Hayes, *Latin America and the U.S. National Interest* (Boulder, Colo.: Westview Press, 1984), Chapter 3.

13. The statement by the head of the U.S. delegation, James Buckley, is in *New York Times*, August 8, 1984, 4.

14. James D. Cockcroft, "Mexico," in Chilcote and Edelstein, *Latin America*, 222–303. Also see John Saxe-Fernandez, "Strategic Dependence and Oil in Mexican-American Relations," *Journal of Conflict Resolution* 17:2 (1980), 119–133.

15. Cockcroft, "Mexico," 250–253.

16. Ibid., 255.

17. Ibid., 260.

18. Bruce M. Bagley, "Mexico, the Promise of Oil," in Hayes, *Latin America*, 123–170.

19. Ibid., 123–126, 141–142.

20. For background of Brazil's politics, see Peter Flynn, *Brazil: A Political Analysis* (London: Ernest Benn, 1978); and Riordan Roett, *Brazil, Politics in a Patrimonial Society* (New York: Praeger, 1978).

21. T. L. Skidmore, *Politics in Brazil, 1930–1964: An Experiment in Democracy* (New York: Oxford University Press, 1967); Albert Fishlow, "Flying Down to Rio: Perspectives on U.S.-Brazil Relations," *Foreign Affairs* 57 (Winter 1978–1979), 387–405; and Jules Davids, *The United States in World Affairs, 1964* (New York: Harper & Row, 1965), 201–207.

22. Phyllis R. Parker, *Brazil and the Quiet Intervention, 1964* (Austin: University of Texas Press, 1979); this is the best study of the coup. Also see Lars Schoultz, *Human Rights and United States Policy Toward Latin America* (Princeton, N.J.: Princeton University Press, 1981), 173.

23. Quoted in *New York Times*, April 4, 1964, 1.

24. For a survey of these steps toward democracy, see *New York Times*, August 19, 1984, 10.

25. A dependency analysis is presented by a Brazilian economist, Theotonio dos Santos, "Brazil: the Origins of a Crisis," in Chilcote and Edelstein, *Latin America*, 415–490.

26. Quoted by dos Santos, ibid., 470.

6
THE DEMOCRATIC MISSION AND HUMAN RIGHTS

THE DEMOCRATIC TRADITION

Another theme in U.S. foreign policy in the twentieth century has been the proclaimed goal of spreading democracy. The U.S. assumption that there are universal values shared by everyone has given U.S. policy a global relevance. The Declaration of Independence states "that all men are created equal; that they are endowed by their Creator with certain inalienable rights." Moreover, these rights are taken as "self-evident" truths, requiring no demonstration of proof. This definition of beliefs has imparted a particular character to U.S. policy, a sense of representing the longings of people everywhere for liberty and equality. Nearly all U.S. citizens would agree that the basic principles outlined in the Declaration provide a foundation for the U.S. political system and a rousing statement of their beliefs, but it is another matter altogether to treat the Declaration as a guide to foreign policy.

In the nineteenth century, there was little evidence to suggest that democratic ideals played a central role in the formation of foreign policy, but by the end of the Spanish-American War in 1899, the beginnings of the notion that the United States had a special democratizing mission in the world were evident. President McKinley's rationale for the annexation of the Philippines, for instance, was influenced by reference to the "white man's burden" and the moral obligation of the United States to protect the Filipinos from paganism. As explained in Chapter 2, the primary reasons for the United States' embarking on the war with Spain and on the road to imperialism had more to do with questions of power and trade than with social idealism. However, the problem remained of reconciling this sudden leap into imperialism with traditional beliefs about the U.S. role in the world. After all, the U.S. experiment in democracy had been unique. The United States, presumably, was not like any other nation and, in fact, had long before rejected such European behavioral traits as imperialism and power politics.

Policymakers, faced with this contradiction between the realities of U.S. power and the faith in the country's uniqueness, had no choice but to rationalize foreign policy as being consistent with U.S. traditions. Just as the United States was different from other nations, its purposes in foreign policy would therefore be different. As the twentieth century progressed and U.S. power expanded, it became increasingly necessary to explain behavior in terms of democratic ideals instead of narrow, selfish political or economic goals. Of course, not all policymakers viewed the democratic mission as the driving force behind U.S. policy, but it does appear to have influenced the attitude of such presidents as Woodrow Wilson and Jimmy Carter. The sense of mission also provided a noble cause in which the public could take solace.

The consequences of defining U.S. policy in terms of the democratic ideal are not all positive. An ideal can provide a sense of purpose to a foreign policy; it gives direction, and it may provide a rallying point for people in various parts of the world, but it is merely an ideal. However, as the United States discovered after World War I, democracy does not necessarily flourish because its benefits are "self-evident." What may seem appropriate at home may be seen abroad as a self-righteous attempt to transplant a political system that has little relevance to other countries. Thus, the United States' self-anointment as the guardian of democracy is no guarantee of the successful promotion of democracy.

Such a mission can, however, have an impact on the people in the United States—and on people elsewhere. First, when U.S. political leaders attempt to justify their policies in terms of democratic values, they run the risk of setting up the public for a major disappointment if democracy is not achieved. No matter whether or not policymakers actually believe their rhetoric, the costs of a public loss of faith are serious. Such a disillusionment contributed to U.S. isolationism after World War I, and it contributed to a similiar bitterness following Vietnam. One of the goals for which the United States had ostensibly entered the war in Vietnam was to defend democracy, but when the actualities of the war seemed so different from those ideals, there was a general loss of faith in the government's cause.

In addition, rationalizing policy in terms of democracy tends to place an unusual burden on diplomacy. Diplomacy implies compromise, but how can U.S. officials compromise on principles such as freedom and democracy? Former Secretary of State Dean Rusk, for example, asserted that the history of mankind has been a long struggle between freedom and tyranny in which the "winds of freedom" are destined to prevail. Today, he continued, freedom is represented by the United States, tyranny by the Soviet Union. The United States is on the side of history; it stands as the "hope of the world," according to Rusk. In fact, he claimed that the United States had repudiated Lord Acton's famous axiom on the corrupting effect of power. ("Power tends to corrupt; absolute power corrupts absolutely.") And further, Rusk offered what may well stand as the definitive statement on the official U.S. approach to revolutions: Legitimate revolutions, he said, are those modeled after the U.S. one. "It lies within our power," he declared, "to apply to the world community the lesson of our unique national experience."[1]

This discussion is a prelude to an examination of three cases in U.S.–Latin American relations where the sense of democratic mission was a strong determining factor in U.S. policy. It should be kept in mind, however, that democratic ideals are never far from the surface in popular assessments of U.S. behavior, and policymakers are constantly bedeviled by this problem. Although it is often necessary to sell a policy in terms of democratic principles, when its outcome does not result in democracy, the problem of maintaining credibility may loom quite large.

The manner in which the U.S. government has tended to treat democracy in its Latin American policy process is instructive. The achievement of democracy has often been classified as a *means*, not as a *goal* of policy. In other words, democratic states would be more likely to contribute to the long-term noncommunist stability in the region, but the actual achievement of that status has not always been identified as a specific objective of U.S. policy. The goals are to maintain the independence of Latin American states and to minimize the influence of the Soviet Union in the area. Democracy can be included with military and economic aid as a means to achieve those goals.

The Dilemma

For U.S. policymakers dealing with Latin America, a recurring dilemma has been how to promote democracy and refrain from intervention. Certainly, the United States is criticized for its tendency to intervene on the side of nondemocratic forces in order to maintain a friendly status quo. And yet, the pursuit of democracy may also require interference in another country's domestic politics. For many in Latin America, U.S. intervention for *any* reason is unacceptable. A critical question therefore, in assessing U.S. policy, is whether the

United States should act as aggressively to change a military government (such as Augusto Pinochet's in Chile) as it did to undermine an elected one (Allende's) in the same country? Or, if policymakers decide that intervention to save a nondemocratic government is unwise and unjust, should the same considerations apply when the United States is confronted with the possibility of intervening to defend a democratic government?

Resolving this dilemma is not easy. This chapter demonstrates the problems and contradictions that emerge when the U.S. government does decide to act in its foreign policy according to the principles of democracy. Three cases will be examined: Wilson's attempt to depose a nondemocratic leader in Mexico, Kennedy's policy to promote political reforms, and Carter's campaign on behalf of human rights. In none of the cases was the United States successful in achieving its stated goals. The implications of this outcome vary, but they suggest that either the pursuit of democratic principles was too difficult a task in Latin America or the U.S. government was not sufficiently committed to achieving them. In any event, these principles remain a component of an understanding of U.S.–Latin American relations.

WILSON AND MEXICO

The troubled history of U.S.-Mexican relations got off to a bitter start when Mexico was defeated by the United States in 1846 and lost California and what is today the U.S. Southwest. The treatment of the defeated Mexicans was harsh and included a dramatic entry of U.S. troops into Mexico City in 1847. The next few decades were not pleasant ones for the Mexican people. From 1876 to 1911, for example, the country was ruled by one of Latin America's most effective dictators, Porfirio Díaz. With the support of a strong police force, Díaz governed by personal decree and with the help of a small group of close friends. He secured the loyalty of the large landowners and in turn guaranteed their prosperity. In central Mexico, for instance, 95 percent of the rural families owned no land, and most of the country's wealth was concentrated in less than 3 percent of the population. From the U.S. perspective, Díaz's stable and secure Mexico was an attractive place for investments and business. U.S. citizens owned over 40 percent of Mexico's private property in 1910.

Díaz was finally deposed by the Mexican Revolution of 1911. In the ensuing struggle for power, elected revolutionary leader Francisco Madero was overthrown and shot in 1913 by General Victoriano Huerta, who had the open support of the United States. The Taft administration had been concerned about the revolution's impact on

U.S.-owned investments and property and expressed sympathy for the attempt to restore more orderly conditions in the country.[2] Huerta, however, was unable to establish control, and a virtual civil war erupted, further threatening U.S. lives and property. Taft, meanwhile, handed the problem over to the newly inaugurated Woodrow Wilson.

Wilson, renowned for his moralistic approach to foreign policy and his commitment to democracy, made his Mexican policy very clear. As Robert E. Osgood has written, Wilson was determined not to follow the selfish policies of dollar diplomacy, but instead to persuade the people that only if they "perfected their own international behavior could they hope to fulfill their mission of uplifting the rest of the world."[3] True to his principles, Wilson departed from the Taft policy and refused to recognize the "butcher" Huerta, who had so ruthlessly overthrown a legitimate government; Wilson also showed little concern about the fate of U.S. investments. He imposed an embargo on arms shipments to Mexico and warned U.S. citizens of the danger of remaining in the country. Wilson would have nothing to do with the morally repugnant Huerta regime.

Wilson's insistence in 1913 that Huerta step down and that free elections be conducted had little impact on the Mexican leader, nor did the president's efforts to back Huerta's main opponent, Venustiano Carranza, who appeared to resent any sign of U.S. interference. Therefore, in March 1914 Wilson dispatched two U.S. warships to Tampico harbor apparently in an effort to persuade Huerta to take U.S. demands seriously.[4] This action provoked the following events: On April 9, 1914, a group of U.S. sailors, in Tampico to buy supplies, was immediately arrested by Huerta's army. The sailors were soon released, but Huerta refused to comply with the U.S. admiral's demand that the general submit a formal letter of apology and show his contrition by saluting the U.S. flag. A few days later, in Veracruz, another U.S. sailor was briefly jailed, and again Huerta refused to apologize and salute the U.S. flag.

Wilson, on April 20, took the issue to the U.S. Congress. He pointed out that because the admiral's ultimatum to the Mexican government had not been met, it was time to take forceful action. (The United States, actually, did not recognize the Mexican government.) After two days of debate, Congress authorized the use of force against Mexico. The first shots came on April 21, when 800 U.S. troops seized the port of Veracruz to prevent the docking of a German ship reportedly carrying arms for Huerta. After a bloody battle with Mexican forces, the U.S. forces occupied the entire city.

In the meantime, anti-Huerta forces were gaining strength under Carranza and his ally Francisco Villa. The opposition forces, however, refused a U.S. offer of cooperation, rejected offers of foreign mediation, and insisted that the Mexicans alone would take care of Huerta. They did. In mid-July, Huerta left office and fled to Europe. Carranza took over the presidency in August. Not a model democrat, Carranza was refused recognition by the Wilson administration until October 1915, when Wilson grudgingly accepted the reality of the nondemocratic Mexican government. U.S. troops left Veracruz in November 1914 after seven months of occupation.

The revolutionary instability in Mexico continued, however. Forces friendly to "Pancho" Villa resisted government control in the north, and while fighting Carranza's troops there, Villa led his forces on raids across the U.S. border. In January 1916, eighteen U.S. civilians traveling in Mexico were shot by Villa's forces, and on March 9 Villa attacked the little town of Columbus, New Mexico, killing nineteen U.S. citizens. On receiving word of the raid, Wilson sent General John J. Pershing and nearly 7,000 U.S. troops into Mexico with orders to capture Pancho Villa. This American Expeditionary Force chased the now famous "bandit" 350 miles into Mexico, but did not find him. Instead, Pershing ran into Carranza's Mexican Army and was ordered by the Mexican president to stop his invasion. An infuriated Wilson ordered 150,000 U.S. troops to the Mexican border. Eventually, the two sides agreed to negotiate, but no formal agreement could be reached: Carranza insisted U.S. troops withdraw first, and Wilson, in turn, insisted that the United States had a right to pursue bandits who attacked U.S. towns. Nonetheless, Wilson did withdraw the troops, beginning in January 1917, as the war in Europe began to threaten the United States.[5]

Wilson's interventions had not brought democracy to Mexico nor compelled the Mexican government to comply with his demands for apologies. Instead, Villa and Carranza emerged as heroes because of their successful defiance of the U.S. Army. Wilson did, however, avoid identifying the United States with the dictatorial Huerta.

Throughout the 1930s and 1940s, U.S.-Mexican relations went through a number of serious trials as Mexico sought to gain control over U.S.-owned property and investments. For the most part, the now largely democratic government has been successful, and although relations with Washington have yet to be fully trusting and cordial, Mexico's stubborn stands against its giant neighbor have given it a distinctive air of independence and self-confidence.

KENNEDY AND THE ALLIANCE

The Principles

The Alliance for Progress was discussed in Chapter 1 as contributing to the Western Hemisphere Idea. It represents as well an effort by the United States to apply democratic principles to its policy in Latin America. John F. Kennedy spoke of a new era in Latin America when he began to implement his regional aid program in 1961. The interests of the United States were to be identified with the forces for reform and change, for democracy and representative government. The success of the United States in preventing another Cuba rested on the triumph of democracy and the defeat of dictators.

Because success also depended on effective U.S. training of counterinsurgency forces and military assistance, Kennedy's policy could not be accused of being merely rhetoric and economic aid. And yet to give substance to the principles of the Alliance, Kennedy made it clear that the United States would not give aid to governments uninterested in political and economic reforms, nor would he recognize and aid governments that came to power by "unconstitutional" means such as a military coup. The Alliance's goals rallied support throughout the hemisphere and spoke to a yearning for some effort to promote democracy.

Kennedy's policy sounded both ideological and practical. It was ideological in its reverence for democratic ideals; it was practical in its assessment that only through responsible and representative governments could the prospects for radical revolutions be diminished. It was a policy backed up by money and action, and in its initial stages the effects seemed dramatic. Reform programs were drawn up by Latin governments, and aid was directed to projects designed to relieve conditions of poor health, poverty, and illiteracy.

The Alliance promised ten years of concentrated economic assistance, $1 billion per year in U.S. government aid, plus $1 billion a year in private development investment. It was the Marshall Plan concept applied to a developing area. It would fight communism by a massive infusion of dollars tied to popular government and the growth of economic opportunity for the masses. Its tone was a marked departure from previous U.S. aid programs that had tended to focus on security and private enterprise.

The Tests

As one might expect, however, developments in Latin America turned out to be more complex than anticipated. Neatly formulated programs, so wise and perceptive in their announcement, too often were destroyed in the difficult political and historical forces of reality. As strong as Kennedy's verbal and economic commitment to democracy may have been, his Alliance slowly succumbed to the facts of Latin American politics and the demands of national security.[6] For example, even though Kennedy had pushed forcefully for elections in the Dominican Republic in 1961 and 1962, no major effort via economic aid or diplomatic support was extended to help Juan Bosch stay in power. To the White House and Congress, Bosch, his election notwithstanding, was just too unreliable and too easy on the Left to generate serious support. Bosch was overthrown by the military in September 1963.

Kennedy's support for democratic processes was put to its first real test in Argentina, when in March 1962 the military canceled election results and threw out the president, Arturo Frondizi, ending four years of democratic rule. The apparent cause of the coup was the military's fear of the consequences of the *Peronista* victories in the March elections. (The *Peronistas* were followers of former President Juan Perón and organized into a populist, working-class, and nationalistic political movement.) Initially, the Kennedy administration was ready to suspend diplomatic relations with Buenos Aires but held back when the Argentine military persuaded the White House that constitutional procedures were being followed in the naming of the senate leader as president. Although this maneuver turned out to be a sham, the United States extended recognition and continued aid to the government.

Three months later, in Peru, Kennedy confronted a similar choice. On July 18, 1962, the military seized control of the government to prevent populist Haya de la Torre from coming to power following his victory in the June 10 elections. Washington had issued a number of warnings to the Peruvian generals that the United States would not recognize the coup, but in light of what had happened in Argentina, the military leaders were not deterred. This time, however, the takeover was greeted by a quick U.S. break in relations and a suspension of both economic and military assistance. Within a month, most Latin American governments had recognized the new government; the United States followed suit on August 17 and restored aid soon after. Washington, unwilling to continue to pressure the military to restore democracy, had by this time made it obvious that political and social reforms were not going to receive top billing in the Alliance for Progress. The U.S. plea for democracy was, after all, just rhetoric.

The consequences for the rest of the region are succinctly described by Edwin Lieuwen, "The year 1963 was an open season for bagging constitutional governments."[7] In March the military took control of the Guatemalan government and suffered only a three-week suspension of U.S. aid. In July the Carlos Julio Arosemena government in Ecuador was replaced by a military junta. Although incompetent and alcoholic, Arosemena was the constitutional president. His removal was greeted with relief in Washington.

In response to the Dominican coup in September 1963, mentioned in Chapter 3, the United States did cancel aid in an apparent attempt to draw the line on military takeovers. It did the same in reaction to the Honduran military's seizure of power in October. Assistance to the Dominican Republic did not begin to flow again until after the 1965 intervention; aid to Honduras was gradually restored in the mid-1960s, but not because of the arrival of democracy.[8]

Although Kennedy's aid effort did bring a temporary hope for improvement to the lives of the poor in various parts of the hemisphere, it did not usher in an age of democracies. This failure, of course, was not entirely Kennedy's fault. Even the United States cannot overcome, in a year or two, decades of political and economic inequalities. Total economic assistance through the Alliance for Progress did reach the promised $1 billion per year target for the 1962–1965 period, as Kennedy managed to increase the amounts substantially to $1.067 billion annually as compared with the Eisenhower administration's average of $480 million. More importantly, security assistance also increased: from $51 million a year during the Eisenhower terms to an annual average of $90 million for 1962–1965.[9]

Counterinsurgency

Of more lasting impact on Latin America was the concurrent Kennedy-Johnson strategy of fighting guerrilla movements with military assistance and advice and with police training and intensified intelligence operations. Designed to control internal threats, these programs did contribute to the survival of democratic regimes in Venezuela and Peru, but they also encouraged the suppression of popular movements in other countries. The Kennedy administration's fascination with covert operations and counterinsurgency is well documented.[10] Its assassination efforts against Castro and other destabilizing operations in Cuba even after the Bay of Pigs are testimony to Washington's determination to fight the communist threat.

The concept of the Green Berets as the vanguard of the U.S. attempt to halt "wars of national liberation" was applied in Latin America through the training of military forces in the strategy and tactics of counterinsurgency warfare. The battleground for the United

States in the 1960s, in the view of Washington, would be in the Third World; communist efforts at liberation via insurgency could not be allowed to succeed. Thus more sophisticated, better equipped and trained armed forces emerged throughout Latin America to both quash incipient revolutionary movements and protect democratic governments, but they also guaranteed a more powerful voice for the military in the political future of the region.

CARTER AND HUMAN RIGHTS

A more recent manifestation of the view of U.S. foreign policy as a means of pursuing the global cause of democratic values is the human rights campaign of the 1970s. Often credited with the effort to make human rights a central feature of U.S. policy, Jimmy Carter's administration essentially gave direction and impetus to a movement well underway before his January 1977 arrival in Washington. The notion that human rights were important had grown out of a sense, reflected in congressional hearings and investigations and in academic circles, that the world had entered a new post–cold war era in which the traditional priorities of security and military power were giving way to concern for the worldwide human condition.

A Global Orientation

For the most part, this new perspective on world politics of the 1970s contended that with the ending of the cold war the United States had to turn its attention to a different set of problems relating to the Third World, economic development, and human rights. The battles over national military and political interests that had so characterized the Soviet-American contest were being replaced by a new consciousness. It was argued, for instance, that given the parity in nuclear weapons and the achievement of the agreements at SALT I, military competition between the superpowers was increasingly irrelevant to the real problems of the world. The critical issues were those of the global community, such as the management of natural resources, environmental control, economic development, and the liberation of people from economic deprivation and political repression. Because the Third World especially would be the arena of the great struggles of the next few decades, it was imperative that Washington recognize the priority of the issues that the Third World peoples were facing. The world was becoming so interdependent that concerns over such problems as human rights could be ignored by the United States only at a high cost in lost influence.

This was the new global agenda; it transcended nation-state boundaries, and because Latin America as part of the Third World came within the umbrella of this new perspective, the problems of the region could not be dealt with by the old style nationalistic, cold war–oriented policies of the past. The United States was now required to address the needs of the people of the region, not necessarily the needs of the nations, much in the way all of the Third World would be approached. As Carter asserted in 1977, "We will put our relations with Latin America on a more constructive basis, recognizing the global character of the region's problems."[11]

Coupled with this shift in policy emphasis, the United States was in the process of reconstituting its self-confidence following the war in Vietnam. Particularly trying was the sense of moral confusion and doubt about traditional democratic values that emerged after the war, the revelations of CIA assassination plots, and Watergate. For Jimmy Carter, the human rights issue provided a means to distinguish his campaign from that of the Nixon-Ford-Kissinger administrations. Blessed by this propitious convergence of moral issues in the mid-1970s, Carter was remarkably successful in mobilizing popular sympathy for his cause.

Carter's discovery of the human rights issue seems to have come rather late, however. There was no specific mention of human rights in his 1976 book, Why Not the Best?, although he did call for a "moral" foreign policy. It was not a noticeable issue in his campaign until September, when he pled for the United States to give attention to governments that torture or arrest people for their beliefs or that deny people the right to emigrate.[12] In his inaugural address, Carter's pledge was quite firm: "Because we are free we can never be indifferent to the fate of freedom elsewhere. . . . Our commitment to human rights must be absolute." To emphasize his new approach, he declared that "the world itself is now dominated by a new spirit. People more numerous and more politically aware are craving and now demanding their place in the sun—not just for the benefit of their own physical condition, but for basic human rights."

Human rights has an instinctive appeal to the U.S. public. The issue has a familiar ring that evokes well-established virtues and goals. Moreover, it involves universal values that apply to all people, to those fighting tyranny anywhere, not just to those in the United States. A human rights drive was an opportunity to restore U.S. faith in its own values and, for a change, to take action to help others. The United States would break with past habits of supporting dictators; now a new standard of conduct for U.S. policy would prevail. As a president openly committed to liberal democratic values, Carter actively sought to link U.S. relations with other countries to the manner in which they treated their own citizens. It was an attempt to go beyond declaratory principles to the imposition of penalties on governments that did not comply with some reasonable consideration of basic human rights.

Origins

The original push for human rights came not from Carter, but from the U.S. Congress at least three years prior to the 1976 campaign. Thus, any examination of the human rights effort in Latin America must begin with the struggle by the House Foreign Affairs Subcommittee on International Organizations and Movements, chaired by Representative Donald Fraser of Minnesota. A series of hearings held by the Fraser subcommittee in 1973 focused attention on the human rights issue as no prior event had been able to do, and it led to the first legislative steps to link human rights to foreign economic assistance.

The congressional efforts built on steps tentatively taken as early as 1961. In the Foreign Assistance Act of that year (Part II, Chapter 1), the president was called on to consider respect for individual rights and responsible government when carrying out aid programs. Revisions of the act in 1973 included a provision—little noticed at the time— that "the President should deny any economic or military assistance to the government of any foreign country which practices the internment or imprisonment of the country's citizens for political purpose." This was followed by amendments to the 1974 Foreign Assistance Act and by the Harkin Amendment to the 1975 act, which placed restrictions on aid to countries "engaged in a consistent pattern of gross violations of human rights."[13]

The Ford administration rejected requests from Congress in 1975 to specify which countries receiving U.S. military assistance were guilty of continued "gross violations" of human rights. The administration's response was that there were so many oppressive governments around the world that it was impossible to identify those which might be more oppressive than others. The refusal to specify abusers was viewed in Congress as a violation of the law. To the Department of State, though, such a "distinction of degree" would not serve the security interests of the United States; instead, "quiet but forceful diplomacy" was a more appropriate way to make progress on human rights.[14] In 1977, just prior to its departure, the Ford administration did report a number of human rights abuses to Congress, but insisted that military aid should continue, regardless of violations, to such countries as Argentina, Haiti, and Peru.[15]

In 1976, amendments to Section 502B of the Foreign Assistance Act and to the Military Sales Act provided rather strict restraints on the Executive's ability to extend military aid to human rights violators. The president was directed to conduct security assistance programs in ways that would "promote and advance human rights and fundamental freedoms." And further, Section 502B prohibited the granting of military aid to any government guilty of "gross violations of internationally recognized human rights." The acts also included requirements that the Department of State report to the Congress annually on the observance of and respect for human rights in each country receiving economic or security assistance.[16]

The first effort to impose sanctions for human rights abuses was aimed at Chile in 1973 and came from Congress despite resistance from the White House and the Department of State. The president was directed to ask the Chilean military government of Augusto Pinochet to protect the human rights of both its nationals and its foreigners and to guarantee fair treatment of political prisoners. In 1974, Congress set a $25 million limit on economic aid to Chile but left vague restraints on military assistance. Higher ceilings were placed on economic and military assistance in 1975, but it was a futile venture into foreign policy for Congress—the Ford administration found a number of ways to circumvent the restrictions. As Lars Schoultz pointed out, this effort to control aid to Chile "will probably stand for some time as the classic example of executive branch contempt for congressional directives on foreign aid."[17]

In a 1976 debate with Secretary of State Henry Kissinger over human rights violations in Uruguay, Rep. Fraser argued that the administration not only seemed to "minimize" the abuses, "but has yet to admit any knowledge of [them]. " Kissinger responded that aid should continue despite the reported violations so as to protect U.S. security and to enable the United States to "influence" the government.[18] Congress, nonetheless, did halt military aid to Uruguay.

Carter's Policy

By the time of Carter's arrival, the human rights movement had picked up full steam. In Europe human rights had been the focus of the negotiations on the Helsinki Agreement from 1973 to 1975; in the United States the movement had generated concern for the emigration of Jews from the USSR and for Soviet treatment of dissidents. In the Third World, the movement highlighted U.S. relations with dictators and brutal regimes that habitually ruled by torture and imprisonment and Washington's refusal to separate itself from repressive governments such as those in South Africa, the Philippines, South Korea, and Iran—plus a number in Latin America.

With human rights now supported by both the Executive and Congress, a number of concrete steps were taken to implement a policy for Latin America, primarily by linking aid to the improvement of human rights. Almost immediately, economic aid to Uruguay was cut drastically. Military aid to Argentina was reduced. New aid programs for Chile and Nicaragua were reduced significantly, and along with modifications of programs for repressive governments in Bolivia, Guatemala, and Haiti, provisions were made to try to guarantee that the aid would reach those who were most needy. The obvious dilemma for the president and Congress was how to punish governments without causing the masses to suffer in the process. Some critics argued, however, that this was a false dilemma, since existing aid programs to dictatorial regimes seldom percolated down to the masses. Aid to the needy also provided a loophole should the administration wish to continue aid to a friendly government in spite of human rights violations.

As the Carter team soon discovered, the implementation of a symbolic and moral policy in conjunction with protecting other U.S. interests failed both to satisfy everyone and to fulfill its own high ideals. Only six months into its term, the Carter administration began showing signs of backing away from its strict standards. Assistant Secretary of State for Inter-American Affairs Terrence Todman, after he visited Chile in July 1977, claimed that General Pinochet had made progress in complying with human rights expectations. Evidence of this was Pinochet's changing the name of the country's secret police, a decrease in the number of Chileans who mysteriously disappeared, and a call for elections in nine years.[19]

Later in the year, however, these favorable comments did not prevent the United States from voting against a Chilean request for a $24.5 million loan from the Inter-American Development Bank (IDB) for roads and bridges. The loan was, nonetheless, approved. A request from El Salvador for a $90 million loan from the IDB, delayed because of human rights violations, was eventually approved when it was determined that the government had eased up on some of its repression.

More dramatic a departure from declared policy was Carter's signing of a $2.5 million military sales arrangement with the Somoza regime in Nicaragua after other forms of aid had been suspended. Although the actual shipment of arms did not take place, Carter indicated that Somoza's lifting of a state of siege and the apparently improved behavior of his National Guard warranted a sign of encouragement. Carter's attempt to reinforce Somoza's positive steps was not, in the view of human rights advocates, likely to produce genuine change. (The Nicaraguan case is discussed in more detail below.)

On the other side, however, the bureaucratic machinery for enforcing human rights compliance was taking shape. Late in 1977 the Department of State, under the leadership of Deputy Secretary Warren Christopher, began to assert more influence over policy. When Todman, for example, approved a $10 million loan for Chile to purchase U.S. wheat, Christopher and his allies in the Bureau of Human Rights and Humanitarian Affairs were able to block completion of the deal. In addition, the United States tried to halt Argentine loan requests at the IDB, but to no avail. The bank approved a $36 million loan, plus two others for $54 million and $65 million.[20]

As a sign of the complexity of the politics of human rights, however, and perhaps as a sign of times to come, the United States did eventually approve a loan to Chile, in April 1978, for $35 million for the purchase of surplus U.S. grain. The signing of the contract was accompanied by virtually no publicity.[21]

At the end of 1977, a report by the private Council on Hemispheric Affairs concluded that Carter had made only modest progress in improving human rights. The report was critical of the administration's failure to "get tough" with private banks and corporations that continued to extend credit and loans to repressive regimes. According to the report, Carter had a long way to go to overcome the violations in such places as Argentina and Chile. "Few regions in the world," the report said, "rival the Western Hemisphere in the scale of brutality and acts of inhumanity practiced by governments in the area to insure the submissiveness of their populations."[22]

Haiti, the poorest nation in the hemisphere, with 90 percent illiteracy, a per capita income of $120 per year, and a ruthless government run by "president for life" Jean-Claude Duvalier, was singled out for praise by the Carter administration for improvements on human rights early in 1978, apparently to help justify a continuation of $20 million in relief aid.[23]

The human rights policy did receive a boost from the prospect of elections in a number of Latin American countries in 1978. In part, the news seemed to affirm progress toward democracy, but a closer look reveals that in many of the elections military officers were the leading candidates or military juntas were still in control behind the scenes. In Guatemala, the three candidates were army officers. In Brazil and Panama, indirect elections would choose military leaders as presidents, and in Bolivia, the leading candidate was a military officer. However, in Costa Rica, Colombia, the Dominican Republic,

TABLE 6.1
Changes in Military Aid Requests for Selected Latin American
Countries, 1976-1979 (in millions of dollars)

Country	1976	1979	Percent Change
Argentina	34.9	0.0	-100.0
Bolivia	11.9	6.7	- 43.6
Brazil	61.1	0.0	-100.0
El Salvador	6.6	0.014	- 98.4
Guatemala	3.6	0.003	- 99.9
Honduras	6.6	2.2	- 66.6
Nicaragua	6.5	0.153	- 97.6
Paraguay	8.8	0.467	- 99.6
Peru	20.9	7.0	- 66.5
Uruguay	17.1	0.0	-100.0

Source: Adapted from Lars Schoultz, Human Rights and United
States Policy Toward Latin America, Princeton, N.J.: Princeton
University Press, 1981, p. 265.

Ecuador, and Venezuela, civilians won elections. The impact of the
human rights campaign was obviously a mixed and muddled one.

Congress Continues the Struggle

The battle continued in Congress to find a means to tighten
control over military assistance by requiring, not just urging, compliance
with human rights before any military aid or credit could be granted.
Military aid was especially unsettling because it appeared to be
directly connected to the survival of authoritarian regimes and because
it offered no demonstrable benefit to the people. By 1978, Congress
had succeeded in amending the International Security Assistance Act
explicitly to prohibit military aid to major violators. By the end of
the year it had significantly reduced or cut off completely aid to
Argentina, Chile, El Salvador, and Nicaragua. Guatemala, Brazil, and
Uruguay refused to accept aid with human rights conditions attached.
A brief sampling of the dollar amounts of military aid to Latin
America reflects the impact of the legislation and Carter's compliance
with at least most of the guidelines. Military aid to the region as a
whole *decreased* from $233.5 million in 1976 to $54 million in 1979,
a decline of 77 percent. Table 6.1 indicates specific years.
Congress's action was a notable shift from previous inertia on
military aid to the region. There appeared to be a genuine effort on

behalf of human rights and democratic reforms rather than merely rhetoric on U.S. enforcement of human rights legislation. The new action was certainly greeted with enthusiasm by democratic governments and by dissident groups in the hemisphere, who could now see some prospect of reversing the pattern of repression throughout the region. The Carter campaign, coupled with congressional action, was a reaffirmation of U.S. values and in keeping with the traditions established by Woodrow Wilson. Human rights were identified as being synonymous with U.S. national interests. The Carter policy, according to a Brazilian editor, promised to restore U.S. moral authority and to bring relief to the suppressed in Latin America.[24]

Assessment

As we have seen, however, there were still contradictions and dilemmas. Criticism of human rights abuses in Brazil, Guatemala, and Uruguay, for example, provoked those governments into rejecting nearly all U.S. aid on the grounds that the sanctions constituted intervention in their internal affairs. Enforcement of the Carter policy implied interference, regardless of noble intentions. Resentment among even moderate Latins arose because of what appeared to them to be U.S. self-righteousness, as the president discovered on his visit to Brazil in 1978. Hoping to dramatize his stance on human rights and to demonstrate a defiant independence from the host military government, Carter arranged an unscheduled meeting with six Brazilian dissidents, including an archbishop active in the human rights movement.[25] This event, even if only symbolic, was viewed in Brazil as a serious affront to the regime, and it was generally seen as inappropriate behavior for a visiting head of state. It demonstrated the potential problems inherent in implementing a policy that called for changes in the way people were governed.

The Definitional Problem

Additionally, there was confusion over the meaning and application of a human rights policy. In the United States, human rights were usually defined as civil and political rights, with a specific concern that governments refrain from torture and unjustified arrest and imprisonment. Moreover, the United States has traditionally judged the legitimacy of a government by whether or not it was elected in an open, competitive election, and it has typically assessed the level of democracy in a country according to the opportunities for dissent.

These are important values in Latin America, but of equal importance to many groups in the region are social and economic rights.

Desirable as free elections and free speech may be, it is also vital for people to have some sense of economic and social justice, to have a chance for employment, for land ownership, for equal economic treatment regardless of race or class. Health care, education, jobs, and a minimum standard of living for the masses would take priority over the "luxuries" of democracy enjoyed by developed societies. Although the United States has given some recognition to these rights, the emphasis has clearly been in the political arena.

Fair application of human rights standards also proved difficult. Latin America was the most frequent target of U.S. sanctions, and yet major human rights violators in South Korea and the Philippines were still receiving U.S. aid, and few penalties were imposed on authoritarian governments in Africa or Asia. It was easy for the Carter administration to single out Latin America. The region was an area where there was little security risk and a region in which the United States had numerous alternative instruments of influence that could be used if aid were cut off. In contrast to other developing areas, in Latin America, U.S. political, economic, and military interests and channels were so pervasive that a reduction of aid would not prevent the exercise of power.

Consequences

If the goal of Carter's policy was to improve the human condition in Latin America, it is accurate to say that he had only marginal, short-term success. Human rights abuses received attention and some governments did adopt modest changes in their behavior. The Department of State's annual report to Congress suggested that by 1979 improvements could be found in only a few countries.[26]

The Nicaraguan Case

One perhaps unanticipated impact of the human rights drive was its effect on the opposition to the Somoza regime in Nicaragua. The U.S. insistence, beginning in the mid-1970s, that the government show respect for civil liberties, that it halt its arbitrary arrests and imprisonment, that it control the actions of the National Guard, and that it allow the opposition to speak out, served first to undermine the legitimacy of Somoza and second to give hope to his opponents. Somoza was an easy target for the Carter administration. A personalized dictatorship that controlled virtually all the country's economy and military provided a ready-made demonstration of the sincerity of the human rights policy. Since the reign of the Somoza family had so long been linked to U.S. support, for Carter now to attack it for human rights violations raised serious doubts about Somoza's claim to power and about his ability to remain in office. By the end of 1978, for example, virtually all military assistance to Nicaragua was being withheld.

Giving credibility to the case against Somoza was a 1978 report by the OAS Commission on Human Rights detailing abuses by the Nicaraguan government and National Guard.[27] Washington's emphasis on human rights had helped launch a hemisphere-wide campaign to expose major violations and to find the means to correct them.

At the same time, the growing opposition to Somoza could take heart from the U.S. position. Now that Washington was encouraging human rights, there was a chance it would not oppose Somoza's overthrow. When the oppressed are given hope and some prospect of victory, it is easier to mobilize them into political action. And, largely through the leadership of the Sandinistas, the resistance to Somoza spread until July 1979, when the regime collapsed. It is likely that the Carter administration did not fully anticipate the consequences of its policies. In fact, Washington had not indicated that it saw the solution to Nicaragua's problems in Somoza's overthrow. The original objective, instead, was a "reformed" regime, one more respectful of press freedoms, dissent, and free elections. The readiness of the White House to accept what might be considered cosmetic changes is demonstrated by a 1978 letter from Carter to Somoza congratulating the Nicaraguan leader on his government's promise to respect human rights. "The steps toward respecting human rights that you are considering are important and heartening signs," Carter wrote.[28] However, the administration did, later, try to arrange the departure of Somoza when it became clear his power had eroded.

As the opposition forces were gaining momentum and the dictator's tenure appeared to be ending, Carter began to seek ways to preserve some semblance of order in the country by forestalling a total revolution. In the summer of 1979 Secretary of State Cyrus Vance, for example, proposed sending an OAS peacekeeping force to Nicaragua to arrange an orderly settlement. Other members of the OAS unanimously disapproved of this idea for multilateral intervention.

When Somoza's fall was inevitable, the Carter administration argued that the National Guard should remain intact so as to prevent disorder and bloodshed in the country—and to protect against a radical takeover. This attempt to separate the Guardia from Somoza was inconsistent with the realities of Nicaragua in 1979, and to critics, it would have led to a perpetuation of the old order with all its inequities and repression, in other words, Somocismo without Somoza. The effort ultimately failed because the National Guard was disbanded and its leaders exiled upon the revolution's victory.

Actually, the combined effect of the fall of Somoza and the collapse of the Shah of Iran in early 1979 had led the Carter administration openly to reconsider the wisdom of its human rights policy. Were the pressures on friendly governments to reform becoming a security risk for the United States? The impact of the Shah's fall was brought home by the forced U.S. evacuation of military installations in Iran and by the November 1979 seizure of the U.S. embassy in Teheran by radical Moslems. The increasingly anti-imperialist rhetoric of the Sandinistas seemed to Washington to spell similar trouble in Central America, particularly in El Salvador. Now, the Carter team was giving first priority to what it perceived as security issues, and aid to governments such as the one in El Salvador, threatened with revolution, was increased. By the end of the Carter term, the interest in human rights had declined considerably from its high point of 1977. The bureaucratic and legislative machinery to do something about the problem was still in place, but the will to implement the policy had weakened. Security was taking precedence.

Argentina

The unexpected impact of the OAS report about Somoza's human rights abuses encouraged the organization to extend its work to other cases, and Argentina was one of those selected. In November 1980 the Inter-American Commission on Human Rights presented a special report indicting the Argentine government for its role in the unexplained disappearances of at least 5,818 persons. The report held the highest-ranking military officers in the government responsible for the decision to combat terrorism by violating the most basic standards of human rights.[29] This report was followed by a moving exposé of conditions in his country by Argentine journalist Jacobo Timerman. Imprisoned for his attacks on the ruling junta, Timerman, in his book, spoke of the uncontrolled vigilante behavior of the military officers, who, he claimed, were more comfortable with slogans from Hitler than those from Jefferson. He also criticized the government's public relations campaign to persuade the United States that the struggle against communism was being won in Buenos Aires.[30]

Ironically, the Carter administration in early 1980 found itself approaching Buenos Aires to request Argentine support for the grain embargo against the Soviet Union in retaliation for the invasion of Afghanistan. Washington had little leverage, however. Even if Carter had been willing to call off the human rights campaign, Argentina would not have been persuaded to pass up the much-needed opportunity to expand its exports of wheat and soybeans.[31] With the election of Ronald Reagan in November, the human rights drive faded. Reagan's campaign statements criticizing the application of the human rights policy in Latin America implied that, with his election, military regimes would not be under pressure to reform, but instead would join the United States to contain communist terrorism. One of his first acts was to lift the ban on military aid to Argentina.

Interest Groups

Another aspect of the effort to promote human rights is detailed in Lars Schoultz's study of U.S. human rights policy in Latin America: the role of U.S. interest groups.[32] According to Schoultz, the best intentions of Congress and Carter to impose penalties on repressive governments were consistently undermined and evaded by private interest groups in collaboration with certain U.S. government agencies and a few key committees in Congress. If economic aid or military sales to Latin America were threatened, legislation would be modified to provide loopholes. Alternative sources of funding or credits could be found through agencies other than AID to finance arms purchases or loans. Coalitions of private businesses would regularly lobby and find an avenue to protect their friends in Latin America whenever Congress or the administration seemed to be closing a loophole or tightening guidelines. Thus, even if human rights advocates had succeeded in securing a more systematic control of aid and credits, the politics of the process suggests that their effects would have been minimal, far short of their goals and expectations.

THE REAGAN APPROACH

Although the Reagan administration did not promote human rights as a foreign policy centerpiece, it used democratic principles to rationalize its actions in Latin America. Reagan's view of human rights is highlighted by his attempt to move away from a strict interpretation of the concept. Note his statement on November 6, 1980: "I think all of us in this country are dedicated to . . . human rights. But I don't think that you can turn away from some country because here and there they do not agree with our concept of human rights."[33]

Policy Statements

In a memo prepared for the president-elect's transition team on Latin American policy, the new administration was warned against naming ambassadors to the region who were "social reformers" and "advocates of new theories of social change." It went on to call for a "more balanced" and "less publicly confrontational" policy on human rights. It recommended that emphasis be given to terrorism as inhuman repression and that human rights concerns not be allowed to "paralyze or unduly delay decisions on issues where human rights concerns conflict with other vital U.S. interests."[34]

Later, in November 1981, a Department of State memo outlined additional directions for the administration's human rights policy. The document claimed that human rights, defined as political and civil rights, were "at the core" of U.S. foreign policy. Policy, nevertheless, was to follow two tracks. A positive track would emphasize U.S. beliefs and values, especially in comparison to those of the USSR, and strongly condemn acts of terrorism. The negative track called for taking "into account the pressures a regime faces and the nature of its enemies. . . . Human rights is not advanced by replacing . . . a corrupt dictator with a zealous Communist politburo."[35] It was not a proposal to throw out the human rights effort, but to give it more balance and to keep it from undercutting security interests.

Reagan's assistant secretary of state for human rights and humanitarian affairs, Elliott Abrams, declared in a debate with Congress over aid to El Salvador that too often critics did not ask about the human rights abuses by guerrillas or about the humanitarian impact of a cutoff of aid. The 1982 elections in El Salvador demonstrated, he said, the government's commitment to democracy, and therefore the Congress should not hinder its progress by denying economic support.[36]

Relations with Congress

The backing away from the Carter crusade was a prominent feature of the struggle over aid for El Salvador. The administration's initial requests were cut in half by Congress, and continuation of the assistance was made contingent on presidential confirmation every six months that the government there was improving its human rights record. The administration complied with those conditions and managed to keep economic and military assistance flowing, but when the certification procedures came up for renewal in November 1983, the president vetoed the bill. The White House rationale was that the certification process would "distort" U.S. efforts at reform.[37] In contrast, the Department of State was criticizing the Salvadoran government for its inability to control right-wing death squads.

The administration's first report to Congress, in 1982, on the global human rights situation did find considerable violations in Latin America but argued that the conditions in El Salvador were improving and contended that the Latin Americans, who were "supporters of the West," were often discriminated against in international human rights assessments. Cuba, for example, deserved more condemnation as a "Marxist-Leninist state closely allied and dependent on the Soviet Union."[38]

Reagan recommended restoring military aid to Guatemala in August 1983, despite reports of excessive brutality by the government and the slaughter of thousands of Indians by private and official military forces. Attempts were also made in November 1983 to increase economic assistance to Guatemala, but Congress turned down both requests. The military regime there had been deprived of U.S. military aid for over five years and had received only modest economic assistance. From Reagan's perspective, however, the absence of democratic traditions, the continuing threat of leftist terrorists, and the Cuban-trained subversives in the country dictated that the United States deal with reality. The Guatemalan government may not be democratic, he asserted, but it was a bulwark against totalitarian ideology.

The Kirkpatrick Formula

The Reagan approach has been well articulated by Jeane Kirkpatrick, the administration's first ambassador to the United Nations.[39] She drew a distinction between "traditional autocrats" and "revolutionary Communists" in an attempt to justify U.S. support for certain nondemocratic regimes. To Kirkpatrick, a communist government rests on totalitarian control of an entire society, typically by means of a single ideology (or "truth"), carried out by a single political party and protected by a pervasive and secret internal security apparatus. In a totalitarian society, all activities, from art to education, from military to business, must conform to the needs of the society at large. There is no prospect for genuine change, since the state defines what is permissable and what is not.

Accordingly, a traditional autocratic society, though not democratic, does not disrupt habitual family and personal relations. The society may be tightly controlled for the benefit of a ruling elite or dictator, but the means of control are not ideological and do not penetrate all areas of society. The authoritarian may rule by force but does not rely on the enforcement of a belief system by the secret police.

The view was reinforced by Samuel Huntington, who drew a similar distinction between "right-wing authoritarian" regimes and "left-wing totalitarian" ones. The former, he asserted, are "almost always less pervasive than" the latter. Huntington went on to contend that U.S. intervention in Latin America has been responsible for the promotion of human rights, democracy, and "the freest elections and most open political competition in the history" of such countries as Nicaragua, Haiti, and the Dominican Republic.[40]

Spain, under Franco, was a case of an authoritarian government that gave way to democratic reform. The imposition of a totalitarian ideology on Cuba, however, has virtually foreclosed the possibility of a pluralist democratic change. Thus, as distasteful as it may be for the United States to associate with authoritarian regimes such as those in Pinochet's Chile or Duvalier's Haiti, the alternative may be to see them go communist and be lost to democracy forever.

The Elections Issue

Another component of Reagan's use of the democratic mission is his invocation of elections as a measure of legitimacy.[41] Reagan contended that elections such as those held in El Salvador in 1982 and 1984 distinguished that country's political system from the system in Cuba, where no elections had been held. He also questioned the fairness of the 1984 elections in Nicaragua. The importance of elections in sanctioning U.S. support for a government cannot be underestimated; it appeals to a strong tradition. Even in the midst of the Vietnam War in 1965, the Johnson administration insisted on elections being held there in order to give credence to U.S. assertions that a democracy was being defended. So it was in El Salvador, where about 80 percent of the electorate turned out in 1982 and 1984 despite the civil war.

The difficulty in relying on elections as a criterion for judging a government's worthiness arises from four problems. First, there are doubts about the fairness of the electoral process in Latin America. The parties and candidates eligible to run are often severely restricted so that, as in the Salvadoran case, those left of center are not even on the ballot. High turnouts are likely to be as much a result of fear as a sign of popular approval for the government. In El Salvador, voting was compulsory, and identity cards were marked as confirmation of having voted. Heavy fines and suspicion of their loyalty awaited those who could not prove that they had cast ballots. In small towns where local military officers could monitor voting and where secret ballots were not guaranteed, the incentive to vote for the "right" candidates is rather obvious. Moreover, the lack of democratic institutions such as a free press made the election vulnerable to abuse, even if outsiders were observing the official polling.

Second, because of years of governmental abuse, the electoral process is widely distrusted, and elections are not perceived as a genuine test of legitimacy. Consequently, the U.S. demand for elections in Cuba, for example, has tended to fall on unsympathetic ears. Elections were held from time to time under Batista, but instead of bringing about an improvement in life, they seemed to be used to entrench even further the elite's power. Thus, in the Cuban view, a revolutionary force that comes to power with popular support and that remains true to the cause need not conduct elections to prove its right to rule. There is, then, no inherent value in voting. Elections, it is argued, could disrupt the revolutionary process, a process requiring discipline and commitment. Although such an attitude was present in Nicaragua, the ruling Sandinistas provided for national elections in 1984 as a means of demonstrating popular support.

Third, elections may not even deal with the real power in a country. Too frequently in Latin America civilian leaders are in power only symbolically. Actual authority resides with the military and land-owning oligarchies, who do not stand for election, but whose influence is paramount.

Fourth, the United States ran the risk of undermining its credibility by placing too much emphasis on elections being held, for example, in Nicaragua, when Washington appeared oblivious to the absence of direct elections in such allied countries as Brazil and Chile. The Reagan administration successfully avoided the domestic political trouble that this apparent double standard is capable of producing.

Emerging from the Reagan years, therefore, was a continuing congressional commitment to keeping U.S. policy in tune with human rights, on the one hand, and an Executive convinced that giving humanitarian concerns a central role to play was detrimental to real U.S. security, on the other. The Carter policy in Latin America was in part explainable in terms of the democratic mission, but Reagan's was not—although much of the legislation and rhetoric remained in place.

CONCLUSIONS

There is a persistent thread in twentieth century U.S. foreign policy that cannot be ignored, that of the United States as the defender of democratic values. This mission's effectiveness has been discussed, yet it is also important to consider how well this role explains U.S. policy. For the Carter administration, the democratic mission does serve as a means of explanation. It serves as a partial explanation for the Wilson and Kennedy policies. For the Reagan administration, this perspective is useful in a negative sense: to demonstrate how policy did *not* conform to a human rights explanation. And yet, even in regard to the Reagan policy we are faced with the persistence of democratic rationalizations. Elections continue to be employed as a measure of legitimacy for governments in Latin America. Whether or not those values are invoked arbitrarily or selectively, they are a reminder of the need to offer the impression that U.S. policy does not deviate too far from traditional ideals.

Dilemmas

Given the inescapable influence of the democratic mission, there are dilemmas in applying its ideals to Latin America. The following discussion will show why these values are an insufficient explanation of policy.

On the one hand, U.S. identification with repressive military governments has often produced little more than short-term benefits. Latin American resentment of U.S. help to dictators has rebounded negatively, as in the cases of Cuba and Nicaragua. The Mexicans seem to have found a way to work out a cooperative relationship with the United States in spite of early U.S. support for dictators and Wilson's intervention. Thus, the argument can be made that in the long run it would pay the United States to be more considerate of human rights and less enthusiastic about military juntas and oligarchs. Then, when revolutions do occur, the United States would not be identified with the old order, but would, instead, be in a position to establish friendly ties with the new, presumably popular governments. Kennedy's Alliance for Progress, as a means of avoiding Castros by first preventing Batistas, reflected this approach.

On the other hand, the attempt to transplant U.S. political values to Latin America has produced resentment on the part of those who do possess power in the region. As Kennedy discovered, nondemocratic governments can successfully defy U.S. pressure for reforms. Carter, too, found governments in Brazil, Argentina, Chile, and Guatemala willing to do without U.S. aid rather than loosen their grip on their societies by complying with human rights standards. Because human rights are laden with moral and ideological overtones, it is difficult to sit down and negotiate compromises. Even in today's El Salvador, U.S. attempts to control human rights abuses by the military meet with little success in spite of El Salvador's presumed client status.

The dilemma of the democratic mission is compounded by the security argument. Policymakers such as those in the Reagan administration who doubt the efficacy of a human rights policy point to its destabilizing effects in Nicaragua and El Salvador. Those suspicious of a human rights policy claim that demands that friendly governments rush into democratic reforms have provided an opportunity for well-organized leftist revolutionaries to take advantage of the instability in order to seize power. The result has been to turn an ally into a threat. Moreover, over the past forty years, support for military governments has generally worked to the advantage of the United States. This is the pragmatist's response: If it works, don't change it. Although Cuba and Nicaragua are "losses," they contend, those are the only two that have turned to the other side, and their "turning" could have been prevented by a stronger U.S. response.

According to this pragmatic view, the lesson is clear. Democratic values may be important politically, but the security interests of the United States can best be served by tolerating—even supporting—military governments. This may be a short-term policy, but what alternative makes sense? It is too risky to permit revolutions or adopt policies undermining the only groups realistically capable of exercising noncommunist power in Latin America.

The Carter administration, of course, did try for a time to identify U.S. security with democratic values. It was argued that since, in the long run, revolutions and the process of democratization would likely come to Latin America, U.S. interests would be furthered by going with the wind and trying to control it rather than going against it. Attempting to halt this impulse for change would serve only to polarize societies and guarantee that the eventual victors—the revolutionaries—would imitate the Cuban model and have nothing to do with the United States.[42]

In the final analysis, there are costs and risks to following either approach. Ignoring human rights and the revolutionary trends can isolate the United States from the masses who may well control the future of Latin America. It is, however, important to recognize the consequences of pursuing a human rights policy in Latin America. It may encourage instability, and it may be undone by forces in U.S. domestic politics. But it may also get the United States off a path that could lead to increasing alienation and isolation as the revolutionary movements pick up momentum.

One thing is certain: Democratic values will continue to play a role in U.S. policy. They will be involved in the formulation and implementation of aid programs, for example, because of the unavoidable link between U.S. domestic politics and foreign policy. Critics of the democratizing mission may bemoan this tendency and may argue that the United States should not be concerned about how other people are governed, but the reality of the U.S. political process suggests that policymakers will have to take the human rights issue into consideration whether they want to or not.

NOTES

1. U.S. Department of State, *Bulletin* 47 (October 15, 1962), 547 and, *Bulletin* 49 (July 29, 1963), 155. Also see Ernest K. Lindley, ed., *The Winds of Freedom: Selections from the Speeches and Statements of Dean Rusk* (Boston: Beacon Press, 1963), 21, 46.

2. Howard Cline, *The United States and Mexico* (New York: Atheneum, 1963), 133–134.

3. Robert E. Osgood, *Ideals and Self-Interest in America's Foreign Relations* (Chicago: University of Chicago Press, 1965), 177.

4. Kenneth J. Grieb, *The United States and Huerta* (Lincoln: University of Nebraska Press, 1963), 142–145, 152–154. Also see Robert Quirk, *An Affair of Honor* (Lexington: University of Kentucky Press, 1962), and Arthur S. Link, *Wilson and the New Freedom* (Princeton, N.J.: Princeton University Press, 1956), Chap. 11.

5. Graham H. Stuart, *Latin America and the United States* (New York: Appleton-Century-Crofts, 1955), 150–155.

6. For a review of the Kennedy and Johnson policies on this issue, see Edwin Lieuwen, *Generals and Presidents* (New York: Praeger, 1965), and Cole Blaiser, *The Hovering Giant: U.S. Responses to Revolutionary Change in Latin America* (Pittsburgh: University of Pittsburgh Press, 1976), 241–258.

7. Lieuwen, *Generals and Presidents*, 117.

8. For a further analysis of the Alliance, see Jerome Levinson and Juan de Onis, *The Alliance that Lost Its Way* (Chicago: Quadrangle Books, 1970).

9. Agency for International Development, *U.S. Overseas Loans and Grants, 1945–1969* (Washington, D.C.: 1970), 32.

10. Senate Select Committee on Intelligence Activities, *Alleged Assassination Plots Involving Foreign Leaders* (an Interim Report), 94th Cong., 1st Sess. (Washington, D.C.: 1975). Kennedy's interest in "unconventional warfare" is reflected in David Halberstam, *The Best and the Brightest* (New York: Random House, 1972). Also see Richard Alan White, *The Morass: United States Intervention in Central America* (New York: Harper & Row, 1984).

11. For the text of Carter's speech at the UN, see *New York Times*, March 18, 1977, A10.

12. *New York Times*, September 9, 1976; also see Jimmy Carter, *Why Not the Best?* (New York: Bantam, 1976), 140–141; and Arthur Schlesinger, Jr., "Human Rights and the American Tradition," in William P. Bundy, ed., *America and the World, 1978* (New York: Pergamon, 1979), 503–526.

13. The legislative acts are PL93–189 and PL93–559. Lars Schoultz, *Human Rights and United States Policy Toward Latin America* (Princeton, N.J.: Princeton University Press, 1981). This study is the most reliable and thorough source for U.S. human rights policy in Latin America.

14. Reported in *New York Times*, November 19, 1975, 1.

15. *New York Times*, January 2, 1977, 1.

16. House of Representatives Committee on International Relations, *International Security Assistance Act of 1976* (Hearings), 94th Cong., 2d Sess.

(Washington, D.C.: 1976), and Senate Committee on Foreign Relations, *International Security Assistance and Arms Export Control Act of 1976* (Report), 94th Cong., 2d Sess. (Washington, D.C.: 1976).

17. Schoultz, *Human Rights*, 198–200.

18. House of Representatives Subcommittee on International Organizations, *Human Rights in Paraguay and Uruguay* (Hearings), 94th Cong., 2d Sess. (Washington, D.C.: 1977), 71.

19. U.S. Department of State, *Bulletin* 77 (December 5, 1977), 815–821; also see Tom Wicker, "A Green Light for the Junta," *New York Times*, October 28, 1977.

20. *Washington Post*, December 17, 1977, A17.

21. *Christian Science Monitor*, April 28, 1978.

22. Reported in *Baltimore Sun*, December 24, 1977.

23. *Wall Street Journal*, February 3, 1978, and *Washington Post*, November 21, 1977.

24. Elio Gaspari, "Carter, Si!" *New York Times*, April 30, 1978.

25. *New York Times*, April 1, 1978, 3.

26. U.S. Department of State, *Country Reports on Human Rights Practices for 1979*, submitted to the House Committee on Foreign Affairs and the Senate Committee on Foreign Relations, 96th Cong., 2d Sess. (Washington, D.C.: 1980), 239–426.

27. Organization of American States, Inter-American Commission on Human Rights, *Report on the Situation of Human Rights in Nicaragua* (Washington, D.C.: 1978).

28. A copy of the letter, along with a commentary, is provided in Anastasio Somoza's own account of his downfall: See his *Nicaragua Betrayed* (Boston: Western Islands, 1980), 144–145. Also see the analysis of Carter's policy in Thomas W. Walker, "Nicaragua and Human Rights," *Caribbean Review* 7 (July-September 1978), 24–29.

29. Organization of American States, Inter-American Commission on Human Rights, *Report on the Situation of Human Rights in Argentina* (Washington, D.C.: 1980).

30. Jacobo Timerman, *Prisoner Without a Name, Cell Without a Number* (New York: Knopf, 1981).

31. *Washington Post*, January 25, 1980, A16, and January 26, 1980, A17; *New York Times*, January 18, 1980, 8.

32. Schoultz, *Human Rights*, Chap. 2.

33. *New York Times*, November 7, 1980. Also noteworthy is the "Santa Fe Document," a paper prepared for candidate Reagan that called for a stronger attack on human rights violations by Cuba and Nicaragua and for more understanding of the security situation in Chile, Argentina, and Guatemala: The Santa Fe Committee, "A New Interamerican Policy for the 80's," (Washington, D.C.: Council for Interamerican Security, May 1980).

34. Memo from Pedro A. Sanjuan to Ambassador Robert Neumann (Office of the President-elect) (Washington, D.C.: n.d.), 1, 7.

35. Text of the memo is reported in *New York Times*, November 5, 1981.

36. Elliott Abrams, "El Salvador: Are We Asking the Right Questions?" *New York Times,* July 29, 1982.

37. *New York Times,* December 1, 1983, 8.

38. U.S. Department of State, *Country Reports on Human Rights Practices for 1981* (Washington, D.C.: 1982).

39. Jeane Kirkpatrick, "Dictatorships and Double Standards," *Commentary* 68 (November 1979), 34–45.

40. Samuel Huntington, "Human Rights and American Power," *Commentary* 72 (September 1981), 37–43.

41. For an analysis of the problems associated with elections, see Tom J. Farer, "Manage the Revolution?" *Foreign Policy* 52 (Fall 1983), 96–117; and Glen C. Dealy, "The Pluralistic Latins," *Foreign Policy* 57 (Winter 1984–1985), 108–127.

42. For a good summary of the Carter definition, see Richard Feinberg, "The Recent Rapid Redefinitions of U.S. Interests and Diplomacy in Central America," in Feinberg, ed., *Central America: International Dimensions of the Crisis* (New York: Holmes & Meier, 1982), 61–63.

7
THE STRATEGIC PERSPECTIVE

A third element in the global approach is the strategic perspective, which treats events in Latin America as connected to the struggle between the United States and the Soviet Union. People with this viewpoint see problems in the context of containing communism and as tests of U.S. credibility. Two cases that illustrate the strategic perspective are examined here: Castro's Cuba and Allende's Chile.

THE COLD WAR SYNDROME

Anticommunism

The emergence of the United States as one of the world's two superpowers after 1945 brought with it the tendency to look at events everywhere as part of the continuing struggle with the Soviet Union. At the height of the cold war in the 1950s the intuitive response of people in the United States to revolutions, changes in governments, and shifts in international alignments was to calculate their impact on the Soviet-American balance. Events were not neutral. They benefited either the United States or the USSR. In such a world, there were no shades of gray and no countries left untouched by the contest between democracy and communism for the "hearts and minds" of the people of the world.

It is little wonder then that events in Latin America became tied to that cold war framework. As we saw in the case of Guatemala in 1954, Secretary of State John Foster Dulles's dichotomous view of the world may have led him to conclude that since the activities of the Arbenz government were not supportive of U.S. interests, they must, logically, be opposed. Dulles employed the same approach to Egypt's president, Gamal Abdel Nasser, in the 1955 and 1956 struggle over Nasser's assertion of "neutralism." In Dulles's eyes, neutrality was impossible. Nations had to decide which side they were on: Fence-straddling was immoral and the United States would not assist governments that engaged in it. (Thus, the Sandinistas' more recent assertion that Nicaraguan foreign policy was nonaligned struck at a long-standing U.S. perception that such a posture was not friendly to the United States.)

The threat from communism, according to the "cold warriors," was especially troublesome because it could be so subtle, so indirect that its dangers could not be seen until it was too late. It wasn't that Communists were necessarily responsible for revolutions or even that they were popular leaders, but rather, the argument went, that they were clever subversives with well-organized and disciplined cadres that could move into positions of power and control in any revolutionary situation. The Communists' subversive takeover of Czechoslovakia in 1948 was proof of their capabilities. It would not, therefore, take mass support for communist activities for them to seize control from well-meaning but innocent revolutionaries and turn nationalist discontent into a victory for the Soviet Union. Such a prospect was, by definition, a challenge to the United States.

The overall policy formulated to deal with the communist threat was containment. By restricting communist, and particularly Soviet, expansion, the United States and its allies hoped not only to defend the free world but also to convince the aggressors that since they could not succeed, the only alternative was to cooperate. Initially designed in 1947 for application in Europe, by 1960 containment had become a global policy, guiding U.S. reactions to events even in the Third World.

U.S. Credibility

In addition to the preoccupation with Soviet communism, the cold war syndrome could be extended to another aspect of the strategic perspective, that of credibility. Stability in the world, it was argued, depended on the reliability of the United States as an ally, as a protector of weaker states. U.S. commitments, therefore, had to be honored, even at the risk of war. Should the Soviet Union—or any other aggressor—sense that the United States would not back its commitments with force, world order would be seriously undermined. Consequently, much of U.S. policy during the cold war was designed to establish and maintain the credibility of U.S. commitments not only to allies but to any country threatened by the Soviet Union. This policy eventually led to Vietnam—and may help explain U.S. actions in Latin America.

This viewpoint is based on a traditional balance-of-power assessment of the U.S. role in the world, one expressed at various times throughout the cold war by government officials, particularly, secretaries of state Dean Rusk and Henry Kissinger. It is a view strongly influenced by the experiences of the 1930s, when the failure of the democracies to stand firm against early German and Japanese aggression has been blamed for the later outbreak of a much larger war. Convinced by that experience, U.S. policymakers were determined, after World War II, that aggression would be halted in its early stages in order to prevent a major war. The containment policy governed U.S. actions into the 1980s; it was predicated on the necessity of an early demonstration of a will to resist Soviet aggression, whether direct or indirect. For containment to be effective, the threat of U.S. retaliation had to be credible. Once the commitments to resist aggression had been made, no wavering was possible. To back down in face of aggression would convince the enemy that the United States had no will to fight. As a result, U.S. allies would no longer trust U.S. protection, the Soviets would no longer be deterred from expansion, and the existing world order would come tumbling down.[1]

How did this apply to Latin America? According to the strategic viewpoint, because U.S. behavior was constantly being judged by allies and enemies alike, it did not matter where the tests took place, but how the United States responded. Of course, if the challenge occurred in its own hemisphere, then Washington would be under tremendous pressure to prove its mettle, to stand up to aggression or any threat linked to the Soviet Union. Thus, events in Latin America at times were treated as tests of U.S. global credibility, as indicators of how the country might react to threats in Europe or Asia, not as mere challenges to U.S. hegemony in a neighboring territory. U.S. policy in Latin America, therefore, became a process of signaling intent and interest.

Synopsis

The strategic perspective begins with the assumption that U.S. decisionmakers do not deal with Latin America on the basis of criteria different from those they would use to assess events elsewhere. U.S. actions in the region may take on distinctive qualities, such as a more frequent use of intervention, but the rationale for the acts, the criteria employed in evaluating them are not noticeably different from those governing U.S. behavior in other parts of the world. This is not to say that these rationales are always based on an accurate perception of a problem or an objective assessment of the threat, for they may not be. What is important, however, is to understand the influence of cold war ideological and power considerations in directing U.S. policy in Latin America after 1945.

We have seen the impact of anticommunism in shaping the U.S. responses to Guatemala in 1954, to Fidel Castro, and to the 1965 Dominican revolt. It has had a more explicit influence on U.S. attitudes toward the revolutions in Nicaragua and El Salvador. Those cases will be studied in Chapter 8. Before turning to them, however, two other illustrations of strategic criteria deserve to be examined.

CUBA: THE MISSILE CRISIS AND BEYOND

The U.S. obsession with Cuba that we considered in Chapters 2 and 3 has continued into the 1980s. It may constitute today what Jorge Dominguez labels "Cubaphobia," an exaggerated fear both of Cuba's potential for spreading revolution and of its ties to the Soviet Union.[2] The most explicit definition of the strategic role of Cuba came in the 1962 missile crisis, but the continuing propensity for U.S. policymakers to see Cuba as a key player in the great powers' global struggle was also important.

The missile crisis has been subjected to extensive discussion and analysis. It stands as a major case study in crisis decisionmaking; it marked a turning point in U.S.-Soviet relations and led to the signing of the Nuclear Test Ban Treaty. Eyewitness accounts, memoirs, documentaries, and scholarly studies have provided a wealth of material for the student of diplomacy, decisionmaking, and nuclear deterrence.[3] The crisis has also become a landmark in U.S. policy toward Latin America, for it has come to serve as a symbol of the danger that can arise from Soviet penetration of the region. A Cuba under Castro might have been a problem for the United States, but a Cuba with Soviet nuclear missiles was a direct threat to the national security and a challenge to the stability of the global strategic balance. After the failure of the Bay of Pigs invasion, Washington seemed resigned to Castro's continued presence in the Caribbean, but the reaction to the installation of Soviet missiles there revealed just how limited its tolerance was.

The Crisis

In brief, the crisis developed in October 1962, when U.S. officials discovered that the USSR was in the process of installing, in Cuba, missiles with the capability of delivering nuclear warheads to the United States and Latin America. The discovery shocked the Kennedy White House, in part because it was such an unexpected move and in part because it threatened to disturb what had been seen as a stable nuclear deterrence.

Kennedy decided the missiles had to be removed. To back up his demand, he imposed a naval quarantine around Cuba, placed U.S. military forces on alert, and issued an ultimatum to Soviet Premier Nikita Khrushchev that declared that any missile fired from Cuba would be considered as having come directly from the Soviet Union. To emphasize his determination, Kennedy announced his intentions to the nation in a dramatic television address. After thirteen days of tension, Khrushchev agreed to dismantle and remove the missiles. The superpowers had pulled back from the brink of a nuclear disaster. As Secretary of State Rusk stated in a meeting at the White House during the crisis, "We're eyeball to eyeball and I think the other fellow just blinked."[4]

In any event, Khrushchev proposed a deal to Kennedy in which the Soviet Union would withdraw the missiles if Washington would pledge neither to invade Cuba nor to allow others to attack. Kennedy took the chance that such a deal would work and wrote Khrushchev that the United States would "give assurances against an invasion of Cuba" once the missile withdrawal was confirmed.[5] Although the exchanges between the two leaders were not so simple as they appear here, Khrushchev did accept the proposition and the two sides pulled away from the edge. Castro was not pleased at the removal nor at appearing as a pawn in great power politics, but there was the implicit "no invasion" promise from Washington that probably would not have been given had there been no missile crisis.

Effects

For the United States, the missile crisis provided an opportunity to discredit the Cuban revolution. Clearly, it was argued, Castro was in power only because of Soviet props. He had betrayed the revolution's quest for independence; Cuba was no better off in 1962 than it had been in 1958. Castro was a Soviet puppet, Cuba, a Soviet satellite state. This was certainly no model for the rest of the hemisphere to follow. Such an argument may have had some short-term benefits, but Castro survived 1962, and although his dependence on the USSR remained quite visible, his revolution still represented, in Latin America, an envied symbol of defiance.

As a superpower, the United States is bound to consider the impact of local events on its global position. In the missile crisis there was no doubt about the strategic implications of the Soviet move; it could not be viewed as a regional or local incident. And yet, the intensity of the U.S. reaction and the price it was apparently willing to pay to remove the threat revealed the special place Cuba and the

Caribbean have in U.S. foreign policy. For the Soviets to gain a nuclear advantage was bad enough, but to do it in the shadow of Key West, Florida, and in collaboration with the revolutionary Castro was to guarantee a strong response. The cold war had hit Latin America full force. It was a sobering experience although its lasting effect outside the United States is difficult to assess.

Kennedy, of course, was not inclined to forget the hemispheric impact of the Soviet intrusion. In his crisis speech of October 22, the president pointed out that, in addition to reaching Washington, Soviet missiles in Cuba could also attack Mexico City and Panama. The Soviet buildup, he stated was "deliberately provocative in an area well-known to have a special and historical relationship to the United States and the nations of the Western Hemisphere."[6] A strategic struggle was at work, but the president's words were also a reminder of the sphere-of-influence considerations that have traditionally shaped U.S.–Latin American relations.

Détente with Carter

Although neither the USSR nor the United States allowed Cuba to escalate into another direct superpower confrontation during the 1970s, little progress was made toward reconciling U.S.-Cuban relations. Castro was still perceived as a pariah when Jimmy Carter took office in 1977.

Under Carter, however, relations with Cuba began to relax. An "interests sections" was opened by the United States in Havana—in lieu of formal diplomatic relations—and Cuba did the same in Washington. The ban on travel of U.S. citizens to Cuba was lifted, and agreements on fishing rights and maritime boundaries were signed. Discussions were also opened on the release of political prisoners and on trade. To Washington, Castro's increasing moderation seemed to warrant a reassessment of the relationship. Even the continued presence of Cuban troops in Angola (southern Africa) was not seen as a divisive issue.[7] Andrew Young, U.S. ambassador to the United Nations, may have overstated Washington's official view when he characterized the Cuban troops in Africa as a "stabilizing" factor, but he did reflect the growing interest in repairing the link with Havana.

By 1979, however, this optimism began to wane, and again, Cuba was in the forefront of great power politics and an issue in domestic politics. The debate over the presumed presence of a brigade of Soviet combat troops in Cuba in the summer of 1979 brought an end somewhat unexpectedly to the nascent modus vivendi with Castro and demonstrated—again—how volatile were Cuban-U.S. relations.

By the time Reagan took over, relations with Cuba had gone from promising to bad to utter confusion. Cuba was being blamed by Carter for stirring the revolutionary cauldron in Central America, for complicity in establishing a communist government in Grenada, for helping subvert the Nicaraguan revolution and was condemned for not pulling troops out of Africa and for undertaking an extensive military buildup under Soviet tutelage. The case against Cuba had been well constructed by the time the Reagan administration took office with its own anti-Castro agenda.

The Continuing Cuban Problem

Cuba's place in the U.S. psyche probably far exceeds its actual importance, but the island has become such a headache for Washington that it cannot be treated as merely a Latin American problem. The removal of Cuban troops from Angola, for example, became a condition for U.S. and South African participation in an arrangement for the independence of Namibia. Castro's assertion of leadership in the nonaligned movement and his support for revolutions in Central America were constant reminders of Washington's inability to influence Cuban policy.

Working out an understanding with Cuba has been hampered by misgivings on the part of both Washington and Havana. Washington's reluctance to open relations stemmed, obviously, from the perception of Cuba as a trouble-making proxy of the Soviet Union. Why reward this kind of behavior? Alternatively, there were signs that the Cubans were hesitant about establishing the ties that might corrupt. Although improved trade with the United States might be of economic benefit, suspicion remained that the impact of an association with capitalism could undermine the hard-fought gains of the revolution. Moreover, in Havana's view, the price the United States was asking was too high. Cuba could not give up its newly achieved status as recognized leader of popular revolutions.

To illustrate this last point, Cuban military advisers and troops, teachers, nurses, and doctors have had an extensive worldwide role far beyond what one would normally expect from a country of only 10 million people, with a military force of 153,000. As early as 1961, Cuban advisers were in Ghana to train guerrillas and in 1963, Cuban arms and technicians assisted Algeria in its war against Morocco. About 250 Cuban advisers were in Congo-Brazzaville in 1965 and a few in Guinea-Bissau in 1966. Small groups of advisers and soldiers have also been in Tanzania, Sierra Leone, and Somalia. And, of course there have been 20,000 soldiers in Angola; 16,000, in Ethiopia. In the Middle East, Cuban military personnel have spent time in South Yemen and Iraq.[8]

In addition to training Latin American guerrillas in Cuba itself, Cuban advisers, teachers, and medical personnel have worked with revolutionary forces in such places as Bolivia, Colombia, Peru, and Venezuela, as well as in Nicaragua. Security advisers have assisted the governments of Guyana, Jamaica, Grenada, and Nicaragua.

The Cuban leadership is unlikely to back away from this heady role in international politics, for as Ché Guevara once said, "the duty of revolutionaries is to make revolution." Nonetheless, these efforts have seldom, with the possible exception of Angola, had a decisive impact. Typically, they have been short-lived and symbolic operations. But they do give credence to the U.S. contention that revolution is a major Cuban export that is serious enough to challenge U.S. global interests.

The Soviets too have extracted considerable benefit from Cuba's external involvement. Association with Cuba gives weight to Soviet claims that it too is a revolutionary power, sympathetic to the interests of the Third World. In this regard, Cuba's value to Moscow extends beyond the concrete benefits of bases and troops to its symbolic reassurance of the legitimacy of the communist cause. Cuba has become a valuable political and military asset for the Soviet Union.[9]

In the Reagan administration, two general assumptions about Cuba itself seemed to prevail. One was that the Cuban government is tightly organized along the Soviet model, with a well-trained and disciplined secret police system, much like the Soviet KGB. The developments in Grenada and the rapid growth of internal security forces in Nicaragua, with Cuban and East European advisers, reinforced the impression that Cuban "advice" was not entirely benign. The Soviets and their allies have demonstrated over recent years a sophisticated capacity for organizing the kind of security and police forces that enable regimes in the Third World friendly to the USSR to stay in power. For Washington, this was an ominous, although not proven, development and one that tended to shut off an easy path to cooperation.

A second aspect of the Reagan approach was the perception that in spite of Cuba's totalitarian ideology, there was still widespread popular disillusionment in the country. The United States, therefore, should try to keep that spark of resistance alive. Inspired no doubt by pressure from Cuban exile groups in the United States, the Reagan administration let it be known that it did not take for granted the permanent "enslavement" of the Cuban people. Representative of this concern was the building of a powerful medium-wave radio station to broadcast the "truth" to the Cubans. Named *Radio Martí* after the Cuban liberator, José Martí, this station was a direct effort to propagandize the Cuban people. The rationale was that Radio Havana broadcasts destabilizing propaganda throughout Latin America; therefore, the Cubans could not claim immunity. The station's power was sufficient to reach all areas of Cuba with programming on AM, the most popular band. Opposition to the station came from those who thought it ineffective and a waste of money plus those who saw it as unnecessarily provocative. When the station began broadcasting in May 1985, Castro immediately cut off talks with Washington about refugee and travel issues.[10]

Wayne Smith, former chief of the U.S. interests section in Havana, was critical of Reagan's attempt to intimidate Cuba with threats of invasion and punishment.[11] This, he argued, reinforced Castro's view of an implacably hostile United States, so determined to unseat him that no trusting negotiations on any topic were possible. Moreover, Smith contended that Reagan's approach was flawed by its presumption that a "quick fix" was possible in Cuba and that pressure and propaganda would compel the Cubans to behave themselves. Such a rapid change was impossible, Smith said, but the attempt to achieve it was further off target because of faulty perceptions about Cuba's role in the Central American revolutions.

Specifically, the Reagan administration dismantled the Carter arrangements with Cuba. The 1977 fishing agreement was not renewed, restrictions on travel to Cuba were reimposed, and negotiations on such issues as the future of Central America were dismissed as pointless—or worse, dangerous. As Smith noted, the White House saw talking to Castro as displaying a sign of weakness that the Cubans might be tempted to exploit. And when U.S. troops discovered documents in Grenada in 1983 intimately linking Cuba with that island's Marxist government, the image of Cuba as the patron of one-party communist states in Latin America seemed confirmed.

The problem for the United States in dealing with Cuba is that the issues separating the two are not simply bilateral but involve a series of interrelated global problems, stretching from revolutions in Latin America to civil wars in Africa, and from the Soviet-American military balance in the Caribbean to the demonstration of U.S. will in a world presumably uncertain about it.[12] Virtually any action by Cuba today can be guaranteed to jolt the United States into a negative response. Because of the strategic consequences, Washington is simply not going to risk the making of another Cuba in Latin America.

ALLENDE'S CHILE

Few cases have generated more resentment of U.S. policy in Latin America than the Nixon-Kissinger role in the overthrow of Chile's Salvador Allende. The issues seemed to encompass the full range of friction between North and South America: widespread U.S. interference in Chile's politics, including assassination plots; involvement of U.S. business interests that had close ties to the White House; a destabilization campaign; and possible complicity in a coup that overturned years of democratic government in Chile and ushered in over a decade of rule by a brutal military regime. This episode also stands as one of the most extensive cases of U.S. intervention in Latin America outside of the Caribbean/Central American area.

Background

For nearly the entire 150 years of its existence, Chile had a government based on constitutional law and democratic procedures. Prior to 1973, there had seldom been any direct military interference in politics. There was a competitive political party system, with parties ranging from the National party on the right to two Marxist parties, the Socialists and the Communists, on the left. The Radicals and Christian Democrats were in the center. All parties expressed a willingness to work in the context of a parliamentary system. In the 1960s, the Christian Democrats controlled the presidency, while various coalitions held forth in the congress.[13]

Chile's democratic traditions were complemented by a more complex social system than one usually finds in Latin America. There was a large middle class and an absence of sharp cleavages based on race, language, and family heritage. Although economic inequities did exist, Chile was not poor. Its copper mines have generated considerable income and have been a major source of foreign currency earnings. Copper's impact has lessened somewhat today, however. Most of the copper industry in 1970 was controlled by major U.S. corporations such as Anaconda and Kennecott. By 1970 growing economic problems brought on by inflation, a poorly developed agriculture sector, and rising popular expectations of prosperity caused many voters to begin to turn to the left.

Salvador Allende, a Marxist, did not suddenly burst onto the scene in 1970.[14] He had been a presidential candidate four times and a member of the congress since the late 1930s. Allende was no gun-toting, bearded revolutionary, but he did propose drastic changes in

Chile's economy. As the candidate of a Socialist-Communist alliance in 1958, Allende came close to winning the presidency but lost to right-wing candidate Jorge Alessandri. In the 1964 election, Christian Democrat Eduardo Frei won an overwhelming victory that was warmly endorsed by the United States. Allende received 38.9 percent of the vote in that election.

Prior to the election of 1970, the Christian Democratic party's unity had deteriorated, the Right was mounting a comeback, and the Left was broadening its appeal in the face of worsening economic conditions and campaigning against foreign ownership of the national economy. Even President Frei had announced plans to control foreign investment, and in June 1969 he began negotiations for nationalizing the copper industry. He also signed a trade agreement with Cuba in 1970. The military was becoming concerned about inflation and neglect, and in 1969 there were plots for a coup, one of which was to be led by General Robert Viaux. Nothing came of the plots. Viaux was "retired" but found an ally for his cause in the CIA, which by 1969 had begun to develop covert plans to prevent Allende from winning the election.

In 1970, Allende ran under the Popular Unity label, which brought together a number of parties including the Socialists and Communists, as well as the center Radicals. The Popular Unity program included plans for expropriating the copper mines, the banking system, major industries, and service monopolies such as the telephone system.[15] Given Frei's recent policy shifts to the left, the Allende program did not appear to be such a major departure for the Chileans; for U.S. businesses, however, it was a blueprint for disaster.

In the race against Radomiro Tomic, a Christian Democrat, and rightist Jorge Alessandri, Allende received 36.2 percent of the vote. Alessandri won 34.9 percent, Tomic, 27.8 percent. Because no one received an absolute majority, the election, in keeping with the Chilean constitution, was decided by the congress. Reflecting the will of the voters, the congress voted in favor of Allende: 153 to 35, with 7 abstentions. On November 3, Allende took office as the first elected Marxist president in the Western Hemisphere.

U.S. Preventive Action

Allende's accession to power came about in spite of considerable efforts by U.S. business and government to prevent it.[16] In the 1960s the U.S.-owned telecommunications giant, International Telephone and Telegraph Company (ITT), had channeled hundreds of thousands of dollars to center and right-wing parties to encourage their success and thus to protect the company's extensive holdings in Chile. The CIA had turned down ITT's request for help in funding Alessandri's 1964 campaign, but the agency did fund anti-Allende propaganda. In June 1970, the CIA was authorized by the White House to spend $390,000 to prevent a "communist" victory in the upcoming elections. As national security adviser, Henry Kissinger was reported to have said: "I don't see why we have to let a country go Marxist just because its people are irresponsible."[17] In contrast, William Colby, who would later be CIA director, called the White House's "spoiling" scheme in Chile "a rather foolish decision."[18]

The resulting effort attacked the economic nationalism of both the Christian Democrats and the Left, with little noticeable effect, just as the attempt to associate Allende with Castro failed. Allende had made it clear that although he was a Marxist Socialist, he was not a Communist, not a party member, and attempts to paint him as such proved unsuccessful.

With the Allende plurality in the September election, ITT stepped up its anti-Allende activities and contributed to the perception that the situation warranted direct U.S. intervention. The company lobbied throughout Washington, and as its own documents show, its officers were prepared to finance a CIA operation, at the cost of $1 million, to prevent Allende from coming to power.[19] The specter of the CIA working for ITT was presumably too much even for the Nixon White House and the proposition was squelched.

However, in spite of some resistance from the CIA, the Department of State, and the U.S. ambassador in Santiago, Edward Korry, the White House proceeded to direct the CIA to keep Allende out of the presidency. Korry, unaware of much of the CIA's covert plans for Chile, told Washington that it was up to the Chileans to deal with the problem, not the United States. He also warned against backing unpredictable characters like General Viaux.[20] Word also went out from Washington for U.S. diplomats and military officers who had served in Chile to renew their contacts with friendly groups there, particularly the armed forces. The CIA's estimate was that an Allende victory would result in serious economic losses for U.S. companies and that it would "create considerable political and psychological costs" for the United States but that there was no threat to U.S. security or to the global military balance.[21]

The White House, and especially Kissinger, were caught by surprise by the turn of events in Chile. According to Kissinger, the State Department had focused disproportionately on the modest impact on U.S. business of an Allende victory and not enough on the strategic consequences. This, he suggested, led to a passive attitude toward events in Chile. The "geopolitical" effect of an Allende election was too serious for complacency, "We did not find it easy to reconcile ourselves to a second communist state in the Western Hemisphere."[22] As a continental power, Chile was marked as a definite threat to vital U.S. interests.

Although Kissinger admitted to a lack of knowledge about Latin America, he insisted that Allende's election to the presidency would be "the last democratic election" for Chile. Allende, he claimed, "represented a break with Chile's long democratic history"; his election was the result of "a fluke of the Chilean political system."[23] The United States, Kissinger asserted, was justified in its efforts to keep Allende out of power. His only regret was not having been warned sufficiently in advance so that effective preventive measures could have been taken. Allende's ties to Cuba and the Communist party constituted a problem that had global implications for U.S. security.

The Schneider Assassination

United States actions in Chile were to follow two tracks. The first consisted of covert activities such as propaganda, bribery, and threats to persuade the congress not to confirm Allende. This track's ultimate aim was to find a way for Eduardo Frei to remain in power. Ambassador Korry, presumably acting on instructions from Washington, delivered the following warning to Frei on the consequences of Allende's selection: "not a nut or bolt will be allowed to reach Chile under Allende. . . . We shall do all within our power to condemn Chile and the Chileans to utmost deprivation and poverty."[24] Frei did not respond, but the threat proved not to be an empty one.

The second track, of which Korry was not informed, was to encourage a direct military takeover. Although the CIA had calculated that this scheme would not work, presidential pressure forced the agency to pursue it. Nixon suggested that the CIA be prepared to spend $10 million if necessary. (That amount of money was never authorized nor spent, however.) The CIA director, Richard Helms, gave the plan only a 10 percent chance of success.[25] Although this maneuver was probably too late, Nixon was determined to keep the "Communists" from taking power.

The obstacle to the second track's goal of a military coup was the opposition by the Chilean commander in chief, General René Schneider, who had no intention of interfering with the constitution. The logical course for the CIA to follow, then, was to remove Schneider from the scene in the hope that less-principled officers would intercede. Thus began a clumsy effort to collaborate with two different groups willing to kidnap Schneider and provoke a coup. One group was headed by retired General Viaux, the other by the Santiago area commander, General Camilo Valenzuela. The United States indicated that it would recognize a military government should one come to power.

On October 19, an attempt by the Valenzuela group to kidnap Schneider failed as did a second attempt the next day. On the morning of October 22 a U.S. officer delivered U.S. machine guns to these plotters. Soon after, Schneider's car was stopped, and the general shot when he tried to defend himself. He died on October 25. There was no evidence that he had been killed by the U.S.-supplied weapons, but it was proven that the killing had come at the hands of people whom U.S. agents had been advising.[26]

Kissinger blamed Viaux for the assassination but insisted that U.S. hands are clean. Viaux, he said, was advised by the CIA on October 17 that the kidnap plan was cancelled. The Valenzuela group was not called off, however, according to Kissinger, because the White House was not aware that it was operating with CIA assistance.[27] In any event, it is difficult to trace direct U.S. responsibility for the general's death.

The removal of Schneider did not produce the desired coup. Two days after the shooting, Allende was confirmed as president. The White House was convinced by this time that it would be impossible to work out an accommodation with Allende. His radical statements, the openings to Cuba, and his collaboration with the Communists guaranteed a long period of hostile relations with Washington. Diplomatic relations between Chile and Cuba were established on November 12, and Castro visited Chile in 1971. Evidence of Allende's radicalism was his creation of a personal security force, his appointment of Communists to his cabinet, and his aggressive policy of expropriating private enterprise without "fair" compensation.

The Big Squeeze

In Nixon's 1970 instructions concerning Allende to CIA Director Helms, the president directed that the economy of Chile be "squeezed until it screamed." That is a fair representation of the intentions of the Nixon administration after November 1970. The actual conduct of the policy was somewhat less than a total squeeze, but it was certainly not benign.

In the wake of the announcement of Allende's nationalization program, the United States did reduce its loans to Chile (direct AID grants had been phased out as unnecessary in 1968) but continued

168

the Food For Peace programs (in excess of $16.8 million over three years). Military assistance and the Peace Corps programs were also continued. The Hickenlooper Amendment, in which the U.S. Congress insisted that all aid be halted to any country expropriating U.S. property without prompt and fair compensation, was not invoked. Some debt repayments to the United States were rescheduled and Washington did not, in this early stage, oppose Chilean loan requests at the Inter-American Development Bank (IDB). Trade between the two countries was not forbidden either. Gradually, however, the economic screws were tightened, and Chile did suffer.

The Nixon-Kissinger response to Allende's programs was derived from two concerns: their impact on U.S. investments and their influence on the U.S. strategic position. U.S. holdings in Chile were considerable—worth about $1 billion. Included were three copper companies, three iron mines, ITT's control of the national telephone system, subsidiaries of about fifty companies such as Du Pont, Coca-Cola, and Esso, plus branches of two major U.S. banks.[28] They were all targets for nationalization, and under Frei, as mentioned above, negotiations for a takeover of two copper companies had already begun.

Allende's plan called for the government to compensate the copper companies for the original cost of their investments, less depreciation and excess profits. Compensation would be paid over thirty years at an interest rate of 3 percent. Since the copper operations were so large and so central to Chile's economy, Allende sought a constitutional amendment, which required congressional approval, for the takeover. The companies were also a symbol of Chile's dependence on the United States. The fact that the amendment was approved *unanimously* by the congress on July 11, 1971, indicates the depth of support for Allende on this issue.

In any event, the details of the copper seizure still required negotiations with the affected companies. In the eyes of the Chileans, it was the U.S. companies that owed money, not the Chilean government. The excess profits extracted from the mines and workers, it was argued, more than made up for the cost of nationalization. It was at this juncture that U.S. economic pressure began to build. The National Security Council had already in November 1970 approved a plan for drying up Chile's credit; therefore, in August 1971 when Santiago applied for a $21 million loan from the U.S. Export-Import Bank for the purchase of three Boeing jetliners, the request was held up at the suggestion of the While House.[29]

After July 1971, no further IDB loans for Chile were approved, largely due to U.S. pressure. No new World Bank loans were made to Chile, and credits from U.S. private banks dropped to $32 million in 1972 from $220 million in 1970. By November 1971, Chile was unable to meet payments on its foreign debts. However, loans and credits did flow to Chile from various sources, including $200 million from Western Europe and $446 million from Eastern Europe, the Soviet Union, and China.[30] The latter loans, of course, only confirmed White House suspicions that Chile was drifting toward dependence on communist states.

Economic problems were rampant in Chile by 1972. Inflation was high, running at a rate of 163 percent per year, truckers were on strike, as were, at different times, shopkeepers, bank employees, lawyers, doctors, gas workers, and bus drivers. Food shortages led women to march in the streets, banging their pots and pans in protest. Allende's honeymoon with the electorate had ended, and in a key by-election in January 1972 opposition candidates were elected. In the March congressional elections, Allende's Popular Unity coalition won 44 percent of the vote, compared to 56 percent for the opposition.[31] It was not an overwhelming endorsement of Allende's policies, but neither was it a total rejection because the vote represented an 8 percent gain over 1970 for Popular Unity.

The purpose of reviewing the internal economic and political situation in Chile lies in its relationship to U.S. policy. First, although Chile did receive outside funds, the U.S. credit squeeze contributed to Allende's economic problems. Allende's own policies and budget deficits were inflationary, and this helped generate opposition to him. There was support for his nationalization program, but the confrontationist style of his politics, coupled with a deteriorating economy, increased the polarization in the country. Nonetheless, there was no widespread demand for him to leave office before the end of his term, and Allende was conducting his government generally within the laws of the country.

To Washington, however, the picture was different. The expropriation arrangements were grossly unfair, and there was fear that if Allende got away with his program, other governments in Latin America would be tempted to follow his example. Moreover, Chile's economic problems were pointed to as proof of the foolishness of the socialist policies and confrontational politics to be expected from a minority Marxist president. Chile's loss of outside capital was due, according to Washington, to Allende's default on his government's debts and to the government's poor credit rating. U.S. banks and investors were simply not going to put their money into a country where free enterprise was not safe. Chile's problems, Kissinger declared, were not the result of any "economic warfare" launched by the U.S.[32]

Covert Action

Although most attention seemed to be focused on economic relations with Chile, to Nixon and Kissinger the key issue remained the strategic impact. The administration's case was outlined by Kissinger as follows:[33] First, there was Castro's month-long visit at the end of 1971 that saw the Cuban and Chilean leaders join in condemning U.S. imperialism and capitalism. At the same time, Allende was seeking stronger presidential powers, presumably enroute to "dismantling democracy," but even Kissinger acknowledged that Allende was doing this through proper congressional and legal channels. Moreover, most of Allende's proposals failed because of political opposition and court challenges. Other "ominous developments" cited by Kissinger included the suppression of dissent, political patronage to leftists, and aid to groups from Cuba and Eastern Europe.

Allende's policies did foster political discontent in Chile, which served only to weaken, not enhance, his power. Kissinger, however, saw totalitarianism around the corner and accused Chile of following a "classical revolutionary pattern" at home and abroad. Confrontation with the United States was the Chilean theme, he claimed, as at the end of 1972 Allende visited Cuba, Algeria, and the Soviet Union. Nixon's doubt about Allende's foreign policy was expressed when he commented that U.S. relations with the Chileans depended "not on their ideology, but on their conduct toward the outside world."[34]

In sum, the case for Chile's strategic threat was not very substantial. Allende may have sought revolution. He was certainly more radical than previous Chilean presidents, and his public posture against the United States was obviously not very cooperative or trusting. And yet, he had not succeeded in his domestic goal of transforming the economy, and his foreign policy adventures were largely symbolic. Moreover, he complied, for the most part, with the laws and democratic procedures of the Chilean political system.

Washington's response, however, was based on an assessment of Chile as a geopolitical threat. In addition to the economic pressures, the Nixon administration spent $1.6 million in 1971 and 1972 to support an opposition newspaper and nearly $1 million to fund opposition political parties.[35] The "destabilization" of Chile may not have come about entirely because of U.S. actions, but they were clearly not acts designed to "stabilize."

As Kissinger reported, the United States systematically sought to "isolate" Chile politically and economically. Late in 1972, it was decided to continue covert aid to opposition groups in view of the 1973 congressional elections in Chile, and $1.4 million was appropriated for that purpose. In spite of the growing problems in Chile, the administration did not think the military would intervene; thus, according to Kissinger, no plans were made in Washington to encourage a coup d'état.[36]

The Overthrow

By the spring of 1973, the Chilean economy was reeling. There were continuing strikes by truckers and copper miners, plus increasing political tensions fueled by the six-day closing of an opposition newspaper. In the midst of this confusion, on June 29, about one hundred army troops launched an attack on government buildings in Santiago. The rebellion was quickly quelled—the bulk of the armed forces remained loyal to the constitution. The uprising, however, did give impetus to efforts to include the military in a program for restoring order in the country, and Allende did bring a number of officers into his cabinet in August. The Christian Democrats intensified their criticism of Allende's tendency to rely on confrontation rather than accommodation to solve problems.

Allende's relations with the military worsened, however, and the country appeared to be near anarchy. Most likely, the military's decision to take over the government came on September 7, 1973, when the navy, persistently critical of Allende, was joined by the army commanders, General Carlos Prat (who had just resigned from the cabinet) and General Augusto Pinochet.[37] The air force joined later. The coup began early in the morning of September 11, when the military called for Allende to resign. He refused, and the armed forces surrounded the presidential palace. After three hours of negotiations, the air force bombed the palace. Soon after, army troops stormed the building. Allende died in the process. Whether his death resulted from suicide or the guns of the army is not known. There is evidence to support both conclusions.

U.S. Role and Reaction

Much has been made of alleged U.S. complicity in the coup and in the death of Allende.[38] Evidence for direct U.S. involvement in the takeover is minimal, but U.S. military officials did have close contact with Chilean officers. Moreover, it was well known that the Nixon administration would welcome Allende's removal (but not necessarily his death). In fact, a recent account of the fall of Allende by the U.S. ambassador in Santiago in 1973 asserted that Washington had made it very clear that a coup would be welcome.[39] In any event, the U.S. encouragement of the economic chaos, the political tensions, and the anti-Allende campaign certainly contributed to an atmosphere that could justify—even promote—a military takeover.

Kissinger, nonetheless, was adamant in his denial of U.S. involvement.[40] He noted the official instructions to the embassy to keep out of the crisis that was building against Allende. To Kissinger, named secretary of state in 1973, Chile was of "peripheral concern" to Washington. Although he expressed regret for the excesses of the military junta that took power, he saw the coup, on balance, as a necessary event, brought on by Allende's own incompetence and radicalism, not by the United States.

In the United States, there was widespread presumption of U.S. involvement. That the military government under General Pinochet imposed a repressive rule on Chile without criticism from the White House did little to assuage the impression of U.S. complicity in Allende's demise.

An Assessment

Whether or not the United States was directly involved in the coup, the Nixon administration had been determined to make life difficult for the Allende government. The intensity of U.S. concern could not be attributed entirely to Allende's economic nationalism and socialist policies. The expropriation did affect a sizeable number of U.S. companies, and if Allende had been successful, other governments might well have been encouraged to try their hand at nationalization. Kissinger insisted that too much was made of Allende's "democratic origins" when, in fact, his 36 percent plurality could not be interpreted as a mandate for revolution. Such phony rhetoric about democratic legitimacy, he claimed, obscured the reality of Chile's drift to the Soviet-Cuban orbit.

For the White House, the presence of a hostile, revolutionary Marxist government in the hemisphere was a threat to U.S. power and prestige in the world. Allende emerged at the time the United States was trying to extricate itself from Vietnam and still save face. Not to move against Chile would serve only to weaken further U.S. credibility as a global power. Although such a bloody end to Allende's presidency might not have been expected, it was clear that Washington was set on making Chile pay for its selection of a Marxist president. Perhaps others would get the message that those in Latin America who chose an unfriendly path would pay a very high price for their deviancy.

Nixon and Kissinger may have made light of Chile's democratic traditions, but those traditions were still intact on September 11, 1973.

More than ten years later, there was no sign of democracy in the country. Washington's interference in Chile confirmed Latin perceptions of U.S. hegemony and of their countries as mere pawns in the game of great power politics.

NOTES

1. This issue is analyzed in Stephen M. Walt, "Alliance Formation and the Balance of World Power," *International Security* 9 (Spring 1985), 3–43.
2. Jorge I. Dominguez, "It Won't Go Away: Cuba on the U.S. Foreign Policy Agenda," *International Security* 8 (Summer 1983), 113–128. Also see Tad Szulc, "Cuba's Emergence, America's Myopia," *New York Times,* May 5, 1985, E27.
3. The best accounts of the crisis can be found in: Graham Allison, *Essence of Decision: Explaining the Cuban Missile Crisis* (Boston: Little, Brown, 1971); Robert F. Kennedy, *Thirteen Days* (New York: Norton, 1969); Elie Abel, *The Missile Crisis* (New York: Bantam, 1966); and James A. Nathan, "The Missile Crisis: His Finest Hour," *World Politics* 27 (January 1975), 256–281. Also see the recently published "White House Tapes and Minutes of the Cuban Missile Crisis," *International Security* 10 (Summer 1985), 164–203.
4. Quoted by Abel, *The Missile Crisis,* 134.
5. Ibid., 177.
6. "The Soviet Threat to the Americas," U.S. Department of State, *Bulletin* 47 (November 12, 1962), 715–716.
7. The Carter view is summarized by Myles R. R. Frechette, "Cuban-Soviet Impact on the Western Hemisphere," U.S. Department of State, Current Policy no. 167 (Washington, D.C.: April 17, 1980).
8. For a review of Cuba's aid to revolutions, based in part on a 1977 U.S. Department of Defense study, see John M. Goshko and Walter Pincus, "Sense of Duty Behind Cuba's Global Role," *Washington Post,* September 21, 1979, 1, 27.
9. The Soviet-Cuban link is explored in Mark N. Katz, "The Soviet-Cuban Connection," *International Security* 8 (Summer 1983), 88–112; and Jiri Valenta, "The Soviet-Cuban Alliance in Africa and the Caribbean," *World Today* 37 (February 1981), 45–53. Also see U.S. Department of State, "Cuban Armed Forces and the Soviet Military Presence," Special Report no. 103 (Washington, D.C.: August 1982).
10. A summary of the debate about Radio Martí is in *Miami Herald,* July 2, 1982, GA; and *New York Times,* May 21, 1985, 1.
11. Wayne S. Smith, "Dateline Havana: Myopic Diplomacy," *Foreign Policy* 48 (Fall 1982), 157–174.
12. William M. LeoGrande outlines the nature of these conflicts in "Cuba Policy Recycled," *Foreign Policy* 46 (Spring 1982), 105–119. A new approach is proposed in Edward Gonzalez, *A Strategy for Dealing with Cuba in the 1980s* (Santa Monica, Calif.: Rand Corp., no. R2954-DOS/AF, December 1982).

13. For Chile's political system prior to 1970, see Federico Gil, *The Political System of Chile* (Boston: Houghton Mifflin, 1966).

14. A good survey of the political and economic conditions contributing to Allende's rise and fall is Paul E. Sigmund, *The Overthrow of Allende and the Politics of Chile, 1964–1976* (Pittsburgh: University of Pittsburgh Press, 1977).

15. Ibid., 88–90.

16. Details of these activities are contained in: Senate Select Committee on Intelligence Activities, *Covert Action in Chile, 1963–1973* (a Staff Report), 94th Cong., 1st Sess. (Washington, D.C.: 1975); also see Senate Committee on Foreign Relations, Subcommittee on Multinational Corporations and U.S. Foreign Policy (Hearings), *The International Telephone and Telegraph Co. and Chile, 1970–71*, 93rd Cong., 1st Sess. (Washington, D.C.: March, April 1973), Parts 1 and 2.

17. Quoted by Roger Morris, *Uncertain Greatness* (New York: Harper & Row, 1977), 241.

18. William Colby and Peter Forbath, *Honorable Men* (New York: Simon and Schuster, 1978), 302.

19. Senate Comm. on Foreign Relations, *The International Telephone*, 433–437.

20. Thomas Powers, *The Man Who Kept the Secrets: Richard Helms and the CIA* (New York: Washington Square Press, 1979), 293–294.

21. Senate Select Committee on Intelligence Activities, *Alleged Assassination Plots Involving Foreign Leaders* (an Interim Report), 94th Cong., 1st Sess. (Washington, D.C.: 1975), 229.

22. Henry Kissinger, *White House Years* (Boston: Little, Brown, 1979), 654–663.

23. Ibid., 654.

24. Senate Select Comm., *Alleged Assassination Plots*, 231.

25. Powers, *The Man Who Kept the Secrets*, 300.

26. Senate Select Comm., *Alleged Assassination Plots*, 244–246. Also see Colby and Forbath, *Honorable Men*, 304.

27. Kissinger, *White House Years*, 673–677.

28. Reported in *New York Times*, September 14, 1970, 59. For extensive discussion of the expropriation issue, see Dale L. Johnson, ed., *The Chilean Road to Socialism* (Garden City, N.Y.: Doubleday, 1973); and Theodore H. Moran, *Multinational Corporations and the Politics of Dependence: Copper and Chile* (Princeton, N.J.: Princeton University Press, 1974).

29. Senate Select Comm., *Covert Action in Chile*, 33; also see Sigmund, *The Overthrow of Allende*, 153.

30. Sigmund, *The Overthrow of Allende*, 174–175, 190.

31. Ibid., 184–186.

32. Henry Kissinger, *Years of Upheaval* (Boston: Little, Brown, 1982), 380–381.

33. Ibid., 380–396.

34. Richard M. Nixon, "U.S. Foreign Policy for the 1970s," (A Report to Congress), *Department of State Bulletin* 60 (March 13, 1972), 361.

35. Senate Select Comm., *Covert Action in Chile*, 29, 60.

36. Ibid., 31; also see Kissinger, *Years of Upheaval*, 390, 395, 403.

37. Sigmund, *The Overthrow of Allende*, 236–240.

38. See, for example, Kissinger, *Years of Upheaval*, 400–404; Robinson Rojas, *The Murder of Allende* (New York: Harper & Row, 1976); and James Petras and Morris Morley, *The United States and Chile* (New York: Monthly Review Press, 1975).

39. Nathanial Davis, *The Last Two Years of Salvador Allende* (Ithaca, N.Y.: Cornell University Press, 1985).

40. Kissinger, *Years of Upheaval*, 403–413. (In contrast, the Costa-Gravas film, "Missing," is a thinly disguised attempt to portray U.S. complicity.)

8
REAGAN'S POLICY

At the heart of the Reagan administration's policies in Latin America was the perception that global strategic interests were at stake in the region. Events in Latin America were subsumed in the U.S. contest with the Soviet Union and in the effort to restore the credibility of U.S. power. In fact, upon the administration's inception in 1981, the Reagan policymakers were determined to reshape and correct a foreign policy gone awry, a policy insufficiently attuned to the overall strategic struggle with the USSR. According to Secretary of State Alexander M. Haig, Jr., the tendency of the Carter administration and of the U.S. public not to think in global terms had, over the years, "cost us dearly."[1]

THE REAGAN-HAIG DEFINITIONS

Approaching Latin America from a strategic perspective was not, of course, unique to the Reagan years, but the intensity of its application aroused controversy because of the revival of what many saw as outdated cold war rationalizations for regional and local problems. Nonetheless, in his first months in office, President Reagan announced a "comprehensive" review of policy on Central America and stated that "important U.S. security interests are at stake in the region."[2] Secretary Haig amplified the mission by declaring that there was "a mass of intervention in this hemishere, through Cuba, the Soviet Union and Libya." He asserted, further, that the region had implications for U.S. interests elsewhere, "We Americans must be as concerned about illegal Soviet intervention in El Salvador as in Africa, in the Middle East, in Southeast Asia and wherever international law is violated and the rule of force is applied."[3]

Cuba, in particular, was singled out as an instrument of Soviet ambitions. A lengthy "research paper" was prepared in 1981 by the Department of State to demonstrate Cuba's "support for violence in Latin America."[4] In this document, the "Moscow-Havana axis" was blamed for Castro's propaganda, training, and assistance on behalf of revolutionary groups throughout Latin America. These activities, the department also said, "could well bring more Cubas: totalitarian regimes so linked to the Soviet Union that they become factors in the military balance."[5]

For Haig, it was necessary for the United States to stand firm against the Marxist rebels in El Salvador because of what it would show the Soviets about the U.S. will. El Salvador was a test case in which the United States had to act decisively and strongly to repel the intrusion of Soviet-aided "wars of national liberation" into "the heart of our sphere of influence." The problems there could turn into another Vietnam, he argued, if the United States allowed this "strategic chokepoint" to fall into enemy hands.[6]

Although the Reagan administration articulated the conceptual and ideological bases for U.S. policy in Central America, the Carter administration in 1979 had already begun to gear up for a more active role in aiding the Salvadoran government and in trying to contain the influence of the Sandinistas in Nicaragua. The first Central American jolt to Washington since the Cuban revolution had been the 1979 victory of the Sandinistas. It forced a major reassessment of U.S. policy throughout the region.

THE NICARAGUAN REVOLUTION

Background

As we noted earlier, the United States has had a long history of involvement in Nicaraguan politics. U.S. intervention in the 1920s and 1930s contributed to the rise of dictator Anastasio Somoza García ("Tacho"), and continuing U.S. assistance helped him and his family stay in power until 1979. (Tacho was assassinated in 1956.)

Somoza's power and that of his sons, Luis Somoza Debayle and Anastasio Somoza Debayle ("Tachito") who took over as president in 1967, rested on the loyalty of a U.S.-organized and trained National Guard and on the family's extensive economic network. The guard and its officers were well cared for and stood by the Somozas until the very end. Their economic empire controlled 25 percent of the country's land, the major port, the beef industry, and a number of factories and commercial enterprises.

Renowned for its corruption, the Somoza regime became increasingly greedy after a 1972 earthquake leveled the center of the capital city, Managua. Unresponsive to pleas even from Washington to use foreign assistance to rebuild the city, Somoza and his guard officers lined their pockets with much of the $32 million in emergency aid from the United States. The earthquake was a turning point. Increased frustration among the masses, coupled with the growing alienation of Nicaragua's middle-class businesspeople and professionals, began to erode the legitimacy and effectiveness of Somoza's government.

The 1979 Upheaval

Dissatisfaction with Somoza did not turn immediately into support for the revolution advocated by such groups as the Sandinista Front for National Liberation (FSLN), fighting in the name of the 1920s rebel Augusto César Sandino. But by 1977 Somoza's power began to wane. Pressure from the Carter administration for human rights compliance raised doubts about U.S. commitment to the dictator, especially after the 1978 assassination of newspaper publisher and Somoza critic Pedro Joaquín Chamorro, which was attributed to Somoza forces. The worsening economy and the brutal attempts by the guard to retain control helped mobilize support for the overthrow of the Somozas, but not necessarily for an FSLN-led revolution. However, the FSLN provided the organization and the guns and led the way to revolution in July 1979. They took control of the nation and have remained in power since then.

Washington had been closely associated with the old order, and its close ties to Somoza did little to engender trust in the United States government. Not only had the U.S. Marines helped put the Somozas in power, but the location of the U.S. embassy, until 1972, next door to Somoza's hillside palace overlooking downtown Managua, reinforced the view of U.S. complicity in Somoza's dictatorship. It was predictable that U.S.-Nicaraguan relations after his overthrow would be difficult.[7]

U.S. Reaction

The Carter administration was initially sympathetic to change in Nicaragua, even if it meant Somoza's departure, but it was not prepared to deal with a total revolution. The ambivalence of its policy led to last-minute efforts to save the National Guard so that order could be preserved. In Nicaragua, this was seen as "Somocismo without Somoza," a totally unacceptable condition. There was also an effort to mobilize an OAS peace force to prevent the FSLN from taking full control, but that too failed.

Carter, although perhaps disappointed by his lack of influence over the revolution, did make an effort to accommodate the Sandinistas.

The new government was immediately recognized, and Carter pledged to respect Nicaraguan sovereignty and to provide aid for reconstruction and development. He also greeted a delegation of government leaders from Managua at the White House in September 1979.

The president's initial aid requests were approved by Congress: $9 million in September, and after a lengthy debate, $75 million in May 1980. In the view of the administration, such aid was essential for maintaining U.S. leverage in Nicaragua. As Secretary of State Cyrus Vance said: "By extending our friendship and economic assistance, we enhance the prospects for democracy in Nicaragua. We cannot guarantee that democracy will take hold there, but if we turn our backs on Nicaragua, we can almost guarantee that democracy will fail."[8]

A skeptical Congress, however, could be persuaded to do little more during an election year. A $45 million aid package for 1981 was delayed, and a request for $5.5 million in military assistance was turned down in June 1980. Increasingly, the view from Washington was of a government becoming too Marxist and too linked to the Socialist bloc to be trusted.

Critics of the Sandinistas pointed to the 7,000 political prisoners reported to be in Nicaraguan jails in 1979 (these were mostly members of the National Guard and Somoza accomplices, who were later released). The critics also noted the Marxists in charge of the FSLN, the educational arrangements with Cuba, the opening of trade with the Soviet Union, and the announced intention of Managua to follow a foreign policy of nonalignment. Clearly, the Sandinista rhetoric was difficult for Washington to accept. Talk of a "Third World orientation," attacks on capitalism and imperialism, support for socialism, and the FSLN hymn that included the phrase, "let us fight against the Yankee, the enemy of mankind," did little to reassure U.S. officials that cooperation was possible.

THE REAGAN CASE AGAINST NICARAGUA

A change in U.S. Central American policy was foretold by the Reagan campaign. The Republican party platform asserted that "we abhor the Marxist Sandinista takeover" in Nicaragua. A group of Reagan advisers, the Santa Fe committee, called for forceful U.S. action in Central America to halt the spread of communism.[9]

For the new administration, the Sandinista revolution was not acceptable on four counts: (1) its aid to the guerrillas in El Salvador, (2) its ties to communist countries, (3) the country's military buildup, and (4) its "totalitarian" ideology. All of these were seen as inconsistent with both stability in the region and U.S. strategic interests, and the four issues have formed the basis for much of the negotiations with Nicaragua in both bilateral and multilateral talks.

Aid to Salvadoran Guerrillas

In February 1981, the Department of State issued a "White Paper" purporting to show the link between the insurgency in El Salvador and an elaborate arms network that extended from Moscow to Vietnam to Cuba and eventually to Nicaragua.[10] The document came under attack for its dubious assumptions and its lack of hard evidence. In fact, it was so discredited that it "became a source of acute embarrassment to the administration."[11]

Nonetheless, the administration was determined to stop the alleged flow of arms to El Salvador. In December 1981 the president signed a "finding" that authorized the CIA to conduct covert military and political action to cut off alleged Nicaraguan support for the guerrillas. The plan, which did not become public until March 1982, called for close to $20 million to create a 500-person paramilitary force for operations in Honduras, El Salvador, and Nicaragua.[12] Argentine advisers would help train these forces, who came to be known as the *contras*, or counterrevolutionaries. Their activities will be discussed in more detail later.

Meanwhile, the effort to build the case against Nicaragua continued. The Department of State, in March 1982, released a document describing Nicaraguan and Cuban backing for the Salvadoran revolt.[13] In essence, the indictment of Nicaragua included two accusations. The first cited the frequent transfers of arms to El Salvador that were coming from Cuba through Nicaragua. Weapons would be airlifted into El Salvador, or trucked across Honduras, or shipped across the Gulf of Fonseca. Even Costa Rica had been used, the report said, as a staging area. The document did acknowledge that the flow of arms had been reduced by the end of 1981 but insisted that it had not ended. The second accused Nicaragua of training Salvadoran guerrillas and providing sanctuary for their leaders. By 1983, however, the Salvadoran revolutionary headquarters and a rebel radio station in Nicaragua had been moved out of the country. Nonetheless, according to U.S. embassy officials in Managua, in June 1984 the Sandinistas were still allowing Salvadoran rebel radios to broadcast military and political information from various sites in Nicaragua.[14]

There were persistent claims by administration officials that Nicaragua's support and sanctuary were critical factors in keeping the Salvadoran rebellion alive, but after 1981 little concrete evidence of arms shipments was revealed despite the constant U.S. surveillance of the Nicaraguan border and the presence of thousands of anti-Sandinista forces in the area. Nicaraguan officials, although conceding that such shipments "may have" occurred prior to 1982, insisted that Nicaragua in subsequent years did not engage in any activity other than moral support for the Salvadoran revolution.[15]

The demand for "proof" of the Nicaraguan aid to El Salvador bedeviled the administration for years. U.S. officials insisted that the arms were transported by mule, backpack, and small aircraft and that they had successfully eluded interception. A Nicaraguan "fishing cooperative" was identified in 1983 as serving as a dispatching point for arms, and in August 1984 U.S. officials revealed what they claimed was "strong support" for the administration's case. The evidence consisted of hazy video tapes and photographs of mules, boats, and canoes presumably carrying arms. Captured maps showed alleged smuggling routes. U.S. General Paul F. Gorman asserted that according to the evidence, El Salvador was "the victim of a pernicious form of aggression by Nicaragua."[16]

Ties with the Communist Bloc

The second component of the administration's case was the Sandinistas' close relationship with Cuba, the Soviet Union, and their communist allies. As noted above, the arms for El Salvador's guerrillas were said to have come through Nicaragua, from the FSLN's communist friends. But the connection went beyond the cooperative effort to "export revolution." In the eyes of the Reagan administration, it extended to a systematic effort to create a Cuban/Soviet base in Central America—a direct threat to U.S. national interests.

To demonstrate this link, administration officials made note of Nicaraguan and Cuban exchanges and of what they saw as the pervasive role of Cuban and East European advisers in the Nicaraguan government and the FSLN's party apparatus.

U.S. officials estimated that in the early stages of FSLN rule, there were more than 6,000 Cuban advisers in Nicaragua, although Managua insisted that most of these were teachers, nurses, and other medical personnel, often working in remote villages. Approximately 1,000 Cuban advisers did leave Nicaragua in November 1983 and more left in 1984. Nevertheless, the U.S. embassy in Managua claimed that close to 2,000 Cuban military advisers remained in the country. In addition, nearly 100 Soviet military advisers were reported to be in Nicaragua and about 70 Nicaraguan pilots and mechanics had received training in Bulgaria and Cuba. A few were being trained in the USSR.[17]

Of particular concern to Washington was the presence of at least several hundred Cuban, East German, and Bulgarian advisers in the Nicaraguan Interior Ministry, the agency responsible for internal security. Under the leadership of Tomas Borge, a member of the Sandinista directorate, this ministry would be, according to U.S. officials, the vehicle for establishing a totalitarian regime through the secret police methods so common in communist states. In fact, it was claimed that a key Cuban police adviser had become a Nicaraguan citizen in order to disguise the ministry's link to Havana.[18]

Cuban and Soviet military assistance was cited by the Reagan administration as hard evidence of Nicaragua's alliance with the Communist bloc. Soviet tanks, armored personnel carriers and rocket launchers, along with East German trucks, were among the early shipments of arms to Nicaragua. By the end of 1984, the Nicaraguan army and militia were outfitted completely with Warsaw Pact equipment from the ubiquitous AK-47 automatic rifle to sophisticated combat helicopters. Modern aircraft, such as the MIG-21, had not been sent, but a number of airstrips were lengthened to accommodate these Soviet fighters.

To demonstrate to the U.S. public the extent of this external support for Nicaragua, the administration televised a briefing by U.S. intelligence officials in 1982 on the military buildup in Nicaragua. Reconnaissance photos showed "Cuban style" barracks, "Cuban style" training facilities, new airfields, and a Soviet/East German military equipment depot. The briefing was reminiscent of the revelations in 1962 of Soviet missiles in Cuba, and it was followed by warnings that if Soviet missiles were installed in Nicaragua, the U.S. response would match that of twenty years earlier.[19]

The peak of concern for Managua's military connections came in November 1984 when reports of a shipment of Soviet MIGs enroute to Nicaragua circulated in Washington. Although no aircraft actually arrived in Nicaragua, administration officials used the opportunity to warn Managua of U.S. determination not to allow a Soviet military base to be installed in Central America. Warnings were also issued against Nicaragua's alleged growing military threat to its neighbors.

In addition to the Soviet military influence, Washington was also convinced that the Sandinistas' close political ties to the international Communist party network directed from Moscow did not bode well for either Nicaraguan or U.S. interests. Although Nicaraguan leaders insisted they had not joined the Communist bloc, Nicaragua abstained on key votes at the United Nations on Afghanistan and on the shooting down of the Korean airliner in 1983. Frequent visits by FSLN leaders to Moscow and open identification with radical movements in Grenada and elsewhere in the Third World further aroused U.S. suspicions.

Documents seized by U.S. troops invading Grenada in 1983 linked the Sandinistas with radical socialist parties in Grenada and Jamaica as well as with the Communist party of Cuba. The papers included notes of a secret meeting in Managua in January 1983 to devise a strategy for persuading the Socialist International to support the "progressive" forces in Latin America. Moderate socialist parties and social democratic parties in Europe and the United States were identified as "enemies" of revolution. Ultimately, the radicalism of the FSLN led to serious splits with West European socialist parties.[20]

Immediately upon coming to power, the Sandinistas joined the Nonaligned Movement and placed their revolution alongside the global struggle against imperialism, colonialism, and capitalism. Nicaragua also consistently voiced support for radical movements in Africa, for the Palestine Liberation Organization, and for Libya's Col. Muammar al-Qaddafi. These positions may amount to little more than rhetorical stances, but they tended to confirm Washington's contention that the radical leadership of the FSLN had no intention of coming to terms with the United States and that the direction of Nicaragua's foreign policy could only lead to a Cuban-style outpost for the Soviet Union.[21]

The Military Buildup

A third area of concern was the size of Nicaragua's military buildup, which, according to the Reagan administration, far exceeded the country's defensive needs and thus posed a threat to stability in the region. Official U.S. estimates of the size of Nicaragua's army ranged up to about 75,000 troops. It is difficult to get an accurate figure on the army's size, but the International Institute for Strategic Studies estimated in 1984 that there were 60,000 regular army forces, including 12,000 reservists, and a militia of 40,000 civilians with small weapons and little training. These figures show an increase over a 1983 army of 47,000 (with 25,000 reservists) and a militia of about 30,000. By comparison, neighboring Honduras had an army of 15,500; Costa Rica had no genuine army at all.[22]

Washington was also alarmed over Nicaragua's acquisition of modern weaponry: sixty Soviet T54/55 tanks, eighty armored personnel carriers, twenty helicopters, thirty surface-to-air missiles and a variety of howitzers, rocket launchers, and antitank guns. As of mid-1985 there were no sophisticated jet fighters.

Despite charges from the administration that this buildup threatened the region, the Nicaraguan government insisted that the increase in military capability was purely defensive. To Managua, the activities of the U.S.-sponsored *contras* and the ever-present threat of a U.S. invasion were adequate justifications for improving the country's defenses. Moreover, because the United States made it virtually impossible for Nicaragua to obtain Western weapons, it had to turn to the Soviet bloc for help. The defensive nature of the Nicaraguan military and the difficulty it would have if it attempted to attack even its neighbors were confirmed by expert military testimony before Congress in 1982.[23]

The Move Toward Totalitarianism

The Reagan administration also condemned the Sandinistas for their failure to move toward the democracy promised in the revolution. For Washington, trust and cooperation with Managua might be possible if certain internal political steps were taken. Elections, of course, were a paramount issue, but nearly as important were press freedom, release of political prisoners, accommodation with the established church, and tolerance for free enterprise economics. On virtually all counts, according to U.S. officials, the Nicaraguan revolution had failed.

1. Although *elections* for a president, vice president, and a national assembly were held on November 4, 1984, the entire procedure, according to President Reagan, was unfair, a "Soviet-style sham." He contended that "a ruling clique of Sandinistas, allied with Cuban and Soviet dictators, have betrayed their citizens."[24] The FSLN won 63 percent of the seats in the assembly as well as the two top executive offices, Daniel Ortega Saavedra as president and Sergio Ramírez Mercado as vice president.

The procedures, however, came in for considerable criticism. The attacks focused on the following points. With martial law in effect for most of 1984, little genuine campaigning could take place until ninety days before the election. Opposition parties did have access to radio and television, but most of the stations were owned and operated by the Sandinistas, who thereby had an obvious propaganda advantage. Charges were made that opposition candidates were harassed by FSLN activitists. Political opponents who were active in supporting the *contras* were allegedly denied the right to run for office. The opposition press was stifled in its criticism of the government, especially on the issue of food shortages. The Sandinistas controlled the registration, the voting, and the ballot counting through the National Electoral Commission. Requests for a delay in the vote to enable opposition groups to organize an effective campaign were denied.[25]

Illustrative of the debate is the case of Arturo José Cruz. Until 1982 Cruz had supported the FSLN and had served as Nicaragua's ambassador in Washington, but he deserted the Sandinistas because of what he saw as their failure to accept a pluralist society. Although a very popular figure in Nicaragua, he was reluctant to give legitimacy to what he saw as a preordained Sandinista victory and thus resisted the urging of the opposition that he compete for the presidency. He was also under pressure from the United States not to participate. At one point when Cruz did show some interest in running, the date for registration had passed and the government refused to extend the deadline any further for his benefit—it had already been extended twice.

Cruz's opposition to the Sandinistas was a major asset for the Reagan administration's policy. Cruz declared that the Sandinistas are "determined to ignore the democratic yearnings of the Nicaraguan people." The FSLN, he said, is "no longer . . . entitled to the benefit of the doubt." There is, he emphasized, a "moral obligation to insist that the Sandinistas restore Nicaragua's liberties and that the Communist world take its hands off our country."[26]

Because of the alleged absence of a genuine and open election, Washington was unwilling to consider the FSLN a legitimate government deserving of trust. And yet, a large number of observers of the election asserted that the procedures were quite fair, that the opposition had ample opportunity to get its viewpoint across, and that the level of criticism of the government was much higher than in previous Nicaraguan elections or in most other elections elsewhere in Latin America.[27] Moreover, the opposition's lack of unity and direction were due in part to the admitted role of the U.S. embassy in persuading leading opponents not to participate in the election.[28] And furthermore, they argued, the fairness of the election was made clear by the fact that even with all of its advantages and a disorganized opposition, the FSLN won only 63 percent of the vote, only slightly more than Ronald Reagan did in 1984.

2. Labeling the Sandinistas as undemocratic in spite of the elections was important for justifying the administration's policy. Government censorship of the only opposition newspaper, La Prensa, was also cited as evidence of the lack of tolerance in Nicaragua. The privately owned, progovernment newspaper, Nuevo Diario, and the Sandinista party paper, Barricada, an openly Marxist publication, were widely distributed and not critical of the government, but La Prensa's publication was often delayed or canceled because of censorship or its distribution hampered by government interference. Pedro Joaquín Chamorro, La Prensa's editor and son of its founder, quit the paper

in frustration at the end of 1984. Nonetheless, *La Prensa* was still in business, and during the election campaign it did attack the Sandinistas on a variety of nonsecurity issues. Such an opposition newspaper did not even exist in countries like El Salvador and Guatemala that were friendly to the United States.

3. An issue that may well be misunderstood in the United States concerns the relationship between the Sandinistas and the Roman Catholic church. Traditionally, *the church* has been identified in Central America with the ruling elites and oligarchies. Nicaragua was no exception; therefore, when the revolution came, the church hierarchy was predictably unsympathetic to the Marxist leanings of the FSLN. Moreover, the revolution did have the support of many priests and church layworkers who had cooperated with the anti-Somoza forces for years, often in Christian "base communities" in the countryside. The FSLN did not strike out against the church in general or against Christianity, and in fact, the new government included four priests, among them the foreign minister, Miguel d'Escoto Brockman.

However, the contest between the established clergy and the revolutionary priests represented a struggle going on throughout Latin America over what is called "liberation theology." It is a division little understood in Washington, where the "church" is considered that which is represented by the Pope and its other prominent leaders. In Managua, the archbishop, Miguel Obando y Bravo, once critical of Somoza, became an outspoken opponent of the Sandinistas. His words carried weight in Washington when he accused the government of violations of human rights and of encouraging the prorevolutionary "popular church" against the official church.[29]

The confirmation for the Reagan administration that all was not right in Nicaragua came with the Pope's visit to Managua in March 1983 and his subsequent attacks on the Sandinistas. Heckling of the Pope by crowds of FSLN supporters and a cool reception by government officials seemed to corroborate the regime's fundamental hostility to the church. Following the visit, the Pope's criticism of the Sandinistas increased as he called their policies "openly harmful to the needs of the Catholic people of Nicaragua."[30]

There were, according to some observers, a number of explanations for the Pope's treatment, but those made little difference to Washington, where the charges that the Sandinistas were intolerant of religion were given additional credit. Although the debate over liberation theology went on, and although it had a major relevance for Nicaragua, it had little impact on changing U.S. assumptions about the problems in Central America.

4. Although the Nicaraguan government claimed to be willing to live with a *free enterprise* economic system, there was, in Washington's view, a gap between the rhetoric and the reality. Property belonging to the Somoza family, their associates, and National Guard leaders was nationalized after the revolution. That represented about 40 percent of the economy and included the country's airline, considerable agricultural land, a brewery, and some manufacturing. In addition, all banks—as in Costa Rica and Mexico, for instance—were nationalized. Private businesses, industries, and farms were allowed to continue, but with government control of imports, currency, and prices, the private sector often received less than top priority treatment compared to the government-owned enterprises. The preferential allocation of resources required in an economically troubled Nicaragua made it difficult for private entrepreneurs to stay in business.

As long as the Reagan administration was successful in characterizing the Sandinistas as totalitarian, the White House was able to get some congressional and popular backing for its effort to get rid of the Nicaraguan regime. By 1985, the administration's case had lost some of its credibility, but later that year Managua's actions seemed to confirm Reagan's contentions. In October, the Sandinistas moved closer to the Cuban model of a tightly controlled society. A state of siege was imposed, apparently in response to growing discontent among owners of small businesses, farmers, and independent labor unions (i.e., those not affiliated with the FSLN). The government also indicated a concern about the increasing *contra* activity inside the country. Stricter censorship was imposed, along with prohibitions of a wide variety of political activity. In addition, expanded aid agreements were concluded with the Soviet Union.

IMPLEMENTING THE POLICY

There were two major manifestations of the Reagan policy toward Nicaragua: (1) support for counterrevolutionary operations and other military activities, and (2) negotiations with the Sandinistas. Additional elements of the policy were (3) economic sanctions, and (4) propaganda.[31]

The Contras

Beginning in December 1981 with the intelligence "finding" on Nicaragua and the president's National Security Directive 17, the Central Intelligence Agency undertook responsibility for organizing covert military action against Nicaragua. Ostensibly this activity was to halt the flow of arms to El Salvador, but it also developed into an operation to harass and threaten the Sandinistas and apparently even to bring down their government.

It was in many respects reminiscent of the covert U.S. action against Guatemala in 1954 and at the Bay of Pigs in 1961. The United States recruited and armed exiled and discontented Nicaraguans, trained them, and put them into paramilitary operations against the Sandinistas from bases in Honduras and Costa Rica. To Managua, these *contras* appeared as the harbingers of a U.S. attempt to overthrow the government or to invade Nicaragua. The *contras* certainly made life more difficult for the Nicaraguans and provided a justification for major increases in the Sandinista military forces.

The number of *contras* grew from about 5,000 in 1982 to 10,000–12,000 in 1984. The loosely organized force was made up of former members of Somoza's National Guard, other anti-Sandinista Nicaraguans, and about 2,000 Miskito Indians from Nicaragua's Atlantic coast. Congressional restrictions, via the Boland Amendment of December 1982 for example, prohibited the use of U.S. funds for the overthrow of the Nicaraguan government, but the aim of those actually fighting was, in fact, to accomplish just that goal. Moreover, signals from Washington seemed to suggest that the administration itself was aiming for an end to FSLN rule, particularly when Reagan labeled the *contras* "freedom fighters."[32]

U.S. aid to the *contras* was in the form of direct funding by Congress (until most of those funds were suspended in 1984), plus arms, advice, and training through the CIA, indirect advising and support from U.S. forces on maneuvers in Honduras, and informal, "private" sources from former Somocistas and other sympathetic groups in the United States. The administration's initial budget of $19 million for covert action was increased by Congress in November 1983 to $24 million, although the White House was asking for $50 million.

Congress proved to be a major stumbling block for sustained funding for the *contras*. Critics of the president's plans questioned the goals of the operation and the credibility of supporting an effort led by ex-Somocistas and doubted the effectiveness of the counter-revolutionary effort. Instead of weakening the FSLN's hold on Nicaragua, the *contras* seemed to be providing an excuse for the party to consolidate its power. Because there were also underlying concerns about "another Vietnam," Reagan's requests were consistently cut or delayed.

A proposal for $21 million in aid for the *contras* for 1984 was killed through congressional inaction, and the spending of $14 million in funds for 1985 was made contingent on further review by Congress.

In spite of intensive lobbying by the administration, the case for the *contras* was not convincing. Their failure to establish a base of popular support, their inability to hold towns, and revelations of their often unsavory methods all worked against White House pleas for support. Nonetheless, it was estimated that over four years, the *contras* received more than $100 million in backing from the U.S. government through a variety of formal and informal channels.[33]

In the wake of the difficulties on Capitol Hill, the administration found other sources to finance the covert war. Private groups were said to have spent more than $10 million for supplies and equipment during the first half of 1984 for the counterrevolutionary effort. U.S. officials insisted that neither the CIA nor any other government agency was connected with this aid but rather that it had come from private corporations and groups such as the Christian Broadcasting Service, the Conservative Caucus, and *Soldier of Fortune* magazine. The issue of private financing of efforts to overthrow foreign governments did raise questions about violation of the U.S. Neutrality Act, but no action was taken to press charges since the administration had no objection to the funding.[34]

Two incidents that helped undermine congressional funding for the *contras* were the CIA involvement in the mining of Nicaraguan harbors and the revelation of a CIA-produced manual that recommended assassinations. Reports that the CIA had helped place mines in three Nicaraguan harbors in the spring of 1984 provoked angry reactions in Congress. The agency was supposed to keep the appropriate committees fully informed—especially because the action went beyond what was understood to be the legitimate role of the *contras* and their U.S. advisers. In addition, the damage to ships of countries friendly to the United States aroused criticism in Western Europe of "reckless" U.S. covert activities in Central America.

The impact of the mining was further complicated by Nicaragua's taking the case to the World Court. In spite of U.S. arguments that it would not accept World Court jurisdiction over this dispute, the Nicaraguans were able to persuade the justices to consider their case that the United States had violated international law by supporting military action against their country. The question of jurisdiction was settled in November 1984 by a 15–1 vote against the United States.

Outrage at the Reagan administration also followed the revelation that a handbook for guerrilla warfare, produced by the CIA, proposed terrorist tactics and assassinations as techniques the *contras* might use against the Sandinistas.[35] The manual set out procedures for "implicit terror," including the killing of informers and "selective use of violence for propagandist effects." It might be necessary, the manual pointed out, "to neutralize carefully selected and planned targets such as court judges . . . police and state security officials." Instructions were also provided on how to kidnap officials and blackmail local citizens.

Although U.S. officials contended that the manual did not explicitly condone assassination and that any allusion to such acts had been purged from the final version of the book, the administration's case on Capitol Hill was seriously undermined. The congressional criticism was aimed at the apparent autonomy of the CIA in producing such a document; Congress also felt that such activities should not be sponsored by the United States and might do the U.S. effort in Central America more harm than good.

The *contra* operations continued without direct aid from Congress, but their effectiveness as an instrument of policy was not persuasive. Washington claimed that backing the *contras* was necessary to halt the flow of arms to El Salvador; the Reagan administration, however, also claimed to see value in the *contras'* ability to harass the Sandinistas, give hope to those opposing the FSLN, and persuade Managua to come to the negotiating table. None of these options received strong support in Congress.

The *contras*, too, have had problems of leadership and purpose, due largely to a membership so diverse that there was no agreement on whether their goal should be a return to a Somoza-style order, the establishment of a pluralist democracy, or merely achievement of rights for certain minority groups such as the Miskitos. In addition, the large number of armed exiles in Honduras raised concern over the *contras'* political impact in that country. And in Costa Rica *contra* activities disrupted life along its border with Nicaragua and increased its need for militarization.

Other Military Activities

Accompanying the covert military actions were stepped-up U.S. military activities in Honduras and the Caribbean. These helped demonstrate U.S. determination to isolate Nicaragua and to remind the Sandinistas of the scope of U.S. power in the region. The Grenada invasion of 1983 was an additional opportunity for the Reagan administration to send a message to Managua on the U.S. willingness to use force to expel Marxist, Soviet-oriented regimes in the Caribbean area.

In Honduras, the United States established a semipermanent network of bases and installations, allegedly to help protect Honduras from a Nicaraguan attack or from internal subversion and to function as a training area for U.S. troops. However, the bases also served as a vivid indication of a U.S. presence in the area and as cover for supplying, training, and assisting both the contras and the Salvadoran army. (The White House and the Congress had informally agreed to place a ceiling of 55 on U.S. advisers in El Salvador, but the number of advisers in Honduras came to nearly 200.)

In August 1983 more than 1,500 U.S. troops, including a contingent of Green Berets, conducted maneuvers in Honduras. By October, the number had swelled to 4,500 in an operation called "Big Pine II," which carried over into 1984.

At sea, the United States intensified its naval exercises in an attempt at "gunboat diplomacy." In the spring of 1982, operation "Ocean Venture" put 45,000 personnel, 60 ships and over 350 aircraft into the Caribbean area. Similar exercises, with fewer troops and ships, were carried out every few months in 1983, and in 1984 another "Ocean Venture" sent 30,000 sailors, marines, and air force personnel on maneuvers off Nicaragua's Atlantic coast. Pentagon officials conceded that these operations were designed as a form of "psychological warfare" against Nicaragua, Cuba, and the Soviet Union.[36]

Negotiations

The second major track of U.S. policy toward Nicaragua was to use diplomacy and negotiations to protect U.S. interests in the region and to effect changes in Nicaragua's behavior. Two approaches were followed: direct bilateral talks and multilateral efforts in collaboration with other states. Both processes were characterized by uncertain terms, shifting conditions, ideological rhetoric, and charges of bad faith and deceit.

The first U.S.-Nicaraguan effort to resolve differences fizzled out in October 1981 when Washington did not make its demands explicit and when Managua refused to respond to only vague, unwritten requests from the Department of State. At this stage, the Reagan administration was insisting on major arms reductions in Nicaragua, an end to arms shipments to El Salvador, and other terms viewed by Managua as tantamount to a national humiliation.[37] As a result, any opportunity for an early rapprochement between the two countries was missed.

The Reagan terms for negotiations became clearer in 1982 when the administration insisted that the Nicaraguans honor their 1979 pledge to establish a democratic government. To negotiate over a country's internal political system is an unusual tactic because it defies the basic concept of national sovereignty. Additional terms gradually came to light. The Nicaraguans were to move toward a "mixed economy" (although they in fact had one), reduce significantly the number of foreign military advisers, and refrain from importing any major offensive weapons. Throughout 1982, however, there was no coordinated presentation of these conditions to the Nicaraguans, nor any systematic answer to their comments on the new U.S. terms. In fact, the decision to include democratization as a negotiating point was apparently taken by the White House without consultation with Secretary of State Haig.[38]

The overall strategy, as outlined in a National Security Council policy paper of April 1982, was to "Step up efforts to co-opt negotiations issue to avoid Congressionally mandated negotiations which would work against our interests." The goal was to "keep the pressure on" the Sandinistas. According to U.S. officials, the Nicaraguans were "clearly feeling the heat. . . . But they could hurt worse. They are not on the ropes."[39]

In Washington, responsibility for directing Central American policy was in confusion as a number of changes in the foreign policy leadership took place. A new secretary of state (George Shultz), a new assistant secretary for inter-American affairs, a new special ambassador for Central America, and ambassadorial changes in El Salvador and Nicaragua provided little basis for systematic negotiations.

The impression in Managua was that the United States was not serious about negotiating even when there was evidence that the arms flow to El Salvador had been virtually halted. In October 1983 Nicaragua's foreign minister, Miguel d'Escoto, made a personal visit to Washington to submit four draft treaties for discussion. Included were prohibitions on both Nicaraguan aid to El Salvador's guerrillas and U.S. assistance to the contras. There was no formal response to his efforts until June 1984 when Secretary Shultz met with Nicaraguan leaders in Managua. Although the meeting led to a rejection of Nicaragua's proposals, it did produce a series of low-level, bilateral talks that accomplished little.

The delays on the U.S. side seemed to stem from bureaucratic rivalry, uncertain leadership, and a general feeling that nothing productive for U.S. interests would come from the negotiating track. Some of the fundamental changes Washington was seeking went beyond what Nicaragua was willing to negotiate.

This attitude was reinforced by the initiatives of four Latin American countries to mediate the dispute in the September 1983 Contadora conference of leaders from Colombia, Mexico, Panama, and Venezuela. Their proposed treaty called for the removal of foreign military advisers, reductions in troops levels, an end to subversion, respect for human rights, and movement toward democracy. Nicaragua endorsed the treaty's principles in January 1984, and in September it announced full agreement with the document. According to Sandinista leader, Daniel Ortega:

> The Contadora proposal does address the need that Central American governments not support movements that have the purpose of defeating governments in place. . . . The United States has stated that mechanisms [for control and verification] do not exist. This is a pretext they are using in their attempt to weaken the proposal.[40]

The Reagan administration, although expressing sympathy for the Contadora process, would not offer an explicit agreement. Instead, it raised a series of reservations, including doubts about whether the treaty could be enforced. For Washington, of course, compliance with the treaty would compel it to withdraw its advisers and installations from Honduras and El Salvador as well as its aid to the contras. Thus, when Nicaragua announced its willingness to sign the treaty, the Reagan administration insisted that such concurrence was premature and that more negotiations were needed to develop a workable and verifiable document.

In a leaked, confidential background paper for a meeting of the National Security Council on October 30, 1984, U.S. policy objectives were explicitly outlined. The paper emphasized the need to mobilize the "Core Four" of Central America (Costa Rica, El Salvador, Guatemala, and Honduras) against Nicaraguan and Mexican attempts to see the Contadora agreement put into force.[41]

The rhetoric of the Reagan administration, as well as its internal deadlock over policy on Nicaragua, made it difficult to envision successful negotiations. With the president labeling Nicaragua a "totalitarian dungeon" and other officials expressing satisfaction with policies that kept the Sandinistas "off balance," little progress toward compromise was taking place. As Rep. Michael Barnes, chairman of the House Subcommittee on the Western Hemisphere, commented, "The administration's objections to the treaty reinforce my belief that it never had any real interest in a negotiated settlement."[42]

Economic Sanctions

Soon after taking office, the Reagan administration put economic pressures on the Sandinistas in the hope of inducing a change in their policies, a movement toward negotiations, or, at best, their fall from power. If the revolutionary government could not deliver employment, decent wages, fair prices, and economic stability, there was a chance that its cause would be so discredited the people would reject the FSLN's leadership. The Nicaraguan government's sensitivity on this issue was reflected in its censoring of any news in La Prensa that referred to food shortages or similar problems.

The $75 million economic assistance program for Nicaragua that was begun and then delayed under the Carter administration was immediately canceled by Reagan in 1981. In May 1983 Nicaragua's allotment of sugar imported into the United States was cut by 90 percent. The White House claimed such a step would reduce the funds available to the Sandinistas for "subversion and extremist violence." Nicaragua's sugar exports—nearly all of which had gone to the United States—had earned about $15.6 million in foreign exchange. Other Nicaraguan exports to the United States in 1982 included beef (worth $32 million), shellfish ($14.5 million), and bananas ($9.5 million). These were not prohibited by Washington.[43]

Administration pressures on U.S. companies led to other reductions in economic ties. Standard Fruit Company, a major U.S. banana importer, pulled its operations out of Nicaragua in 1982. Sale of spare parts and high technology equipment to Nicaragua was restricted. In all, Nicaragua's trade with the United States in the years 1980 to 1983 fell from 31.5 percent to 18.5 percent of its total trade. The value of Nicaragua's exports to the United States dropped from $214 million in 1980 to only $58.1 million in 1984.[44]

The final blow came in April 1985 when Reagan imposed a halt to trade with Nicaragua. Even the Nicaraguan airline was prohibited from flying into Miami. Managua was compelled to look to Europe and the Soviet Union for markets and for the essential goods it had obtained from the United States. By this time, the political impact of the sanctions was dubious. The Sandinistas' survival was not linked to U.S. trade, and the sanctions did not persuade them to capitulate.

Washington also effectively blocked Nicaragua's access to credit and loans from international lending agencies. In the Inter-American Development Bank, where U.S. influence is paramount, almost no loans for Nicaragua were approved after 1981. A similar fate befell the Nicaraguans at the World Bank, and they were denied access to the U.S.-operated Export-Import Bank.

Efforts were undertaken to discourage other Latin Americans, especially oil-producing Venezuela and Mexico, from trading with Nicaragua. Venezuela did cut off oil sales, but U.S. diplomacy was unable to enlist Mexico in the embargo or to persuade Western Europe to cut back on trade. U.S. diplomats did, however, persuade its allies not to fill the gap left by the decrease in U.S. trade. Instead, this gap was replaced by major increases in trade with the Soviet

Union and Eastern Europe (which rose to 15 percent of Nicaragua's total trade) and Japan. Toyotas, for example, had become by 1984 virtually the only model of new automobile imported by the Nicaraguans.

An economic impact was also felt from the *contra* attacks. The *contras* deliberately attempted with guerrilla raids to disrupt coffee harvests. Grain storage silos were blown up and farmers in the north were regularly harassed. A comic book–style manual (*Manual del Combatiente por la Libertad*), prepared by the CIA for distribution in Nicaragua, instructed opponents of the regime on how to disrupt economic activity throughout the country. Included was advice on stealing food, leaving lights burning, sabotaging government delivery trucks, blocking roads, and making Molotov cocktails. It was estimated that *contra* damage to the country's infrastructure was costing Nicaragua over $100 million a year and that by 1984 total material damage from the *contras* since 1979 had amounted to over $1 billion.[45]

The economic squeeze on Nicaragua did contribute to serious problems in the country. Food supplies and distribution were often disrupted. Unemployment remained high, and because of severe import restrictions, small businesses and manufacturing firms could not function effectively. It was even difficult to obtain basic medicines such as aspirin and other medical supplies. Coincidentally, however, the Soviet Union funded the construction of a new children's hospital in Managua and provided a sizable team of doctors and nurses to staff it. The impact of U.S. actions was felt by all Nicaraguans, and although the government was blamed for some of the problems, the revolution was not discredited. In fact, the resentment against *contra* attacks on economic targets gave the Sandinistas an edge in their battle to hold the loyalty of the people and to repudiate the *contras*.

Because the Soviet Union was apparently unwilling and unable to solve Nicaragua's economic problems, the Sandinistas have sought to negotiate with Washington to remove the economic sanctions. The concessions demanded by the Reagan administration, seen by Managua as requiring a dismantling of the revolution, may be so unacceptable that no accommodation can be worked out.

Propaganda

A necessary element in securing popular and congressional approval for a foreign policy is the effective explanation of that policy. "Explanation" aimed at persuasion and representing a highly partisan and subjective point of view can be classified as propaganda. The Reagan administration's efforts to isolate and discredit the Sandinistas frequently fell into the category of propaganda—just as did the Sandinistas' characterization of their struggle with the United States. U.S. officials and press typically labeled the Nicaraguan government as "Marxist." Although that label was largely accurate, given the ideology of the FSLN leaders, such a characterization in the United States led to stereotyping the Nicaraguans as communist puppets of the Soviet Union. The reality was more complex than that, but Sandinista attacks on "Yankee imperialism" and on capitalism and their talk of "liberation" and "revolution" all served to strengthen the Reagan administration's claims. Calling the 1984 elections a "sham" and arguing that Nicaragua should stop "exporting revolution" played on instincts of the U.S. public to distrust Marxist commitments to democracy and peace.

As in the earlier cases of U.S. interventions in Latin America such as in Guatemala in 1954, once a government was linked to communism and thus to the Soviet Union, it became much easier to rationalize interventionist actions. Congress, too, would be put on the defensive if it tried to oppose action to rid the hemisphere of such strategic threats. It was estimated, for example, that the CIA had spent $80 million by 1984 on a variety of propaganda efforts aimed at "destabilizing" the Sandinista government. CIA-sponsored distortions are said to have included misleading reports on the killings of Miskito Indians, the extent of Nicaragua's military buildup, and the role of Nicaragua in El Salvador's guerrilla war.[46]

The effectiveness of the administration's rationale was mixed. Although its policies were not repudiated by Congress, it did not receive consistent support or full funding for the contras. As the administration invoked the analogy of "another Cuba" to frighten Congress into action, members of Congress seemed more attuned to the cautions suggested by a different analogy, that of Vietnam.

EL SALVADOR

The scene for the Reagan administration's first stand against another communist revolution was a small, densely populated Central American country of about 5 million people. By 1981, rebellion in El Salvador was escalating into a major threat to bring down the government and establish a revolutionary regime that in the eyes of Washington would be modeled on the Nicaraguan experience. Since the success of the El Salvador guerrillas, it was argued, stemmed from outside support from Cuba, Nicaragua, and the USSR, it was imperative that the United States demonstrate that such an effort by communist forces to spread their influence would not be tolerated. The new administration would send a clear message to Moscow by drawing the line in El Salvador.

Standing Firm

El Salvador was the administration's test case. Thwarting Marxist guerrillas there would communicate to the world that a new team was in town and that the rules of the game had toughened. The export of revolution and the exploitation of local unrest for strategic gain by the Soviet Union had gone far enough. The State Department's 1981 White Paper on El Salvador (mentioned above) was the administration's first, and not very successful, attempt to prove that the source of guerrilla warfare was the Soviet Union and its allies in Havana and Managua.

Convinced that the insurgents were close to toppling the Salvadoran government, Reagan quickly added $5 million in military aid to the $25 million already appropriated by the Carter administration. Another $26 million would be spent in 1982, along with about $110 million in economic assistance. Both military and economic assistance were nearly doubled in 1983. By early 1984, an additional $65 million in military aid was approved by Congress, and in August the consensus on El Salvador produced another $70 million appropriation for emergency assistance (although the White House had requested $117 million). For 1985, the president was requesting a figure of $350 million in military aid, making El Salvador the largest recipient, by far, of U.S. assistance in Latin America.

Fifty-five U.S. military advisers were in El Salvador, and Salvadoran troops were being trained in both the United States and Honduras. U.S. aircraft also flew reconnaissance missions for government troops. Clearly, the U.S. was committed to the survival of the Salvadoran government.

For Secretary of State Haig, El Salvador was a top priority item for the United States, but he was frustrated by Congress's proclivity to tie aid to improvement in that government's respect for human rights and by the inability of the public to see beyond the immediate issues at stake in Central America. For Haig: "It was typical that Americans would be reluctant to treat El Salvador as a strategic problem with global implications. Historically, we have been slow to think and act in these terms."[47]

Haig insisted on the Cuban connection: "There could not be the slightest doubt that Cuba was at once the source of supply and the catechist of the Salvadoran insurgency." In response to this threat,

Haig argued for a major U.S. commitment rather than an incremental, gradual involvement such as was the case in Vietnam. Haig was not entirely successful in winning this debate in the White House, but gradually or not, Washington was becoming deeply committed.

The Salvadoran Cauldron

Among the difficulties faced by Reagan in convincing Congress to fund fully his policies was the record of the Salvadoran government on human rights. At the time of Carter's arrival in 1977, military assistance to El Salvador had been virtually phased out by Congress because of the country's human rights violations. In 1979, however, Washington began to reassess the importance of stability in Central America and reopened the aid pipeline.

A military coup on October 15 overthrew the repressive government of General Carlos Humberto Romero and showed signs of addressing the political and economic conditions that were giving rise to popular discontent in the country. But such a reformist program was too risky for the established military and economic elites, and in a few months the reformers in the government were dismissed. In response to the growing revolutionary fervor and to the increased guerrilla activity, the revised junta chose to crack down hard on any person or group that appeared to be associated with the "Communists." The nature of the "new order" in El Salvador was revealed by the assassination of the popular archbishop, Oscar Romero, on March 24, 1980. Salvadoran military officers including Major Roberto D'Aubisson were implicated in the killing.[48]

In addition to the military's seizing tight control, numerous right-wing vigilante groups roamed the country, eliminating suspected guerrillas—and large numbers of innocent civilians in the process. During 1980 alone the Salvadoran church estimated that 10,000 political murders were committed, mostly by government forces or right-wing "death squads." Civilian deaths in 1981 fluctuated between 200 and 600 a month, as the government and its allies tried to terrorize the people into compliance. By 1984 the total civilian death count stood at an estimated 40,000.

Violence was not new to El Salvador. A peasant revolt in 1932 was crushed by an army onslaught that killed close to 30,000 people in one month. This came to be known as La Matanza—"The Slaughter." The guerrilla movement of the late 1970s took the name of the rebel leader of the 1930s for their cause: the Farabundo Martí National Liberation Front (FMLN). This organization, formed in 1980, pulled together the five factions fighting against the government. These revolutionary groups also created a unified political organization, the Democratic Revolutionary Front (FDR).

The killings began to attract attention in the United States in December 1980 when four U.S. churchwomen (three nuns and a lay worker) were raped, brutally beaten, and killed by national guardsmen. In January 1981, two U.S. land reform advisers were gunned down by off-duty soldiers at the Sheraton Hotel in San Salvador. As of 1985, only the soldiers tied to the killing of the four women had been tried and imprisoned, primarily due to pressure from the U.S. Congress. No officers who might have given the orders had been charged, and there were no indictments of death squad leaders or participants.

Dilemmas for Washington

Land reform programs, introduced in the 1970s at the insistence of the United States, were aimed at correcting an inequitable and politically explosive landholding pattern that had concentrated ownership of land in the hands of a few powerful elites. Both the Carter and the Reagan administrations attempted to have the programs fully implemented, but too often these efforts were undercut by the Salvadoran military or the private police forces of local chieftains. As a result, both Washington and San Salvador came to depend increasingly on military means to deal with El Salvador's nascent revolution. In fact, unhappy at having to report every six months on the human rights violations there in order to secure military assistance, Reagan, in November 1983, vetoed the attempt to renew that legislation.

Congress, however, was reluctant to buy the administration's full package. Support of a military government that was unable to demonstrate popular support and unable (or even unwilling) to control the death squads was not an attractive option on Capitol Hill. To persuade Congress that El Salvador was deserving of U.S. backing, the Reagan administration invoked two key rationales: The revolution was connected to strategic interests and the government could be democratic and responsible—and elections would be held to prove it.

We have already detailed the administration's strategic perspective and its troubles in proving that arms were flowing from Cuba and Nicaragua. Haig, especially, felt that the source of the unrest was Cuba and that the United States should retaliate against that source and its patron, the Soviet Union. Failure to respond forcefully would, he said, "result in a loss of credibility in all our dealings with the Soviets."[49] As fervently as the administration pleaded its case, it was unable to induce Congress to concur with all of its requests for aid.

The Elections

The White House had better luck in demonstrating the legitimacy of the U.S. commitment by helping to sponsor elections in El Salvador in 1982 and 1984. Convincing Congress to back an elected regime was certainly easier than appealing to unsubstantiated strategic threats. Nonetheless, even on this issue the administration stumbled. The March 1982 elections for a constituent assembly were heralded by the administration as a testimonial of popular support for the government and a rejection of the rebel cause, as well as a vindication of U.S. policy. More than a million voters cast ballots despite rebel attempts to sabotage the process, but the outcome caught the United States by surprise. Roberto D'Aubisson's National Republican Alliance led the way to a victory for the extreme right wing over the Reagan favorite, the Christian Democrat, José Napoleon Duarte. Polarization, not accommodation, continued in El Salvador.

The presidential elections set for the spring of 1984 saw a concerted effort by Washington not only to repeat the huge turnout of 1982, but also to help the more moderate Duarte come to power. For the United States, a successful campaign against the guerrillas required political reforms and a controlled military effort, not the erratic vigilante antics of the death squads. A Christian Democratic victory would also enhance El Salvador's appeal to Congress. The United States closely monitored the campaign and even contributed to the preferred candidates. Duarte's Christian Democratic party, for example, received nearly $1 million from the CIA.[50]

Hailed by Washington as a triumph for democracy, the elections were conducted in full view of hundreds of outside observers. Although there was no overt corruption and rather open campaigning, judgments did vary on the fairness of the election procedures. There was neither a free press nor candidates from the Left. Since voting was obligatory, Salvadorans not having a stamped identity card were quickly associated with the rebels, who had advocated a boycott of the elections. Transparent ballot boxes and other suspicious procedures for handling the ballots raised questions about secrecy. The ballots were counted by computers operated under U.S. supervision, a procedure seen as an assurance of fairness, but in a nontechnological society, those who operate computers have a clear opportunity for influencing results.

In any event, Duarte won the presidency in a runoff against D'Aubisson. The results produced a surge of sympathy on Capitol Hill, especially when Duarte set out to gain control of the military, abolish the death squads, implement land reform, and improve the government's record on human rights.

Progress Assessment

By the end of 1984, the Salvadoran government appeared, for the first time in years, to be making headway against the guerrillas. Duarte's reform efforts, improved performance by the military, and the rebels' failure to expand their support to all parts of the country and to the middle class suggested that the government might survive after all.

In response to this tentative shift in the struggle, Duarte and the guerrilla leaders began a series of exploratory talks to find a way to halt the civil war. At issue were some very complicated problems related to power sharing, but the mere fact that Duarte would talk directly with the FMLN/FDR was a major breakthrough, especially because the government had since 1982 consistently rejected rebel requests for negotiations. It also seemed to have caught Washington off guard. Committed to the military option in El Salvador, the administration had given no sign that it had expected—or even approved of—a negotiated settlement that could give the FDR a share of political power. For years Washington had rejected any negotiations with those who wanted "to shoot their way into power."

Solutions—or even a stalemate—in El Salvador depended on Duarte's negotiating skills and his ability to balance the demands of the radical FDR with those of the established conservative forces. In a country where the Center had had little success, Duarte risked survival by even agreeing to talk. This was the third time Duarte had been in line to lead his country, and any movement toward a serious redistribution of power could again be his undoing. He had been expected to win the 1972 presidential election, but a questionable ballot count denied him the office. He was then thrown in jail and exiled by the military. He had also served as interim president of a military-civilian junta in 1980–1981 that failed to last. On his shoulders rested not only a possible halt in the civil war, but the redemption of U.S. policy as well.

The Future

If the United States succeeded in El Salvador, how long would the accomplishment last? An effective counterinsurgency strategy requires both military and political progress. It may be that U.S. training helped the Salvadoran military hold out against the revolutionaries, but then it may be too much to expect the army to change its traditional character and habits so quickly. Too frequently in the past, the military's brutal actions and corruption have alienated the masses, and if long-term suppression of discontent becomes necessary, a return to previous behavior seems likely.

Dealing with revolutionaries also necessitates political accommodation and change. The guerrillas are not a small group of terrorists, but a well-organized and well-supported coalition of forces. Any political settlement would have to take their demands into account. It was estimated that the 6,000 to 10,000 FMLN forces had the backing of 150,000 to 300,000 people and that they controlled major portions of the northern and eastern sectors of the country. The national army numbered 40,000, plus an air force of 60 combat aircraft and another 7,000 national police and guardsmen.

The rebels, if expected to play by the rules, that is, no violence, must receive something in return—a share of power, the right to participate in government, and restraint by the Salvadoran army. Whether El Salvador's political system is flexible enough to adjust to such an accommodation is very much in doubt. The long history of conflict and angry polarization, the record of killings, and the continuing poverty do not bode well for Duarte, the moderates, and the United States. At best, Washington may achieve some short-term time to begin to address El Salvador's economic, social, and political problems. This would require a shift in attitudes from reliance on military options to dealing with the sources of revolution. This change was, to some degree, recognized by the president's special commission on Central America.

THE KISSINGER PANEL

The culmination of the Reagan effort to build support for its policies came with the publication of the Report of the National Bipartisan Commission on Central America in January 1984.[51] In response to rising criticism of U.S. actions in Nicaragua and El Salvador, President Reagan named a special panel, composed of well-known figures in law, labor, business, government, and education, to examine the problems in the region with the aim of providing advice on long-term U.S. policy. Representative of both Democratic and Republican viewpoints and chaired by former Secretary of State Henry Kissinger, the panel conducted a series of hearings and made several trips to Central America. It produced a 132-page report that generally endorsed the approach being followed by the administration.

Presidential commissions such as this are useful for defusing partisan policy disputes. Although there was dissent from some of the administration's analyses, the report did temporarily quell the congressional debate. Virtually all the members agreed that U.S.

security was directly threatened by Soviet and Cuban exploitation of the economic and political instability in Central America. This strategic linkage formed the unifying theme of the report, but there was acknowledgment of the underlying causes of the unrest.

In spite of the indigenous sources of revolution and the justified demands for correcting centuries of economic and political inequities, the report argued that top priority for the United States was to meet the external threat to the region. Because, according to the report, the Communists were taking advantage of local instability to extend their power, security interests must take precedence over the long-term effort to solve the more fundamental problems.

The commission did call for an extended U.S. commitment to economic assistance and political reform in order to avoid future crises, but in the final analysis U.S. "credibility" required a strong and immediate response on both the military and the economic fronts. Especially important was the "test" to which the United States was being put in El Salvador. Central America is too important an area, the report argued, to allow Marxist revolutions to succeed. "Prudent presidents," one commission member stated, "must take into account such an improbable but highly risky sequence of events."[52]

GRENADA

When opportunity knocks, open the door. Events on the tiny island nation of Grenada during 1983 provided such an opportunity for the Reagan administration to demonstrate the nature of its policy in the Central American–Caribbean region. For Washington, the fortuitous developments in Grenada could not have been invented better in Hollywood: a Marxist government fell apart and was taken over by even more extreme leftists who, in turn, set out violently to control the island. Backed by Grenada's neighboring Caribbean states, U.S. military forces intervened to save the Grenadians from terror and tyranny, and, in the process, also rescue U.S. students at a local medical school. The quick, successful military action sent shudders through Central America where rumors of impending U.S. intervention there suddenly took on a new sense of urgency—as the Reagan administration hoped it would.

This low-risk, high payoff move by the United States may or may not have been a result of a long-planned scheme to rid the Caribbean of a Marxist regime, but the series of unexpected events were ripe for spontaneous exploitation. The decisive action sent what Washington felt were the appropriate messages about the willingness of the Reagan administration to use force. It also buttressed, at least temporarily, popular domestic support for the president's foreign policy. The episode was used to underline the strategic threat working its way through the backyard of the United States.

Why Grenada?

With a population of only 110,000, an area just twice the size of Washington, D.C., and a location at the end of the Windward Islands, just off the coast of Venezuela, the former British colony would seem an unlikely player in major power politics and even less a threat to the United States. And yet, Grenada became a focal point for U.S. policy in 1983 and a symbol of the Reagan approach to Latin America.

Granted independence in 1974, Grenada saw its first elected government, that of Prime Minister Eric Gairy, overthrown in 1979 by a coup led by Maurice Bishop and the New Jewel Movement. Gairy's departure was not mourned. His government had become repressive, especially through the use of a private army known as the "Mongoose Gang." Questions were also raised about Gairy's competence. He had begun to act irrationally; he tried, for example, to mobilize the United Nations to fend off flying saucers.

The Bishop government identified with "progressive" socialist forces in the Third World and established close ties with Cuba and the Soviet Union. They, in return, provided military, political, and security training as well as arms to the Grenadians.[53] This association and the one-party rule made relations with Washington difficult, and when Reagan arrived in the White House, all U.S. aid was cancelled.

Efforts by Grenada to secure international funding for a larger runway at its only major airport were thwarted by Washington on the grounds that such a runway would enable long-range transports from Cuba to land en route to Africa. It might also have provided an opening for a Soviet military presence. A U.S. aid program had originally backed the project as a means of increasing Grenada's tourism. Eventually, Cuba stepped in with the workers to finish the runway—under the supervision of a British construction firm.

Bishop did visit Washington in June 1982 in an apparent attempt to work out some accommodation with the Reagan administration, but he received little sympathy. Both Secretary Haig and the Department of State publicly portrayed Grenada as a client of Moscow and Havana and as a country devoid of democracy. Bishop defended the use of workers from Cuba and advisers from the Soviet Union and North Korea by citing Grenada's poor economic situation. He also contended that the Western model of government imposed by Britain was not appropriate for Grenada.[54]

The October Takeover

Impatience with Bishop's "moderate" revolution, along with a power struggle within the Central Committee of the New Jewel Movement, led to Bishop's ouster and death on October 19, 1983. This upheaval set off a chain reaction climaxed by the U.S. invasion. The takeover had been a bloody one. After a radical faction led by Deputy Prime Minister Bernard Coard and his wife, Phyllis, and backed by the army commander, General Hudson Austin, had seized power on October 17, Bishop and his supporters staged a comeback. They were met by gunfire that killed Bishop and seventeen of his followers; others were imprisoned. Coard's imposition of martial law and his hard-line, radical posture were immediately condemned by Wasn-ington. (The takeover also appeared to have surprised and disappointed Fidel Castro.) In addition, U.S. officials stated that they were concerned about the fate of 650 U.S. medical students on the island.

Although Washington announced that the U.S. invasion was a result of a request from Grenada's neighbors in the eastern Caribbean, it is clear that planning had begun the day after Bishop's death, well before the Caribbean leaders debated the issue. In fact, it was reported that the formal request for help was drafted in Washington.[55] Nonetheless, when the Organization of Eastern Caribbean States (OECS) called for military action against Grenada on the twenty-second, it was obvious that the troops would be from the United States.

The Invasion

Approximately 1,900 U.S. Marines and Rangers landed on Grenada on October 25, 1983. After three days there were 6,000 troops on the island, and except for a few pockets of resistance, the fighting was over. The invasion was protected by an eleven-ship naval task force, including about eighty carrier-based aircraft. Later, nearly 300 police and military forces from the Caribbean states joined the U.S. troops on the island.

Most of the opposition to the U.S. forces came from the 700 Cuban workers at the airport. Initial administration claims had put the number of Cuban "soldiers" at 1,100; later, this was reduced to about 100 "combatants." About 25 Cubans were killed. Grenadian deaths totaled about 44, while U.S. casualties were put at 20 dead, 89 wounded.

The discovery of thirty Soviet advisers and an extensive cache of small arms prompted President Reagan, in a television address, to assert that Grenada "was a Soviet-Cuban colony being readied as a major military bastion to export terror and undermine democracy."

Characterizing the effort as a "rescue mission," he claimed, "We got there just in time."[56]

International reaction outside the Caribbean was negative. The U.N. Security Council voted to "deplore" the invasion, but the resolution was vetoed by the United States. The Organization of American States refused to endorse the action, arguing that such intervention was a contradiction of the OAS Charter. In the United States, however, popular opinion backed the president's action, 53 percent in favor, 34 percent opposed.

The Message

The sound of the invasion was heard throughout Central America, and it was especially loud in Nicaragua. For the Cubans and Soviets, the risks of underwriting client states had increased. The administration's claims of restoring order and democracy, of protecting U.S. lives, and of responding to a Caribbean SOS were lost in the broader strategic message sent by this revival of interventionism. Whether or not the United States was contemplating a similar "liberation" of Nicaragua was immaterial; it was the symbol that counted. In Surinam, for example, leftist leader Lt. Col. Desi Bouterse expelled the Cuban ambassador after the invasion, despite Surinam's close ties to Havana. It was reported that Bouterse suspected Cuban subversion in his country.[57]

Eugenia Charles, prime minister of Dominica and one of the strongest supporters of the intervention, declared that the action should show Fidel Castro "that we will not allow any force in this part of the world to come in and allow people to manipulate." The Jamaican prime minister, conservative Edward P. Seaga, predicted an end to Marxist governments in the region, but his predecessor, socialist Michael Manley, contended that the progressive forces were only temporarily setback in their effort to throw off dependency. As long as the political, economic, and social problems persisted in the Caribbean, Manley warned, radical, Cuban-style solutions would be attempted.[58]

CONCLUSIONS

Although the strategic viewpoint helps explain the Reagan approach to Latin America, it is not the only contemporary perspective, nor does it guarantee a successful policy. Subsuming Nicaragua's revolution and El Salvador's civil war in the great-power contest may reflect a realpolitik, an orientation to the global balancing and jousting

that goes on between superpowers, but it may also be an oversim-
plification of reality. U.S. interests may not be well protected if critical
local or indigenous factors are overlooked.
Should the fact of Cuban and Soviet involvement in Latin American
politics be the primary factor guiding U.S. policy? As the Kissinger
panel pointed out, the United States must pay attention to the strategic
issues; it is too risky to ignore them. However, as the Reagan
administration discovered, it has been difficult to get Congress to
accept that argument as the major rationale for a deep U.S. commitment
in the region. In the next chapter, we will consider some of the
criticisms of interventionism as a globalist U.S. policy, whether it be
on behalf of strategic factors or human rights.

NOTES

1. Alexander M. Haig, Jr., *Caveat: Realism, Reagan, and Foreign Policy*
(New York: Macmillan, 1984), 118.

2. The announcement of this review was reported in the U.S. Department
of State, *Bulletin* 81 (May 1981), 1, 71.

3. Reported in *Washington Post,* December 20, 1981, B1.

4. U.S. Department of State, "Cuba's Renewed Support for Violence in
Latin America," Special Report no. 30, December 14, 1981.

5. U.S. Department of State *Bulletin* 81, 1.

6. Haig, *Caveat,* 118-129.

7. For background on the Nicaraguan revolution, see Shirley Christian,
Nicaragua: Revolution in the Family (New York: Random House, 1985); Thomas
W. Walker, *Nicaragua: The Land of Sandino* (Boulder, Colo.: Westview Press,
1981); Howard J. Wiarda, ed., *Rift and Revolution: The Central American
Imbroglio* (Washington, D.C.: American Enterprise Institute, 1984); and Richard
Fagen, "Revolution and Crisis in Nicaragua," in Martin Diskin, ed., *Trouble
in Our Backyard* (New York: Pantheon, 1983), 125-154.

8. Carter's policy is reviewed by Roslyn Roberts, "Nicaragua: Conditions
and U.S. Interests," Library of Congress, Congressional Research Service, Issue
Brief, no. 1B80013, November 6, 1980. Vance is quoted in *Washington Post,*
September 28, 1979, 17.

9. The Committee of Santa Fe, "A New Inter-American Policy for the
Eighties." (Washington, D.C.: Council on Inter-American Security, May 1980).

10. U.S. Department of State, *Communist Interference in El Salvador,*
Special Report no. 80, Washington, D.C.: February 23, 1981.

11. Wayne Smith, "Dateline Havana: Myopic Diplomacy," *Foreign Policy*
48 (Fall 1982), 161.

12. Reported by Leslie Gelb in *New York Times,* March 14, 1982, 1.
Also see "A Secret War for Nicaragua," *Newsweek,* November 8, 1982, 42-
49.

13. See text of report, "Cuban and Nicaraguan Support for Salvadoran Insurgency," in *New York Times*, March 21, 1982.

14. Interview with author, U.S. embassy, Managua (June 1984).

15. Author's interviews at Nicaraguan Foreign Ministry, Managua (June 1984).

16. *Washington Post*, July 8, 1984, 1. Gorman, commander of U.S. forces in Central America, is quoted in *New York Times*, August 9, 1984, 3.

17. For an analysis of Cuba's policy toward the revolution, see William LeoGrande, "Cuba and Nicaragua: From Somoza to the Sandinistas," *Caribbean Review* 9 (Winter 1980), 11–14; also, Jiri Valenta, "Soviet and Cuban Responses to New Opportunities in Central America," in Richard E. Feinberg, ed., *Central America: International Dimensions of the Crisis* (New York: Holmes & Meier, 1982), 127–159. For reports of the Cuban presence: *New York Times*, August 2, 1983, 6 and November 27, 1983, 8.

18. Reported in interviews by author at the U.S. embassy in Managua (June 1984), and with a U.S. Department of State spokesman (November 1984).

19. For the text of the briefing, see *New York Times*, March 9, 1982; for copies of the photos see Central Intelligence Agency, "Evidence of Military Build-Up in Nicaragua" (Washington, D.C.: March 1982).

20. Paul Seabury and Walter A. McDougall, eds., *The Grenada Papers* (San Francisco: Institute for Contemporary Studies, 1984), 254–258. Also see Nadia Malley, "Nicaraguan Relations with Western Europe and the Socialist International," in Thomas W. Walker, ed., *Nicaragua: The First Five Years* (New York: Praeger, 1985).

21. On Nicaragua's position, see Alejandro Bendaña, "The Foreign Policy of Nicaragua's Revolution," in Thomas W. Walker, ed., *Nicaragua in Revolution* (New York: Praeger, 1982), 319–327. Also see *New York Times*, November 29, 1983, 2, and September 2, 1984, 1.

22. Official U.S. estimates are reflected in a report by Drew Middleton in *New York Times*, May 6, 1984. More reliable figures are found in International Institute for Strategic Studies, *The Military Balance, 1983–84* (London, 1983), 112; and *The Military Balance, 1984–85* (London, 1984), 123–124.

23. Lt. Col. John Buchanan (ret.), "Prepared Statement Before the House Committee on Foreign Affairs, Subcommittee on Inter-American Affairs" (mimeographed), September 21, 1982.

24. Reagan's statement is in *New York Times*, December 5, 1984, 1; Secretary Shultz's views are in the issue of November 5, 1984, 4.

25. For a skeptical assessment of Sandinista "democracy," see Robert S. Leiken, "Nicaragua's Untold Stories," *New Republic*, October 8, 1984, 16–22. Also, Senator David Durenberger, "Expect a Farce," *New York Times*, November 2, 1984, 31.

26. Arturo José Cruz, "Managua's Central Problem," *New York Times*, December 6, 1984, 27.

27. For testimony on the fairness of the election, see "Sandinistas Win Clean Election," *Latin American Weekly Report*, November 9, 1984, 2; and

"Report of the Latin American Studies Association Delegation to Observe the Nicaragua General Election," *LASA Forum,* November 1984. Also see "A Political Opening in Nicaragua," (pamphlet) (Washington, D.C.: Washington Office on Latin America, December 1984).

28. U.S. pressure on the opposition was indicated in the author's interviews at the U.S. embassy in Managua and by John Oakes, "Fraud in Nicaragua," *New York Times,* November 15, 1984, 31.

29. Thomas W. Walker, "Catholic Unity Dissolves in Revolutionary Nicaragua," *MesoAmerica,* September 1982, 7-9; and Tommie Sue Montgomery, "Cross and Rifle: Revolution and the Church in El Salvador and Nicaragua," *Journal of International Affairs* 36 (Fall-Winter 1982-1983), 209-221. Obando y Bravo's views are summarized in *New York Times,* August 1, 1984, 1.

30. Quoted in *New York Times,* July 7, 1984, 4E.

31. William LeoGrande, "The United States and Nicaragua," in Walker, ed., *Nicaragua: The First Five Years;* and Piero Gleijeses, "Nicaragua: Resist Romanticism," *Foreign Policy* 54 (Spring 1984), 122-138.

32. Reagan is quoted in *New York Times,* May 5, 1983, 1. Also see the reported statements of CIA Director William Casey, *New York Times,* May 23, 1983, 1, and his denials, May 24, 1983, 1. The defection of anti-Marxist moderates to the *contras* is discussed by Christian, *Nicaragua,* 267-287.

33. *New York Times,* November 11, 1984, 12, and July 25, 1984, 1; also *Washington Post,* April 21, 1984, 1.

34. *New York Times,* July 15, September 9, 11, and 13, 1984.

35. Tayacan, *Psychological Operations in Guerrilla Warfare.* Translated by the Congressional Research Service (Washington, D.C.: October 15, 1984).

36. Reported in *New York Times,* March 25, 1984, 1; also July 7, 1983, E1, and February 9, 1984, 4.

37. The best account of the negotiating process to date is Roy Guttman, "Nicaragua: America's Diplomatic Charade," *Foreign Policy* 56 (Fall 1984), 3-23.

38. Ibid., 12-13.

39. The National Security Council (NSC) document is reprinted in *New York Times,* April 7, 1983, 16; also see official statements in issue of December 1, 1983, 8.

40. Quoted in *Newsweek,* October 15, 1984, 70.

41. "Background paper for NSC meeting on Central America, October 30, 1984." Copies of this secret document became available following a report of the meeting in *Washington Post,* November 6, 1984.

42. Reagan is quoted in *New York Times,* July 22, 1984, 4E; also December 9, 1984, 8. And Barnes is quoted in *New York Times,* October 3, 1984, 3.

43. Figures from *New York Times,* May 11, 1983, 6. This cut in Nicaragua's sugar quota was attacked by the General Agreement on Tariffs and Trade (GATT), the intergovernmental body that oversees international commerce, as a violation of its trade rules.

44. Sylvia Maxfield and Richard S. Sholk, "External Constraints," in Walker, ed., *Nicaragua in Revolution,* 1982. Also see *New York Times,* May 2, 1985, 6.

45. Jozef Goldblat and Victor Millan, "Conflict and Conflict Resolution in Central America," *Bulletin of Peace Proposals* 15:4 (1984), 1–12. Also see *New York Times*, August 13, 1983, 1.

46. "America's Secret Warriors," *Newsweek*, October 10, 1983, 39.

47. Haig, *Caveat*, 118; and for the following quote, 122.

48. The Salvadoran upheaval is well covered in Cynthia Arnson, *El Salvador: A Revolution Confronts the United States* (Washington, D.C.: Institute for Policy Studies, 1982), and Tommie Sue Montgomery, *Revolution in El Salvador* (Boulder, Colo.: Westview Press, 1982).

49. Haig, *Caveat*, 129.

50. Reported in *New York Times*, May 5, 1984, 8; and May 13, 1984, 10E.

51. *Report of the National Bipartisan Commission on Central America* (Washington, D.C.: January 1984). Members of the Commission were: Henry Kissinger (chair), Nicholas F. Brady, Henry Cisneros, William P. Clements, Jr., Carlos F. Diaz-Alejandro, Wilson S. Johnson, Lane Kirkland, Richard M. Scammon, John Silber, Potter Stewart, Robert S. Strauss, and William B. Walsh.

52. Statement by Carlos F. Diaz-Alejandro, in *New York Times*, January 18, 1984, 23.

53. The New Jewel Movement's close ties with Moscow and Havana are described by the documents seized in the invasion, some of which have been published in Seabury and McDougall, eds., *The Grenada Papers*.

54. See Bishop's interview with Barbara Crossette in *New York Times*, August 7, 1983, 1, 6.

55. Reported by Patrick Tyler in *Washington Post*, October 30, 1983, A14; and by Bernard Gwertzman in *New York Times*, October 30, 1983, 1.

56. See transcript in *New York Times*, October 28, 1983, 5.

57. *New York Times*, November 6, 1983, E1.

58. Barbara Crossette, "The Caribbean After Grenada," *New York Times Magazine*, March 18, 1984, 51ff. Also see *New York Times*, (November 8, 1983, 6.

PART 3
AN ALTERNATIVE PERSPECTIVE

An alternative approach for analyzing U.S. policy in Latin America is one that focuses on nonintervention. Recurring criticisms of U.S. policy have contended that whether Washington treats Latin America as a sphere of influence or as part of a global contest the result has typically been intervention. Such a development is considered contrary to the best interests of both the United States and Latin America. However, as the Bolivian case demonstrates, the problem of interpreting the role of the United States in the hemisphere remains a difficult one.

9
THE NONINTERVENTIONIST CRITIQUE

For many countries in Latin America, the major foreign policy conflict with the United States has been over the question of intervention. From the agreements signed at the Montevideo and Buenos Aires conferences of the 1930s to the Charter of the Organization of American States, Latin American pressure has persuaded the United States to sign formal pledges not to intervene in the internal or external affairs of any country in the hemisphere. And yet, U.S. intervention in a variety of forms has continued and thereby remains the central unresolved issue in U.S.–Latin American relations.

In Chapter 8, we looked at recent events in Central America from the strategic perspective of the Reagan administration. Critics of that approach contended that it provided an inappropriate rationale for intervention, an act that was unlikely to accomplish U.S. goals and that would probably result in further polarization and conflict contrary to U.S. interests in stability and cooperation. The lessons of the past are that U.S. attempts to mold Central American and Caribbean politics often produced regimes that in recent years have been the causes of revolutions. Moreover, as the Cuban experience demonstrated, the capacity of Washington to influence events through the use or threat of force has diminished considerably.

THE NONINTERVENTIONIST THEME

A frequent assertion is that, in general, U.S. intervention in Latin America has served only to worsen the situation for both the United States and the Latin Americans. The arguments typically contend: (1) that U.S. involvement to promote democracy has not produced democracy; (2) that U.S. intervention has resulted in authoritarian regimes that alienate the masses, thus making anti-U.S. revolutions more likely; (3) that U.S. dominance of areas such as Central America has so long thwarted local attempts to carry out moderate changes that violent upheavals are now nearly inevitable; (4) that too often the United States creates problems for itself when it intrudes into the area without proper concern for the inherent political culture and values of the Latin Americans; and (5) that the economic and political impact of the United States in Latin America is so pervasive that it is impossible to understand the politics of many countries without taking it into account.

This criticism of U.S. policy tends to fall into two broad categories. One contends that the United States cannot, because of its power, divorce itself from the hemisphere and thus ought to be involved on behalf of change and democracy and human rights. The second argues that because U.S. interventions of any kind, whether on behalf of dictators or democrats, are likely to protect neither, Washington should allow the political dynamics of Latin America to develop on their own and become involved only when important security interests are threatened. Both contentions are "noninterventionist" in that they are critical of past U.S. interference. Advocates of the first position can be labeled the "democratic progressives"; those of the second, the "cautious realists."

These two perspectives share a common concern about the negative effects of U.S. involvement in Latin America and about the ignorance that usually accompanies that intrusion. Both assert that an informed policy, one more attuned to the realities of the region's politics, would result in a more patient policy, fewer problems for Washington, and in the long term, a more cooperative, mature relationship with Latin America. However, these "schools" disagree on the nature and degree of U.S. involvement, and that disagreement provides the framework for the discussion that follows.

The Democratic Progressives

Representative of the democratic progressives' position is historian Walter LaFeber, who argues that the record of recurring U.S. domination of political and economic life in Central America has set the stage for "inevitable revolutions" in the area.[1] The explanation for revolution, he suggests, can be found in the historical pattern for dependency that has suppressed change for so long that eventually the system explodes—as occurred in Nicaragua in 1979. The failure of U.S. policymakers to understand the dynamic of the region only guarantees that they will be confronted with hostile and irreconcilable forces. According to LaFeber, "U.S. power has been the dominating outside (and often inside) force shaping the societies against which Central Americans have rebelled."[2]

By implication, the solution for the United States is to use its power in a positive way: to encourage a strengthening of democratic forces and a respect for human rights. Instead of suppressing change, the United States needs to tolerate it, even if it is revolutionary. Aligning itself with authoritarian regimes only results in the loss of influence when the revolution does occur. Thus, it is in the national interest of the United States to back away from the unquestioning support of the Batistas and Somozas and tolerate, even support, those who advocate democratic change. Only that attitude will prevent the revolutionary forces from turning to Moscow for help.

The Cautious Realists

In contrast to the democratic progressives, an alternative non-interventionist contention is that U.S. interests would be served by not interfering at all in Latin America, not even on behalf of democracy and human rights. Essentially, this approach calls for an understanding of the political culture and other distinctive characteristics of the region so that Washington is better able to determine an appropriate relationship.

Critical of the democratic progressives, the school of cautious realists asserts: (1) that the role of the United States in Latin American politics is severely exaggerated; (2) that intervention to promote democracy (a strategy implied by the democratic progressives) is a futile and ethnocentric endeavor; and (3) that intervention to protect security interests has likewise offered no assurance of success.[3]

There is, according to this perspective, a tendency in the United States to place too much emphasis on the U.S. influence in Latin America. Although the impact of Washington may be seen in some specific instances, the general course of political change and stability in the region can be explained without direct reference to the United States. The rise and fall of Salvador Allende, for example, or the military regime in Brazil can be accounted for by the political culture and forces indigenous to Chile and Brazil. To see the hand of Uncle Sam directing events in the region is to ignore the strength of local politics and to exaggerate the capacity of the United States actually to exert influence. Conspiracy theories placing the United States at the root of the military and authoritarian regimes in the hemisphere reveal both an ignorance of Latin America and an arrogance about U.S. power.[4]

Resolving the Debate

Is it possible to identify one of the two themes we have been discussing as the better explanation of the relationship of the United

States to Latin American politics? If one accepts the democratic progressives' analysis that the intimate involvement of the United States in Latin America has shaped the political and economic life of much of the region, then U.S. policymakers have an opportunity to redirect Washington's activities in a more positive way. By supporting and tolerating the forces of change, Washington may avoid the painful consequences of confronting hostile, Soviet-aligned revolutions.

The implications of the cautious realists' approach are that because the United States has not determined the destiny of Latin American politics to begin with, attempts to intervene on behalf of democratic change will be futile, just as will efforts to prop up discredited dictators.

Both of these positions have merit. First, it is important to acknowledge that U.S. involvement has affected the political development of many Latin American countries, some more than others. However, it would be foolish to exaggerate this influence to the point where policymakers perceived themselves as completely in control of the course of events. Local political culture and values, along with national traditions, are important variables in the Latin American political scene—and they are not always susceptible to democratic recipes from outside.

Thus in the final analysis Latin American politics have developed in tune with indigenous forces but have been buffeted by and influenced by the power and interests of the United States. This power may be selectively applied, but it is a factor and must be taken into account. After all, it has typically been the established elites and upper classes that have benefited from the order imposed by military governments. The strong link between these ruling groups and U.S. political and economic interests has clearly influenced Latin American perceptions that the U.S. role is quite strong.

The logical question, therefore, is how U.S. power is to be used. Is it to be used to promote change or to aid the old order? Or should it be used as little as possible, since most developments in the region are beyond outside control? In countries more vulnerable to U.S. power, such as those in Central America, would a U.S. decision to accept change lead to revolutionary upheavals detrimental to U.S. security interests?

Obviously, these questions cannot be answered definitively, but they do point to the complexity of U.S. relations with Latin America and to the dilemmas facing policymakers. The case of Bolivia (1952–1964) may be illustrative of the problems of drawing simple conclusions about U.S. influence in the region.

THE BOLIVIAN EXPERIENCE

The tragedy of Bolivia after 1952 can be subjected to several different interpretations. However, it is an instructive case for assessing the impact of both the U.S. actions and the indigenous political and economic factors on the fate of a popular revolution. From one perspective, U.S. policies co-opted and ultimately destroyed the revolution. From another, the revolution failed to achieve all of its aims because of the country's unrelenting poverty and its internal political rivalries. There is probably an element of truth in both of these explanations.

Critics of U.S. policy can point to Bolivia as an example of how U.S. influence can subvert a revolution. Others argue that the U.S. response demonstrated that Washington was able to support revolutions not tied to Moscow or to communism, and that if the Bolivian experiment failed, it was due to local problems, not to U.S. interference.

Origins

The revolution of 1952 was the first twentieth-century popular revolution in a South American country with a predominantly Indian population, and it has remained a distinctive case since then. It was a revolution that grew out of a series of developments culminating in a brief, almost bloodless, takeover of the government. It was not a revolt characterized by years of guerrilla warfare. It occurred, however, in a country seemingly made for revolution.

Prior to 1952, Bolivia was virtually a feudal society, divided between mestizos and Indians. Ninety-four percent of the latter spoke no Spanish, and most owned no land and did not participate in the country's political and economic life. The country's main source of income was the tin mines, controlled by three major foreign companies whose owners neither lived in Bolivia nor left their profits in the country. World War II had enabled the tin barons to earn incredible profits, but this increase in wealth meant little for Bolivia. In 1951 the Patiño family's tin mining enterprise, for example, paid only US$145 in taxes to the Bolivian government—despite the Patiños' reportedly enormous income.[5]

The revolutionary movement coalesced in a political party, the Nationalist Revolutionary Movement (MNR), created in 1940 by a group of intellectuals and activitists led by Víctor Paz Estenssoro, Hernán Siles Zuazo, and Juan Lechín Oquendo. It was influenced by socialist ideas but contained a variety of factions from former Nazis to Marxists. In its effort to improve the situation of the Indian peasants and tin miners, it confronted the old oligarchy of mine owners, landlords, and the military.

The MNR won a surprising number of seats in the legislative election of 1951 and, more importantly, elected its candidate, Víctor Paz, to the presidency, with a plurality of 45 percent. His confirmation as president was prevented by a military coup in May, but the political force of the MNR could not be so easily suppressed. The new political awareness of the peasants and miners and general resentment toward the old order produced such confusion that the junta became disunited and finally fell in face of a violent upheaval in La Paz in April 1952.

U.S. Response

The United States was initially hesitant about the revolution because of uncertainty over the makeup of the MNR and questions about the party's socialist platform that called for the nationalization of the tin mines and for a major redistribution of farm land. After reassurances that the MNR was not tied to Moscow and that compensation would be paid for all expropriated property, Washington recognized the new government in June.

Washington's reaction was quite supportive: It purchased Bolivian tin despite a world surplus and promised an increase in economic assistance. However, these gestures demonstrated how dependent Bolivia was on U.S. help, and because there were no other sources of aid, Bolivia was compelled to meet U.S. conditions: compensation for the nationalized tin mines. Thus, the owners who had enriched themselves on the country's resources were reimbursed about $27 million for their losses—an amount equal to two-thirds of Bolivia's foreign reserves and clearly beyond what Bolivia's struggling economy could afford to pay.[6]

A Dependent Economy?

Bolivia's economy was intimately linked to the international economy. Foreign capital funded the search for oil. The value of its tin exports depended on world prices, which fell after the revolution. The export market also determined the crops grown on large estates. In such a vulnerable economy, the MNR adopted a reformist, rather than a radical revolutionary, strategy. It invited private foreign investors into the country and promised to respect private enterprise. In return, the Eisenhower administration increased economic assistance from $11 million in 1953 to $20 million in 1954 and 1955. Bolivia became the largest per capita recipient of U.S. aid in Latin America.[7]

The production of the tin mines was hampered by a number of factors, some beyond Bolivia's control. In addition to low world prices, the tin magnates had already mined the best ore—what remained was of lower quality and more difficult to obtain. Foreign capital, necessary for new equipment, was unobtainable, and U.S. aid was not to be used for government-owned enterprises. The powerful miners' union, led by Juan Lechín, insisted on hiring more employees than were necessary, although it did refrain from asking for large wage increases.

The extensive land reform program broke up the large estates and distributed private plots to previously landless peasants. Universal suffrage was adopted, increasing the number of voters from 200,000 to 1 million. An effort was made to reduce illiteracy from its 1952 level of 70 percent, and thousands of new schools were built. The revolution had dramatically altered the social and political structure of Bolivia, but the economic problems in the country were so serious that full realization of the revolution's goal of national independence was not being met.

Private Enterprise

In an effort to help the Bolivian government get control of its budget and to stabilize the country's economy, the Eisenhower administration, in 1956, sent a financial adviser, George Jackson Eder, to La Paz to direct the Bolivian treasury. The policymakers and Eder were determined to cut inflation, regularize exchange rates, reduce state subsidies, and establish wage and price controls.[8] It was a program designed to clamp down on the runaway economy and to establish the priority of private enterprise in Bolivia's economic recovery. Continued U.S. assistance depended on Bolivia's acceptance of Eder's policies.

Thus, although Washington was willing to continue underwriting the Bolivian national budget (up to 32 percent at one time), it insisted on stringent financial management and a rejection of socialist solutions. If the revolution were to succeed economically, it would do so, according to U.S. officials, in the context of private enterprise. The struggling tin mines, however, had their subsidies cut, and the miners saw their wages reduced so as to not fuel inflation.

The effects of the stabilization program were a 40 percent reduction in the national budget, increased local taxes and increased rents, a drop in inflation, and predictable exchange rates. On the negative side, unemployment increased, manufacturing production fell 30 percent, and credit was reduced, as was income for all workers except farmers who benefited from increased food prices. The tin miners were hit especially hard by the austerity program.

End of the Revolution

Politically, the stabilization program produced a split in the MNR that never completely healed. Juan Lechín found himself closed out of the party's leadership. Power shifted to the moderate Paz and his vice president, Hernán Siles. By 1964 the party of the revolution had disintegrated, the government was taken over by a military coup, and the country was still locked in poverty.

Despite the social and political changes wrought by the revolution, Bolivia's fundamental problems remained, and for some, the United States shared the blame. Even if the U.S. culpability is exaggerated, it is clear that the stabilization plan forced a drastic refocusing of the economy by applying formulas suitable for a developed capitalist economy on a developing economy just emerging from feudalism. In the 1956–1964 period, U.S. economic aid flowed to Bolivia at the rate of about $50 million a year and did keep the country afloat; it did not, however, assist the country's key industry: tin. In fact, the United States prevented Bolivia from accepting help for the tin industry from East European countries.[9]

Military and security assistance also increased. Originally pushed out of politics by the revolution, the internal security and military forces were given renewed emphasis by U.S. officials, especially under the Siles administration after 1956. U.S. military assistance reached $3.2 million by 1964 and was accompanied by a close collaboration between the CIA and the Bolivian Interior Ministry. The Kennedy policy to control guerrilla movements in Latin America by building up local counterinsurgency forces pushed the Bolivian military into civic action programs that contributed to its political status and consciousness. Thus the coup of 1964, led by General René Barrientos Ortuño, was endorsed by the U.S. military as a means of bringing order to the country.[10]

The Barrientos government lasted more than four years and brought a renewed emphasis on private enterprise and a crackdown on the tin miners' union and its leaders. Private U.S. banks and investors increasingly influenced Bolivia's economy as profits earned in the country were exported. Imports from the United States, including food, increased.[11]

In the years following, the U.S. presence in Bolivia grew. Military assistance doubled from 1968 to 1973–1974. The conservative and repressive regime of Hugo Banzer Suárez (1971–1978) was backed by Washington and Brazil. By the 1980s, a succession of military governments and the widespread corruption growing out of the cocaine traffic seemed to make Bolivia's politics even more erratic. Despite the return to power of old MNR leaders Hernán Siles and Víctor Paz (the latter in 1985), the democratic promise of the 1950s could not be restored. There had been a revolution in Bolivia, but after thirty years, no one seemed to remember what it stood for.

Explanations

Perhaps the revolution was destined to fail. The domestic poverty, the dependence on the international economy and foreign assistance, along with the unresolved internal struggles might have been too much to overcome. In addition, the MNR might not have been sufficiently radical to sustain a complete revolution. Reformist governments might have meant well, but their reluctance to confront the implications of a dependent economy could have undermined the original hope of the revolution for national independence.

And what about the role of the United States? Was it the villain in this tragedy? Washington was clearly a generous supporter of the MNR government in the 1950s. The prompt aid and the purchase of tin might well have prevented the MNR's collapse in 1953. Washington's restraint and its decision not to portray events in Bolivia as part of the East-West contest was a departure from what was happening at the same time in regard to Guatemala and Cuba. Of course, Bolivia was quite far from the United States, and there were no major U.S. economic interests at stake there as there had been in the Caribbean region.

Nevertheless, did the United States deflect the revolution with its involvement? Bolivia's leaders were desperate for aid, thereby giving the United States leverage in turning away the revolution from a radical course. The demands that Bolivia compensate the tin barons, protect the free market economy, and seek private foreign investment while at the same time cutting subsidies to key industries like the tin mines may have imposed an excessive burden on the Bolivians. In addition, the gradual nurturing of the military by the United States resurrected a political force the revolution had sought to neutralize. As a result, U.S. actions, deliberate or not, could well have been a major factor in the revolution's collapse.

In the final accounting of Bolivia's recent history, it is important to recognize the role of the United States. Although Bolivia's internal conditions were the primary factors in this story, outside influence cannot be discounted. As revolutionary movements in the 1980s consider the effects of cooperation with Washington, and as they assess the role of the military, the Bolivian model, even if distorted, is likely to cast a shadow on their planning.

CENTRAL AMERICA: ANOTHER VIETNAM (OR CUBA)

The argument against U.S. intervention was given added impetus in 1984 and 1985 during the battle in the U.S. Congress over Reagan's policy toward Central America. The debate revived concern that the United States might find itself involved in a conflict similar to the one that led to defeat in Vietnam. If any historical analogy seemed to sway the minds of members of Congress during the debate it was that of Vietnam. The president's attempt to invoke the comparison with Cuba did not match the fear that the United States could be dragged into another uncertain war in the Third World when the U.S. public appeared opposed to such a prospect. The White House struggle to secure funding for the *contras* reminded some members of Congress of the process that led to the fateful 1964 Tonkin Gulf Resolution, an act that gave President Johnson a carte blanche to conduct a war in Southeast Asia.[12] In reality, however, is Central America potentially "another Vietnam"? Are those concerns justified?

The central issue giving rise to this concern was Nicaragua. If the United States were to back fully the *contra* effort to overthrow the Sandinistas, U.S. troops might eventually be required, and such an intervention could lead to a prolonged antiguerrilla war in a country where very few people would support the United States. A similar scenario could develop in El Salvador if it were necessary to send U.S. forces to save the government there from the revolution.

Funding the Contras

The Reagan request in April 1985 for $14 million in aid to the *contras* followed a year in which the Congress had not approved any requests for direct support of their efforts. The 1985 request aroused concern in the House and Senate among both Republicans and Democrats that approval of the aid, even for humanitarian purposes, would commit the United States to a cause that could not succeed without U.S. combat troops.[13] According to this view, once the commitment was made, the United States would find itself locked into a path of escalating involvement to rescue an unworthy cause simply because it could not afford to back out of a promise.

Mirroring the language used during the Vietnam War, congressional critics asserted that once a commitment existed, no U.S. president or Congress would find it easy to reverse it, no matter how futile the enterprise. For Senator Patrick Leahy, approval of Reagan's request "is a down payment on eventual American military involvement in Central America, and I don't think there is any military reason to justify it."[14]

In the 1960s, U.S. officials had claimed that perhaps the promises to Saigon should not have been made, but because the United States had given its word and made an issue out of protecting its friends, to desert them would raise doubts about U.S. credibility and the strength of U.S. character.

In fact, President Reagan's portrayal of the *contras* as "freedom fighters," and as "our brothers" fighting for democracy seemed designed to engender sympathy in Congress for just such a commitment. For Reagan, the Sandinistas were duplicating what Castro had done in Cuba "to rid themselves of the other elements of the revolution." If the Nicaraguan government, he argued, "would turn around and say . . . uncle," the real revolution could then proceed.[15] However, critics pointed out that if the rhetoric surrounding the *contras* made their early efforts so critical, what would it sound like when they required even more aid?

U.S. Troops

Administration opponents contended that once the faucet of aid was officially opened again, it would be difficult to turn off, and yet there was considerable doubt on Capitol Hill that the *contras* even with more aid could wage a successful guerrilla war against Managua. Thus it was feared that U.S. troops would be required to salvage the effort, regardless of the White House denials that such a contingency was planned.

Because U.S. military intervention in Nicaragua was not assured of a quick victory, popular support in the United States would be difficult to sustain. A protracted battle in the jungles and mountains, it was argued, against a popular revolutionary force would require the resumption of the draft and provoke the divisive politics that had characterized the Vietnam era.

Congressional reluctance to encourage U.S. involvement came about despite the existence of the War Powers Act. Passed in the wake of Vietnam, this act restricted the ability of the president without explicit congressional approval to send and keep troops overseas in an area of combat. But in light of the refusal of presidents Nixon, Ford, Carter, and Reagan to acknowledge the validity of that act and in view of the president's ability to move on his own, Congress was clearly unwilling to trust the act to restrain the Reagan administration in Central America.

Although Secretary of Defense Caspar Weinberger asserted that U.S. forces would not intervene anywhere without popular and congressional support, doubters in Washington pointed to the suddenness of the Grenada invasion, the various military maneuvers in Honduras, and the increasing seriousness of contingency plans for an intervention as indications that the Pentagon was at least preparing for an invasion. Moreover, Secretary of State George Shultz, although not advocating U.S. military action in Nicaragua, did argue, in contrast to Weinberger, that it might be necessary to use U.S. troops in a limited way even if popular support were not immediately forthcoming.[16]

Given the difficulties six thousand U.S. troops had in subduing a few hundred resisters in Grenada in 1983, there was doubt that the Pentagon could conduct a swift and decisive action in Nicaragua. Thus, Congress agonized over even a modest gesture of direct support for the *contras*.

Another Tonkin Gulf?

The president's troubles were compounded by the similarity of the *contra* case to that of the Tonkin Gulf episode. As Congress had learned later, the events of August 1964 in the Tonkin Gulf had been deliberately distorted and exaggerated by the White House in order to secure approval of a resolution authorizing the president to use force in Southeast Asia.[17] In the days preceding the vote on the president's 1985 request, Reagan indicated that he had endorsements from the Pope and from the president of Colombia for his program. This was later denied by both individuals.[18] Exaggerated claims about Soviet aid to Nicaragua and the imminent arrival of Soviet MIGs also undermined the president's case.[19]

Although members of Congress appeared unsympathetic to the Sandinistas, they were not convinced that Nicaragua posed a threat sufficient to justify even indirect U.S. intervention. The Boland Amendment had restricted earlier aid to the *contras* by requiring that it not be used for the overthrow of any government. In 1985, the president persuaded Congress to end that restriction. "Some of the proposals that have been made in Congress," he said, "have lacked a complete understanding of what is at stake there and what we are trying to do."[20] Clearly, the president's strong convictions and undeviating campaign against the Sandinistas were quite capable of overriding the uncertainty of Congress.

The Ortega Trip to Moscow

The power of symbols in shaping the attitudes of an indecisive Congress is demonstrated by the reactions to the visit to Moscow by Nicaraguan President Daniel Ortega in May 1985, on the day the House voted to deny aid to the *contras*. Ortega's trip seemed to turn the tide against Managua. The Nicaraguans had won a battle in the House and then lost it by what was interpreted in Washington as a deliberate flaunting of their ties to the Soviet Union. As a result, Congress, in July 1985, finally authorized $27 million in "nonlethal" aid for the *contras*.

Reagan exploited Ortega's trip to mobilize support for his cause and to expand his options for deposing the Sandinistas. The mood in Washington was increasingly sympathetic to a direct U.S. intervention, although no consensus had emerged.[21]

Which Analogy?

The Reagan White House insisted that Central America was not Vietnam and that the analogy broke down in part because of the geopolitical differences. Nicaragua and El Salvador were in the U.S. backyard, not halfway around the world. Moreover, the growing influence of the Soviet Union in the area was more directly a threat to the United States than it had been in Southeast Asia. Reagan invoked the Cuban missile crisis as an example of the consequences of the United States' not standing firm against the Sandinistas. Cuba, he contended, was the proper analogy, not Vietnam. According to the president, the dominoes were about to fall in Central America: "If we permit the Soviets, using the Sandinistas, to establish a beachhead on the American mainland to spread their subversion . . . we could turn around one day and find a string of pro-Soviet dictatorships in Central America and a threat to our southern borders."[22]

The image of falling dominoes had been presented by Secretary of State Haig in 1981, when he referred to a communist "hit list" that would eventually include Guatemala and Mexico. Such an eventuality would destroy U.S. credibility and threaten U.S. security. To Reagan, the country could not "walk away from one of the greatest moral challenges in postwar history."[23]

Such rhetoric revived memories of the claims that the defeat of South Vietnam would lead to dominoes falling across Southeast Asia to the point where vital U.S. interests would be threatened. It was a scenario somewhat discredited by 1985 and thus not an effective device for convincing Congress or the public of the need for deeper U.S. involvement in Central America.

Secretary of State Shultz used the Vietnam analogy to explain why the United States *must* become involved in Central America. If a vacuum were left in Central America comparable to the one left in Southeast Asia when the United States pulled out, there would be a serious threat, he stated, to the nation's security. And furthermore, he declared, "Our goals in Central America are like those we had in Vietnam: democracy, economic progress, and security against aggression." Nicaragua, he implied, was just like North Vietnam: "Broken promises; communist dictatorship; refugees; widened Soviet influence, this time near our very borders—here is your parallel between Vietnam and Central America."[24]

Conclusions

The specter of Vietnam haunted the debate because in fact there were sufficient similarities to give the image credence. In South Vietnam, the United States tried reforms and aid to salvage a regime backed by a minority comprised of urban, educated upper classes. The South Vietnamese army, however, was infected by corruption, poor leadership, disloyalty, and an inability—even an unwillingness—to fight a guerrilla war. The conduct of the army and the failure of political and economic reforms only served to alienate the population from the government. Washington did act in El Salvador in a manner apparently designed to prevent these conditions from developing.

The refusal of Washington to recognize the realities of nationalism and revolution in Vietnam caused it to underestimate seriously the determination of the North Vietnamese and Viet Cong to continue fighting. Despite overwhelming U.S. firepower and often heroic missions by U.S. troops and pilots, the "enemy" did not surrender. Moreover, it was often impossible to identify the enemy, to separate soldier from civilian. Having been drawn gradually into a revolution and civil war, the United States tried to define the conflict as an international war. The faulty definition contributed to an inappropriate commitment and a misdirected military effort.

To extend the same kind of commitment to the *contras* or to El Salvador's government would constitute, in the eyes of administration critics, a mistake comparable to that made in 1964. Defining Central American struggles as strategic contests with Moscow and communism instead of as revolutions and civil wars growing out of indigenous factors was to repeat the earlier mistakes of Vietnam. Experience seemed to suggest that once the United States made a commitment, it would not change, it would not back out no matter how futile or untenable the endeavor. Such a view had nothing to do with motives or intentions, because the United States, even with the best intentions, had to face the reality of what could be accomplished. This, it was argued, was the lesson of Vietnam.

To prevent Vietnams, therefore, U.S. policy needed to address the sources of discontent in the region: the poverty, the economic and social inequities, and the political repression. Heading off the conditions that give rise to revolution made more sense than attempting to turn back the clock with appeals to a fear of global communism.

Thus, to many in Congress there were sufficient parallels with Vietnam, from the revolutionary context to the president's rhetoric, to cause Congress to hold back a commitment—for a time. Congress wanted no share of the blame for a Vietnam-style disaster. If the president wanted to take the United States into battle in Central America, the message was that he might be doing it on his own.

However, Congress has never been inclined to want to be blamed for allowing a country to "go communist" either. The fear of being depicted as giving away Central America to communism might well persuade Congress to do what it did during Vietnam and what it has often done in the past: defer to the president. If previous congressional behavior is instructive, compromises will permit Reagan to continue his policies at least incrementally. Congress may not intend it, but the commitment could well grow.

TOWARD A POLICY OF POSITIVE RESTRAINT

Foreign policy is a process of making choices between what is desirable and what is possible. It is a process of confronting both long-term historical forces and contemporary issues of immediate urgency. For the United States, foreign policy involves reconciling an interest in democratic institutions with the demands of protecting the nation's security and its economic interests.

To develop a reasonable policy toward Latin America one must recognize these choices and dilemmas. If anything, recent history has demonstrated that the United States cannot remake Latin America into a region of democratic states, but neither can it blindly support dictatorial repression without ultimately paying a very high price. Latin American politics and culture are not amenable to quick fixes based on simple notions of human rights and freedom; but, as the Cuban and Nicaraguan cases have shown, the absence of an understanding of the U.S. contribution to revolutionary conditions can produce situations where the U.S. sees its security interests as directly threatened.

Nonintervention

Of course, it is appealing to the isolationist impulse in the United States to suggest a policy of absolute nonintervention. Such a course of action could: (1) allow Latin American authoritarian governments to rule without challenge, and/or (2) allow revolutions to take place even if they threaten U.S. interests. However, because the United States is concerned about Latin America, because it does have major economic, political, and security interests in the region, and because one cannot expect the United States suddenly to be uninvolved, a policy that calls for a global superpower to keep its hands off is unlikely to be considered a realistic recommendation.

Policy Requirements

A U.S. policy toward Latin America with a reasonable chance of political acceptance in the United States and a chance of being implemented successfully in the region must start first with the understanding that the United States will be involved in the politics and foreign policies of the Latin Americans. Involvement does not necessarily mean intervention, but the power of the U.S. economy, its security interests as a bloc leader and as a global power, as well as its historical record of interference, suggest a continued strong presence in the region. Wishing away U.S. power will not cause it to disappear.[25]

Secondly, a successful policy must accept the limits of what the United States can accomplish in Latin America. The days of effective gunboat diplomacy and manipulation of governments with promises of aid and trade have passed—despite attempts to keep them alive. Economic sanctions and covert actions did not bring Fidel Castro to heel. The attempt of the Reagan administration to overturn the Sandinista revolution using similar tactics suffered a similar fate. Persuading Guatemala or Argentina or Chile to comply with human rights requirements did not work either. Thus, the United States needs to be willing to accept changes and conditions in the region that may be hostile to some U.S. interests but that do not pose direct threats to U.S. security. The reason: There may be little Washington can do short of major military action to influence those developments.[26]

Third, the United States must recognize that the use of military force has a very limited chance for success in the region. The Grenadan victory was such an anomaly that it would be dangerous to project a general policy on that single incident. The high costs of a military intervention and the likelihood that it would not achieve any lasting political solution will no doubt deter U.S. officials. And, of course, the fear of another Vietnam has limited the prospects for domestic support of such action.

Fourth, the United States cannot escape the history of its involvement in Latin America. As we mentioned at the outset of this book, incidents that people in the United States have tended to forget loom large in the minds of Latin Americans. Whether it is the interventionist record of dollar diplomacy or the contribution to the overthrow of Salvador Allende, the legacy of U.S. intervention colors any dispute between the United States and its hemispheric neighbors.

Even though the actual incidents of intervention cannot explain all of the region's problems, the memories of them tend to overshadow the positive aspects of U.S.–Latin American relations. The cooperation on economic development, the promotion of representative government where it showed promise (in the Dominican Republic, for example), and the recent attempts to address issues of contention such as the Panama Canal have often been lost in the rhetoric of retribution.

Washington needs to be mindful of the consequences of its actions. The appearance of U.S. involvement in establishing military rule in Brazil and of encouraging the rise and reign of authoritarians such as Chile's Pinochet virtually assures a popular rejection of U.S. influence when those regimes collapse. The hostile reception accorded Vice President Nixon in 1958 in Venezuela should serve as a reminder of the cost of embracing dictators such as Perez Jiménez. And furthermore, the recent Latin American reluctance to join in U.S. efforts to depose the Sandinistas points to the continued adherence to the principle of nonintervention.

A fifth policy requirement follows from the fourth: As revolutions occur, Washington needs to raise its threshold of tolerance for national independence. The cry for "national liberation" among revolutionaries may conjure up images of terrorism and a marriage to the Soviet Union, but it also reflects a long-standing desire for many Latin Americans for control over their own destinies. When this search for independence does not involve invitations to the Soviet Union to set up military bases or satellite states, the United States can afford to be tolerant of excessive rhetoric.

And finally, a sixth requirement is that U.S. policymakers recognize the complexities of Latin America. The nations of the hemisphere have a variety of political values and styles. Democratic procedures and traditions may be well established in, let us say, Costa Rica and Venezuela, but have had less impact in Bolivia and Guatemala. Foreign policy orientations also differ, with the global and regional ambitions of Brazil, Argentina, Cuba, and Mexico clearly diverging from the more limited concerns of Ecuador, Peru, and El Salvador. It is not a region susceptible to simplistic policies or to U.S. guidance, no matter how benevolent. Washington's acceptance of the region's diversity may require a tolerance of Cuba's role in Africa as well as an understanding that military influence in politics is not going to disappear overnight from countries such as Honduras and Peru.

A Positive Response

Although these requirements argue for restraint in U.S. policy, there is also a possibility for positive actions. First, there are opportunities for Washington to assist struggling democratic governments such as those in Argentina, Brazil, and the Dominican Republic with assistance in resolving their national debt problems. The potential social disorder arising from a perpetual economic crisis encourages a turn to either authoritarian order or mass upheaval. These two options are not necessarily contrary to U.S. interests, but the record suggests that Washington is better able to establish long-term cooperative arrangements with moderate governments, such as those of Mexico and Venezuela—even if they occasionally show signs of independence—than with narrow dictators and revolutionaries.

Second, when revolutions do occur, there are openings for the United States, if the situation is handled with patience and modesty. If U.S. assistance, whether in the form of aid or trade, is extended in such a manner that the revolution is not completely undermined, the long-term benefits for Washington are likely to outweigh the costs. It was not preordained that the Nicaraguan revolution would be driven to so much dependence on the Soviet Union, but the U.S. conditions for cooperation were so threatening to the Sandinistas that there was no room for compromise. There are risks involved in working with revolutionary governments, but the United States is strong enough to gamble on finding a way toward a relationship of some mutual benefit.

An obsession with strategic and ideological factors is not likely today to produce the subtle, pragmatic responses necessary to protect U.S. interests in the region. In fact, the inability to deal with reality in a positive manner may well perpetuate the unstable conditions Washington has been trying to avoid.

Third, a positive response requires a commitment to popular, democratic forces when possible, instead of the instinctive turn to the military whenever the going gets tough. Supporting those interested in more popular reforms and democratic procedures is not always going to guarantee success—as the failure of the Alliance for Progress demonstrated. However, the alleviation of the pressures for change can contribute to heading off the conditions that could bring about violent anti-U.S. revolutions.

Although U.S. expectations for democratic change must be tempered by the reality of history and culture, the expectations need not be abandoned. Democratic changes may not correspond to the U.S. model, but they can address the problems of many in Latin America. Again, if there is no direct threat to U.S. security, encouragement is likely to be more productive and less costly than a short-term negative reaction.

FROM THE GLOBAL TO THE REGIONAL

As we suggested at the beginning of this book, the United States cannot escape the history of its involvement in Latin America. A wise foreign policy requires an understanding of the impact of past behavior on the Latin Americans and on U.S. perceptions of its role in the region. History may not repeat itself, but it does shape attitudes and reactions.

Over the past century and before, U.S. officials have approached Latin America from a variety of perspectives. The region has been seen as part of a Western Hemisphere community, as a sphere of U.S. influence, and as a pawn in the cold war. Latin America has benefited from periods of good will such as the Alliance for Progress and the Good Neighbor Policy, but it has also endured periods of intervention in the name of such causes as democracy, dollar diplomacy, and anticommunism. No single theme has dominated U.S. policy.

Nonetheless, two broad trends have stood out. There has been a recurring struggle between the regionalist perspective and a globalist one. Treating Latin America as a special region, important for its own sake and for its particular relationship to the United States, was characteristic of the nineteenth and early twentieth centuries. Even in the years after 1945, U.S. policy often corresponded to those sphere-of-influence and hemispheric-community approaches. More recently, critics have urged U.S. officials to pay more attention to region-specific issues as a means of improving U.S. policy.

Globalist perspectives dominated U.S. policy during the cold war era. As the United States emerged as a world power, its views of Latin America changed. The region's importance came to rest on its relationship to the contest between the United States and the Soviet Union. Strategic and ideological interests shaped U.S. actions, not the dynamic forces of the region itself.

Other globalist impulses have influenced policy, too, from the periodic crusades for democracy to the concern over the ills of economic dependency. Although these perspectives may reflect well-meant values, they may be too ethnocentric and normative to contribute to effective policy.

How a situation is defined directly affects the policy choice. It is incumbent upon policymakers, therefore, to consider their assumptions or definitions about Latin America and about the appropriate responses of the United States. Faulty definitions can lead to frustrating efforts to control events in a region not so vulnerable today to outside influence.

The cases used to illustrate the various patterns of U.S. policy generally were dramatic incidents of U.S. intervention. Although the United States was successful in a number of these cases, their long-term impact has been to undermine U.S. ability to protect its interests today. The Chileans, Nicaraguans, Guatemalans, and Cubans, for example, have not been convinced of the benevolence of U.S. policy in the region, and Washington's repeated inability to recognize the negative impact of its actions only serves to create more problems. A more subtle policy, one attuned to the revolutionary dynamics of the region, is more likely to assure long-term accomplishment for the United States than a policy that tries to perpetuate a deteriorating status quo.

NOTES

1. Walter LaFeber, *Inevitable Revolutions: The United States in Central America* (New York: W. W. Norton, 1983).

2. Ibid., 12. Also see James Chace, *Endless War* (New York: Vintage, 1984), Richard Alan White, *The Morass: United States Intervention in Central America* (New York: Harper & Row, 1984), and Robert S. Leiken, ed., *Central America: Anatomy of a Conflict* (Elmsford, N.Y.: Pergamon Press, 1984).

3. The skepticism about the effectiveness of U.S. intervention can be found in: Howard J. Wiarda, *In Search of Policy: The United States and Latin America* (Washington, D.C.: American Enterprise Institute, 1984); Lars Schoultz, *Human Rights and United States Policy Toward Latin America* (Princeton, N.J.: Princeton University Press, 1981); and Abraham Lowenthal, "Change the Agenda," *Foreign Policy* 52 (Fall 1983), 64–77.

4. The influence of political culture is thoroughly discussed in Howard J. Wiarda, *Corporatism and National Development in Latin America* (Boulder, Colo.: Westview Press, 1981); James M. Malloy, ed., *Authoritarianism and Corporatism in Latin America* (Pittsburgh: University of Pittsburgh Press, 1977); and Robert Wesson, ed., *New Military Politics in Latin America* (New York: Praeger, 1982).

5. For a thorough survey of the revolution, see James Dunkerly, *Rebellion in the Veins: Political Struggle in Bolivia, 1952–1982* (London: Verso Editions,

1984); also Richard W. Patch, "United States Assistance in a Revolutionary Setting," in Robert D. Tomasek, ed., *Latin American Politics* (New York: Anchor Books, 1970), 344–374.

6. Dunkerly, *Rebellion in the Veins,* 58. Also see Cole Blaiser, "The U.S. and the Revolution," in James M. Malloy and Richard S. Thorn, eds., *Beyond the Revolution: Bolivia Since 1952* (Pittsburgh: University of Pittsburgh Press, 1971), 53–109.

7. Cole Blaiser, *The Hovering Giant: U.S. Response to Revolutionary Change in Latin America,* (Pittsburgh: University of Pittsburgh Press, 1976), 136.

8. Richard S. Thorn, "The Economic Transformation," in Malloy and Thorn, *Beyond the Revolution,* 183–189; also, George Jackson Eder, *Inflation and Development in Latin America: A Case History of Inflation and Stabilization in Bolivia* (Ann Arbor: University of Michigan Bureau of Business Research, 1968).

9. Blaiser, "The U.S. and the Revolution," 89–90. Also, Agency for International Development, *U.S. Overseas Loans and Grants, July 1, 1945–June 30, 1969* (Washington, D.C.: 1970), 36.

10. William H. Brill, "Theories of Military Intervention and the Bolivian Case," in Paul Sigmund, ed., *Models of Political Change in Latin America* (New York: Praeger, 1970), 56–60; also Dunkerly, *Rebellion in the Veins,* 108–113.

11. Dunkerly, *Rebellion in the Veins,* 125–129.

12. This question is cogently discussed by George C. Herring, "Vietnam, El Salvador and the Uses of History," in Kenneth M. Coleman and George C. Herring, eds., *The Central American Crisis* (Wilmington, Del.: Scholarly Resources, 1985), 97–110.

13. Accounts of this debate are in *Washington Post,* March 2, 1985, 1, 6; and *New York Times,* April 19, 1985, 10. Also see Robert Healy, "A Viet Lesson for U.S. in Central America," *Boston Globe,* April 17, 1985, 17.

14. Quoted in *New York Times,* April 21, 1985, E3.

15. Quoted in *New York Times,* February 23, 1985, 10.

16. For the Weinberger-Shultz discussion, see *Newsweek,* December 10, 1984, 34; and *New York Times,* December 11, 1984, 1, 6.

17. Accounts of the Tonkin Gulf episode are in Joseph Goulden, *Truth is the First Casualty* (Chicago: Rand McNally, 1969); and Leslie H. Gelb and Richard K. Betts, *The Irony of Vietnam: The System Worked* (Washington, D.C.: The Brookings Institution, 1979), 100–104.

18. *New York Times,* April 12, 1985, 3; and April 23, 1985, 30.

19. See "The MIGs are Coming," *Barricada Internacional,* December 4, 1984; and *New York Times* editorial, November 15, 1985, 30.

20. Quoted in *New York Times,* February 22, 1985, 10.

21. *New York Times,* June 6, 1985, 4.

22. *New York Times,* April 15, 1985, 6, and April 19, 1985, 7.

23. *New York Times,* April 21, 1985, E3.

24. George Shultz, "The Meaning of Vietnam," *Current Policy* 694 (Washington, D.C.: U.S. Department of State, April 25, 1985).

25. Among the recent plethora of studies with suggestions on revising U.S. policy in Latin America are Wiarda, *In Search of Policy;* James R. Kurth, "A New Realism in U.S.-Latin American Relations," in Richard Newfarmer, ed., *From Gunboats to Diplomacy: New U.S. Policies for Latin America* (Baltimore: Johns Hopkins University Press, 1984), 3-14; Abraham Lowenthal, "Latin America: A Not-So-Special Relationship," *Foreign Policy* 32 (Fall 1978); and Paul Sigmund, "Latin America: Change or Continuity?" in *America and The World, 1981* (Elsmford, N.Y.: Pergamon Press, 1982), 629-657.

26. For a similar argument, see Lowenthal, "Change the Agenda." A cautionary note for U.S. policy in Nicaragua is presented by Piero Gleijeses, "Nicaragua: Resist the Romanticism," *Foreign Policy* 54 (Spring 1984), 122-138.

SELECTED BIBLIOGRAPHY

HISTORICAL BACKGROUND

Bemis, Samuel Flagg. *The Latin American Policy of the United States.* New York: Harcourt, Brace, 1943.

Connell-Smith, Gordon. *The Inter-American System.* New York: Oxford University Press, 1966.

Langley, Lester D. *The Banana Wars: An Inner History of American Empire, 1900–1934.* Lexington: University of Kentucky Press, 1983.

May, Ernest R. *The Making of the Monroe Doctrine.* Cambridge, Mass.: Harvard University Press, 1975.

McCullough, David. *The Path Between the Seas: The Creation of the Panama Canal, 1870–1914.* New York: Simon and Schuster, 1977.

Mecham, J. Lloyd. *The United States and Inter-American Security, 1889–1960.* Austin: University of Texas Press, 1961.

Munro, Dana G. *Intervention and Dollar Diplomacy in the Caribbean, 1900–1921.* Princeton, N.J.: Princeton University Press, 1964.

Stuart, Graham. *Latin America and the United States.* New York: Appleton-Century-Crofts, 1955.

Whitaker, Arthur P. *The United States and the Independence of Latin America.* Baltimore: Johns Hopkins University Press, 1941.

———. *The Western Hemisphere Idea: Its Rise and Decline.* Ithaca, N.Y.: Cornell University Press, 1954.

Wood, Bryce. *The Making of the Good Neighbor Policy.* New York: Columbia University Press, 1961.

RECENT U.S. POLICY

Blaiser, Cole. *The Hovering Giant: U.S. Responses to Revolutionary Change in Latin America.* Pittsburgh: University of Pittsburgh Press, 1976.

Chilcote, Ronald A., and Joel C. Edelstein, eds. *Latin America: The Struggle with Dependency and Beyond.* New York: Schenkman, 1974.

Hayes, Margaret Daly. *Latin America and the U.S. National Interest.* Boulder, Colo.: Westview Press, 1984.

LaFeber, Walter. *Inevitable Revolutions: The United States in Central America.* New York: W. W. Norton, 1983.

Levinson, Jerome, and Juan de Onis. *The Alliance that Lost Its Way.* Chicago: Quadrangle Books, 1970.
Lieuwen, Edwin. *Arms and Politics in Latin America.* New York: Praeger, 1961.
Newfarmer, Richard, ed. *From Gunboats to Diplomacy: New U.S. Politics for Latin America.* Baltimore: Johns Hopkins University Press, 1984.
Schoultz, Lars. *Human Rights and United States Policy Toward Latin America.* Princeton, N.J.: Princeton University Press, 1981.
Wiarda, Howard J. *In Search of Policy: The United States and Latin America.* Washington, D.C.: American Enterprise Institute, 1984.

CASES

Allison, Graham T. *Essence of Decision: Explaining the Cuban Missile Crisis.* Boston: Little, Brown, 1971.
Bonsal, Philip. *Cuba, Castro and the United States.* Pittsburgh: University of Pittsburgh Press, 1971.
Christian, Shirley. *Nicaragua: Revolution in the Family.* New York: Random House, 1985.
Cline, Howard. *The United States and Mexico.* New York: Atheneum, 1963.
Dunkerly, James. *Rebellion in the Veins: Political Struggle in Bolivia, 1952–1982.* London: Verso Editions, 1984.
Immerman, Richard H. *The CIA in Guatemala.* Austin: University of Texas Press, 1982.
Macaulay, Neill. *The Sandino Affair.* Chicago: Quadrangle Books, 1967.
Matthews, Herbert L. *The Cuban Story.* New York: Braziller, 1961.
Montgomery, Tommie Sue. *Revolution in El Salvador.* Boulder, Colo.: Westview Press, 1982.
Parker, Phyllis R. *Brazil and the Quiet Intervention, 1964.* Austin: University of Texas Press, 1979.
Schlesinger, Stephen, and Stephen Kinzer. *Bitter Fruit: The Untold Story of the American Coup in Guatemala.* New York: Doubleday, 1982.
Sigmund, Paul E. *Multinationals in Latin America: The Politics of Nationalization.* Madison: University of Wisconsin Press, 1980.
———. *The Overthrow of Allende and the Politics of Chile, 1964–1976.* Pittsburgh: University of Pittsburgh Press, 1977.
Slater, Jerome. *Intervention and Negotiation: The United States and the Dominican Revolution.* New York: Harper & Row, 1970.
Timerman, Jacobo. *Prisoner Without a Name, Cell Without a Number.* New York: Knopf, 1981.
Walker, Thomas W., ed. *Nicaragua: The First Five Years.* New York: Praeger, 1985.
Wyden, Peter. *The Bay of Pigs.* New York: Simon and Schuster, 1981.

INDEX